W9-CEX-349

Don't Get Taken Every Time

Don't Get Taken Every Time

The Insider's Guide to Buying Your Next Car

REMAR SUTTON

The Viking Press   New York

Copyright © 1982 by Remar M. Sutton, Jr.
All rights reserved
First published in 1982 by The Viking Press
625 Madison Avenue, New York, N.Y. 10022
Published simultaneously in Canada by
Penguin Books Canada Limited

Library of Congress Cataloging in Publication Data
Sutton, Remar.
Don't get taken every time.
Includes index.
1. Automobiles—Purchasing.   I. Title.
TL162.S96   629.2'222   81-65279
ISBN 0-670-69092-9   AACR2

Printed in the United States of America
Set in Fototronic Century Schoolbook

To Dad

Acknowledgments

If this book is a good one, a large share of credit goes to Mary Abbott Waite. M. A. took a rookie writer's first effort, showed me how to organize it, polish it. At the same time she believed in it—and me. Thanks, sport.

In the course of doing research for this book, I worked and shopped at over fifty dealerships around the country. Thanks to you: Bob Mize, Fred Gay, Harvey Strother, Vic Osman, Tom Molnar, George Warrington, and Mark Singleton. Thanks to you, too, A. J. Hiers.

To Paul Wiser at the MACO Federal Credit Union: thanks for your technical help. Bunny and Holly: you get to do the next one, too, you lucky souls. Ron Massey: thanks for your help with the checklists.

To Jay: my friend when it wasn't easy to be so. To Jay again: for the mixup in bedrooms. And finally to the Duke of Dunwoody, the rarest car person.

Contents

PART I
Forearming

1

A Day in the Life of Killer Monsoon

"Killer Monsoon" is late for the sales meeting again, the daily "ream-'em-out and charge-'em-up" gathering that begins the day at most automobile dealerships in America. Killer's feeling fine today; he's delivering a new car to that nice old couple who came to the store yesterday. The folks never knew what hit them, either; they paid "full-boat," list price, and they're happy, of course. The buyer's order showed a whopping allowance on their trade, and that's what they wanted. It's Killer's best talent, giving people what they want.

The general manager is running the meeting this morning. When that guy's up this early, it's usually going to be a bad session, Killer thinks. And he's right. J. C. looks angry. Don, one of the sales managers, looks solemn. Killer stands by the door until everyone is seated and then strolls down the aisle, nodding, passing out "good mornings" and "how are yous?" to the forty men settled tentatively in their seats. As he passes J. C. and Don, he turns slightly toward them and curtsies, spreading his imaginary dress with both hands, a thin and innocent smile curving his lips. The rumble of laughter in the room turns to silence quickly as J. C. stands, pulls his belt upward over his belly, and inhales, a snorting sound. Obviously J. C. isn't amused. He walks three heavy steps to the podium, grabs both edges with an intensity escaping no one in the room, and begins to talk in loud, clipped sentences.

"Damn it, men. We're down in new-car gross. We're down in used-car gross. Financing is down. Rustproofing is down. We had fifty people on this lot last night. We didn't sell ten cars. And not a damned one of you T. O.'d a soul. [Lots of terms at car stores are peculiar to the business. The Glossary on p. 365 will help you with those that are unfamiliar to you.] The *next* one of you that lets anybody walk without talking to a manager is going to be on his ass out the door!" J. C. begins to upbraid each salesman individually, saying each name as if it were a command, looking first at the man and then the Perk Board on the wall. The board ranks every salesman on unit sales new and used, "front-end" gross, "back-end" gross, deals financed, and bonus cars. Killer is leading in every column; he's not only "Salesman of the Year" again, but the dealership's best closer.

But even the Salesman of the Year isn't immune from a lecture today. Pausing at the end of his roll call, J. C. looks at Killer, who has slipped down in his chair, eyes half closed in boredom. "Hey Killer, wake up!" J. C. slaps the lectern. "This applies to you, too. You may lead the board with two hundred new cars out. But you've been doing too much sleeping. This time last year you had out three hundred new and your average gross was $50 dollars higher. So either you've been dozing or you're over the hill, old man."

"Well, J. C., I guess you better send me to that great car store in the sky. But before you do that, why don't you help us sell some cars? Like, why don't you put a bonus on that beat-up old Lincoln; I get indigestion every time I see it. Maybe it's my age or something." Killer still reclines in his chair, but he's made a smart move. He's changed the subject. He's also changed J. C. into a bear again.

"Killer, you traded the damn thing in," J. C. replies hotly. "But I'm going to be nice today. The first person that brings me a deal, a signed order on that piece of junk, will get a $200-dollar bonus when the S.O.B. drives it off. I'm also paying $50 for the highest gross written today, and the most write-ups today. I'm also going to give a C note to every one of you that writes a good deal on all used cars over ninety days old . . ." J. C. pauses, looks over the room once more, and brings his fist down hard on the podium. "Now, damn it, get the hell out of here and write some deals!"

One of the first men out of the room, Killer heads for the employees' lounge. He pours himself a coffee, drops in six sugar cubes, and sits at a small table by the door. Between sips he looks at his bird-dog list. Jerry, his car-queer friend who just loves to trade cars every six months, might have a new prospect, Killer thinks. Jerry is a barber, one of the best bird-dogs, a guy who tells everyone sitting in his chair what a good deal he can get them "as long as you deal with Bobby DeMarco." That's Killer's real name. "Killer Monsoon" is what the other guys call him, a good description, too. Killer always squeezes every single ounce of profit from every customer. He's famous for "bumping" one guy, raising him, six times.

By ten in the morning, Killer has made his bird-dog phone calls and is standing close to the main entrance of the showroom. He's hot. All these damn new salesmen, the "floor whores," are grabbing all the "ups," and blowing them off the lot without ever really working them. And nothing ticks Killer off more than people blowing sales. "Those new guys don't know how to control anyone," he's always bitching to J. C., "they're costing you money, man." J. C. knows he's right, too. A salesman who works his own deals always costs the house money. One of these days

J. C.'s going to kick ass. But not today. The hangover is bad today.

Killer watches a car pull on the lot. It looks like a clean, nice car, maybe three years old. The people look nice too, a middle-aged couple who obviously don't know what they want, first crawling into a big car and then into a tin can. Killer starts toward them. He needs to set them on that bigger car with the nice bonus. Screw the tin can.

Killer isn't dressed like the hot-shots with their blown hair and snappy shoes. He is a perfect shade of gray in a gray world: slightly rumpled short-sleeved shirt covering an ample belly, a tie that's the wrong width pulled loose at the neck. He needs a haircut—Killer always needs a haircut. He is quiet, almost shy, unassuming in the most disarming way, and friendly without showing his teeth too much. If you met him, you'd instantly feel comfortable and slightly superior.

"Hi, I'm Bob DeMarco; thanks for coming in to see us." He shakes both their hands, paying attention to them equally, watching for the signs that will say which person is the control, the decision-maker of the two. As Killer talks, his eyes constantly move from the couple to their car. "Folks, that's a mighty fine trade-in you have there," he volunteers. "I'll bet it's paid for, too." His observation is an important one. The couple's response will tell Killer what their payment range is if they're still paying. If they say, "Oh, it's paid for, just last month," he'll know the couple has lots of equity, a situation in which good salesmen always make more money. If they say, "We paid cash for it," Killer will know he's dealing with a different type of buyer.

These folks turn out to be the easiest marks, the type who say, "As long as the payment isn't too high, we're not concerned with what the car costs." Killer just loves payment buyers. He'll never mention once during the next hour what the couple's trade-in is worth, or what the difference in the old car and new car will be. He'll just talk payments. "After all, it's the payment that's important, isn't it, folks?" They nod yes. "Well, let me ask you then—if I can get the payments to a level that is satisfactory to you, will you buy the car today?" Well, who wouldn't say yes to that?

Now the three of them are sitting in Killer's office, surrounded by "Salesman of the Month" plaques, pictures of the DeMarco children, and several "Appreciation" scrolls from the local YMCA. The stock card for a pretty silver hardtop is lying on the desk right by a pad of buyer's orders and the two Cokes Killer insisted on purchasing. Both people have driven the hardtop—Killer insisted on that. After a few moments of small talk about the price of cars these days, Killer begins his quiet talk, a gentleman speaking to intelligent buyers.

"Now, I know you folks were paying a $150 per month on your old car. But the new one lists for several thousand more. You understand, then, that it will cost you a little more per month?" Sure, they understand that. "Mrs. Smith [Killer knows by now that she's the real decision-maker], I think we can have you riding in that car tomorrow. If a payment of $325 dollars sounds okay to you."

The couple's faces turn dove-white. She clears her throat. "Mr. DeMarco, there's just no way we can afford that . . . I don't think."

Killer knew that all along, he was just testing. They're not the bolting type, people who run out, or at least try to. They weren't *that* shocked, either. Killer continues talking, lowering in small amounts the payment, reminding them how much will be saved on maintenance, how much will be saved on gas. "Well, Mrs. Smith, I don't really believe the boss will let me get the payment below $250. If you remember how much more this car costs, it's really an excellent payment. If the house—my bosses—will agree, you will actually be saving $2500 dollars, the difference between a payment of $325 and a payment of $250." The two of them like that logic, and they look at each other silently.

"I'll tell you what," Killer adds happily, "I will even *make* the first payment for you. You won't have a payment for two and a half months. I really do want to see you folks satisfied."

And so the Smiths buy the car for $250 per month, and they're happy. The first payment is paid for them, too. Now, what's wrong with this deal? After all, Killer brought the payment down from $325 to $250, plus the Smiths received a free payment.

Everything is wrong. First, Killer knew all along he could sell them the car for $200 per month. And that wasn't a payment pulled out of the air, either. He knew how much $200 per month would buy. Second, Killer didn't lower the payments by cutting his deal. He simply quoted them the first payment based on financing for thirty-six months at the maximum interest rate, while the final payment was based on forty-eight months at the minimum rate. Killer's profit never changed. Third, the couple's car was appraised and had an actual wholesale value of $4500 dollars. But these people were not really interested in the value of their trade-in. "After all," the guy had said, "that 'trading' figure always keeps changing at different dealerships; that's why I stick with something that's simple, like my payment." So, is it Killer's fault the couple accepted $4000 for it, instead of $4500?

And finally, there's the "free" payment. In the car business this technique is usually called the "Christmas Club." Killer didn't reach into his pocket and make that payment; he simply added the amount of the payment to the total car price, then financed the $250 in their contract. Killer gave them a check for $250, sure. When he turned his deal into the finance office, he simply attached a note saying, "First payment financed; cut a check to the Smiths." But the Smiths would simply be paying that $250 back over the next forty-eight months, plus interest.

A nice sale like this calls for a celebration, so Killer makes a quick trip to the little food shop next door and downs a quick beer. Yes sir, this is going to be a fine day.

By twelve-thirty, Killer is sitting up at the used-car department. Most of the regular used-car salesmen go to lunch then, and it's an easy time to catch another "up." The car pulls in before Killer's feet are up on the desk, and a couple jumps out quickly, hurrying around a small used Datsun. These folks are jumping beans, nervous customers convinced they'll be taken wherever they buy. Killer is a master with this type of customer.

"Hi, folks, I'm Bob DeMarco. Boy, I'm glad I saw you! The guys have been trying to sell that car to someone for a month. It's just not a car you would want to own." The people stop walking and look at him. Here is an honest man, just what they've been looking for.

They are a young couple with little credit but a savings account of $2000 dollars. The type of car they purchase isn't important, as long as it's a good car with a "drive-out price" of $2000—tax, title, and tag included. And Killer knows just the car to fit their budget: the Lincoln with the $200-dollar bonus.

"Yes, Tommy, it's a better car than the Datsun. It's also a safer car. Did you read the story in the paper about the wife and two kids who were killed in a little car like this?" Killer looks at the Datsun as if it's infected with a dangerous, highly contagious germ. He pulls a copy of the article from his pocket. This article has switched lots of people from small cars.

Killer prices the Lincoln at $2100, even though it's on the books at $1000. As usual, he raises the asking price to fit the sucker's cash. He lets them drive it by themselves; that's against the rules, but Killer isn't worried about things like that. He knows the couple will be impressed with this kind of trusting attitude. They drive the Lincoln back to the new-car showroom and wander inside, looking for him.

Killer's in his office, already filling out the buyer's order, and he barely looks up as they enter. "Folks, sometimes I want to quit this business. Would you believe the boss says I can't sell the car for a dime less than $2100? That guy never gives up; he wants to take advantage of everyone. I'm going to sell it for $2000 anyway. What you had better do, though, is give me a check for the whole amount. It'll give me more ammunition when I'm arguing with the S.O.B." Of course, Killer hasn't seen the manager. But that's not really important. How can these people be so lucky? Killer is actually on their side. They buy the car.

It won't last them a week before conking out on the freeway. Killer earns the $200-dollar bonus, plus his regular commission. The buyers have no recourse when the car breaks down, either. Killer sold it to them "as is," with no warranty. "At this price, we can't give you a warranty," he had told them. "I'm going to be in trouble with the boss as it is."

Killer likes to take a break in the afternoon. Around five each day he checks out with the switchboard. "I've got to show a car across town, honey. I'll be back by seven." He winks at her. That Killer is such a sport.

The Dead End is a noisy bar, and after two Seven-and-Sevens have done their job, Killer barely hears the waitress. "Hey, Killer!" Cherry nudges his shoulder, drawing him from some other world. "They found you. Your boss is on the phone." Mr. DeMarco is not worried, however. When you are the high-gross man, and have been for years, people may yell and scream and threaten, but they do not fire you. It's one of the nicest realities about the car business: Whatever you've done in the past means nothing. It's what you do every day with the ups that makes you good.

A specialist is needed at the store, that's why J. C. called. One of the new boys has spent three hours with a guy who's on a "tank," one of those twenty-foot, $20,000-dollar jobs no one seems to be buying these days. The guy is an "allowance buyer"—all he cares about is how much he's allowed for his trade. The new boy has already given the car away, cut the deal to $200 above invoice, and he still can't sell the car. It's T. O. time.

It takes Killer exactly ten minutes to sell this man, or rather, for the man to sell himself. The new salesman just didn't know how to find the button. The man gets the allowance he wanted, too. He really does get a fantastic deal on the car. "Give me $5800 in allowance and I'll buy," he keeps saying.

"Sir, even if I do that, you're still going to have mighty high payments," Killer retorts.

"I don't give a damn, I can make payments; you just can't steal my car."

"Well, let me figure here a minute and see what they would be. On this much money, you'd want life and accident and health, right? A man like you knows how important that is. I'd even put some life insurance on your wife, too."

"If you meet my price, of course I want the insurance. I'm not an idiot." Sure.

Killer meets his price. He also puts him on "the chart," the highest interest rate allowed by law. He puts all the insurance in the payment, too. The front-end profit on the sale of this car is zero. But the back-end profit—financing— is over $1700 dollars. Specialists sure can work wonders.

It is a satisfying way to end the evening. Killer walks to the conference room, takes a bright orange piece of chalk, and writes "Killer's O.K. with me—signed Robert De-Marco" across the width of the Perk Board. "Over the hill, hell!" he mutters. Killer walks from the room and heads to his demo. "Just wait until tomorrow."

Our friend Killer is many persons, a composite of all salesmen I have worked with and known during the past ten years. And they are some of the best car salesmen you may have the misfortune to meet. I would like to own the dealership that employed ten like Killer.

By the lights of the automobile business, Killer is an honest man. As a matter of fact, he is an honest man by the lights of just about any business that involves selling. Don't think for a minute your local appliance store, insurance salesman, or even favorite restaurant are pure in their motivations. And, for God's sake, don't think that the "professional" people—doctors and lawyers and the like—are any more noble. How do you check the "gross" on your lawyer's time? Have you ever considered offering your doctor less than his normal payment? The guy would probably threaten you with a proctoscope.

The car business is different, however. Most people don't

lose $10 dollars or $100 dollars when they trade cars. They lose many hundreds or even a thousand. They buy used cars that won't provide them service through the first payment. They overbuy new cars and jeopardize their credit, only to find themselves "hung," unable even to sell their shiny new toys. The car business is one of the last roundups in America, the great slaughterhouse of wheeling and dealing, where millions of people each year willingly submit to being taken. The average man and wife in America pour more than $100,000 dollars down this hungry auto drain during their lifetimes.

It's not that automobile people are inordinately greedy, either. Virtually any dealership in our country will sell you a car for a small profit. It doesn't take the dealer long to receive a replacement. That same dealership will also work hard to find you a good used car and will sell you payment money for little or no profit on its part. None of these nice things will happen, however, unless you ask. Unless you really know what a few things are worth, such as your car and their car, the cost of money. Unless you really know the best times to buy. Unless you really understand the entire car-buying-and-selling process and understand yourself and your own motives.

This book is designed to help you understand all these things and more. It takes you on the other side—the salesman's and manager's and dealer's side. It listens in as the road hogs, dip-shop managers, F and I men, skaters, and whores do their magnificent magical acts. It turns the tables and tells you how to survive and profit. Every single portion of the buying and selling transaction is detailed and explained, step by step. I hope portions of the book will amuse and terrify you. Other portions will require a goodly amount of pencil work and time. But if you will take the time, you will become a knowledgeable buyer and a richer buyer. You will be more than a survivor in this tricky and complex maze.

Even knowledge won't help you, though, if you are a typical car buyer. I have always wanted to have the ostrich declared the national bird of car buyers. It would be the most appropriate symbol: one of those slick color renderings of a bird with its head buried in the ground, tail wagging in the wind. The average car buyer will balance his checkbook three times—no bank is going to cheat him or her out of a dime—then walk right into a friendly neighborhood showroom and blow, waste, throw away forever hundreds of dollars.

Why? Partly because that person doesn't know the business, but mainly because the vast majority of cars are bought by using emotional processes rather than rational ones. If the truth were really known, I would suspect that automobile maufacturers are guilty of spraying their cars with some secret nerve gas left over from World War I, one of those gases that made the enemy laugh as our troops took their weapons and lands from them.

Whatever the reasons for this lack of sense, don't read any further until you can at least guard against these moments of weakness. If deep in your heart, you are already taking this book as an excuse to trade carelessly; if your pulse quickens at the thought of a really luxurious car—after all, you're probably thinking, you'll save enough with the knowledge contained within to justify that purchase—then give this book to someone else. I am burdened with enough guilt without having you on my mind. After many years in the business—as a salesman, finance manager, and dealer—I have an adequate supply of remembrances of shorn lambs.

2
What You're Up Against: The World of Sellers and Selling

KILLER AND HIS "FAMILY"

"I mean to tell you, she was one classy dame, a real lady. And her figure? Oh, God! She had more curves and ripples than a roller coaster!" Killer was talking with his hands more than his mouth, entertaining the guys in their favorite "break room," the clean-up shop located behind the service department. On cold and wet days like this one, everyone seemed to head back there. It was a good place to hide from the boss, J. C. It was also a good place to hide the community bottle. Buzz and Ted, the new guy, were there. Forrest DeLong was there, too. Even Kip had joined the sipping party this day. He was a retired colonel, a quiet type of guy who never really seemed to fit in comfortably with the off-color conversations and endless streams of four-letter words that constitute most in-house discussions at automobile stores.

Ted took the bottle next and sweetened his coffee. He was maybe twenty-two, had moved to town several weeks earlier, and had sold no more than two cars during his first weeks at the store. Ted wiped his lips with his right thumb and began to talk. Maybe it was the juice. Half-and-Half at eleven-thirty would untie any tongue.

"Well, boys, let me tell you something. I don't know whether this business is going to bore me to death or starve me to death. I mean, where are all those big commissions J. C. told me about when he hired me? Hell, I'd do better working for the Boy Scouts or something."

"Ted, from what they tell me at the Dead End, you'd be a better Girl Scout," Killer volunteered. "I understand you chase just about every tail that flies by."

"Hell, yes, I do! After standing around here all day talking with jerks, I've got to have some recreation. How do you guys put up with all the crap around here? If the flakes don't drive you crazy, then it's J. C. or Don. I don't think they know any other words than 'get on the phone, boys,' or 'let me see some deals, boys' or 'let's get some ups in here, boys'—why don't they just record all that bull, play it over the P. A. and go play golf with Davies?"

"Sure," Kip added. "I don't think Davies even likes to talk with *those* guys. Owners don't want to get their pinkies dirty."

Killer raised his hand. "Now, wait a minute. I don't want to hear any of you damn guys talking about my dealer. I want you to know he talks to *me*. Of course, that was last Christmas. And he called me Bill. Then he got confused and called me Will." Killer started laughing. "Maybe I'll give him one of my cards the next time we meet. As a matter of fact, I think I'll ask him to *pay* for my cards the next time I see him."

Killer had hit a nerve. Forrest spoke first. "Hey, Killer, I was going to ask you that. I don't mind paying for my cards, but, hell, I hear we're going to be paying for a lot of things. Like our demos. Don even told me that we're going to have to sell them before we get another one, too. And drive junkers from the used car lot until they're sold."

Killer was high man on the pole at Davies Motors, and he liked that. Everyone came to him for the real scoop on what was happening at the store. "Yeah," he said. "Davies says we've got too many demos in service, and he's also yelling about the money. Within the month, I'll bet we'll all be paying at least fifty bucks for our cars. But that isn't the worst of it. They're raising the pack on all the new cars again, and they're cutting our percentage on financing to three percent."

Killer's words seemed to light a very short fuse in each of the guys, and Forrest was the hottest. "Like hell he is! I'll be damned if I'm going to hang around this place and put up with that. Hell, there are a lot of other stores in this town." Forrest's hot head was probably one of the reasons he was a vagabond in the business, spending one or two months at one dealership and then lighting across town at some other. But he wouldn't be missed. There would probably be a hundred DeLongs at Davies Motors in the next twenty-four months. The Forrest DeLongs of the world may make up the vast majority of automobile salesmen, and they may sell lots of cars in the aggregate, but they are always the low men on the scale of respect.

At the opposite end of the scale was Kip, the Colonel. Kip had been at the store for five years, running the fleet operation, and was never a part of the pack. He rarely took a drink with the guys, either. But, at this particular moment, he served a really important function at this meeting of the Half-and-Half Club. He heard the door open as they were talking, quickly silenced the group with a "shhh," then walked quietly around the corner. He returned double-speed, looking like some kid caught in the closet with his sister. "It's J. C.!" he whispered. Everyone quickly lit up cigarettes, hoping perhaps the smoke would cover up the smell of Jim Beam, or maybe even throw a wall to make them invisible. J. C. sauntered around the corner and ambled toward them, as if he were simply taking a Sunday stroll. No one spoke as they stood there, waiting for the explosion.

J. C. just looked at them, his lips moving apart enough to make a smacking sound—like some wild animal's anticipation of the bite to come. "Well, boys." J. C. looked from man to man, no expression betraying his thoughts. He looked at Killer last. "I sure could use some Half-and-Half—my coffee's cold."

It was an unexpected comment. But that's why most of the guys liked him. J. C. was a real bastard at times, but just as the guys were ready to write him off, he would say or do something like that. No one could really figure J. C. out. No one cared to at the moment, though. They all sat on the floor, their feet pulled up, bodies in a semicircle.

Buzz broke the ice. "Well, J. C., if you'd send someone for marshmallows, we could have a campfire." His comment broke them up.

"Hell, yes," J. C. said. "I tell you what, we could get a van and go to my cabin. We'd probably sell as many cars there as here today." J. C.'s statement didn't really seem like a cut—it sounded more like the truth. Business had been lousy, real lousy, for the past two weeks, and no one had gotten more heat than J. C. "Boys, I'll tell you what. I think all the ups have just packed up and left town. I talked with some of the other stores a while ago, and none of them are doing any business."

It's the damndest thing about the car business. Customers either come in in droves, filings to the magnet, or they don't come in at all. After a few years, people in the business accept that fact. Or, at least, the employees do. The dealers of the world never accept it, and that's where the heat always comes from first.

The coffee Thermos was sitting on empty and the Jim Beam down to a third when the real war stories began. The new kid, Ted, started them rolling. "J. C., I don't mean this to sound bad or anything, but doesn't anything exciting ever happen in this business? I thought selling clothes was bad, but, unless you sell someone, the days get awful long."

"Hey, J. C.—Ted doesn't know about the Smith thing. And from what I hear, he'd *better* know about it." Mention of the "thing" didn't bring a smile to anyone's face. It had made headlines around the country, really big headlines in the scandal rags, and no one felt it was typical of the business. But God, had it thrown a wrench in the operation of All-City Motors, a well-respected and successful dealership in a neighboring state.

J. C. didn't look at any of them as he began to talk but quietly laid out the story, as if he were reading some bedtime story to a group of kids. "It was bad, real bad." He stopped just long enough to take one final sip. "A new salesman, the guy had been at All-City maybe three months, was sitting in the lounge when he got a page to the showroom. His name was Ed Vista. There was a man waiting there to see him—from what everyone said, he was a real nice person, too, real friendly. Well, anyway, Ed thought the guy wanted to buy a car, and he took him into a big closing office just off the showroom, one with glass partitions. Shirley Kubek in the office was standing outside and just happened to be looking at Ed's face when he turned snow-white and started to stand up. The guy sitting across from him stood up first, and Shirley said, just as Ed raised his hand, the guy raised a gun and shot him in the head." J. C. looked around the room and continued. "Then the guy just sat down. All hell broke loose; the place went crazy. Joe Weeks, the owner, heard it and came down there, but the guy was still holding the gun, so he cleared out the showroom and waited on the police. The guy was so damned calm, he introduced himself to the cops and even tried to shake hands with them."

J. C. had a manner, a certain way of sounding and gesturing in some enormously kind fashion whenever he talked about bad things, and as he continued, his face and arms seemed to evoke the senselessness of this incident better than the words. "The guy finally told the police Ed was having an affair with his wife. No one knows if that's true or not, she won't say. But, hell, the salesman may have been a little crazy, but he had a wife, too. He also had a son not much younger than my youngest." He shook his head. "I mean to tell you, this is a crazy world." J. C. sat there, scratching the back of his neck, twisting his head as if to loosen the very tight screws that seemed to push into every nerve.

"J. C.?" Ted broke the quiet. "I was telling the guys what a hard time I'm having making any money. At the rate I'm going, I'll be dead and gone to hell before I see one of those W-2's you told me about—you know, the $40,000-dollar years?"

J. C. grinned and reached over to Ted, grabbing him around the neck in a bear hug. "Son, be patient. Why, you're sitting in the room with one of those guys right now. Killer, tell him what you made last year."

Killer blushed just enough to look modest and stretched his arms out. "Hell, J. C., I've had better years than the last one. But I made $75,000 dollars, which isn't bad, I guess." You can bet your B. P. on that statement. Killer was in the top tenth of one percent in the country last year. He continued to talk. "But, hell, it took me fifteen years and a lot of work to get to that. And I spend nearly $10,000 a year on things for my regular customers, too. Plus, I really do work, you know." He smiled, and started to speak again before any of the guys could stop him. "And yes, I do sell *lots* of cars at the Dead End. Who ever said drinkers don't buy cars, anyway?"

Smart move. Killer's visits to the favorite automobile watering hole were one of the worst-kept secrets in the business. But Killer really didn't want the conversation changed to that subject. He had just started a tale about how the business *really* used to be when Don Burns, one of the new-car managers, came walking around the corner.

Don showed no surprise but started talking quickly. "Excuse me, fellows, but there are some ups on the lot and, J. C., Davies is on the phone. I told him you were in the closing booth with some customers." It was a good breaking point in the camp meeting, and the group stood up and almost in unison, reached in their pockets for the nice little bottles of Binaca Mouth Freshener. J. C. started laughing as he pushed down the little nozzle and closed the meeting between sprays. "Well, boys, if you'll excuse me, I've got to call my broker. It looks like Binaca stock is going up again."

It had been a nice morning, and the guys headed back to the showroom single-file. "Hey, Buzz." Don Burns walked up behind him, pulling him back a little as the others went on. "Buzz, I hate to tell you this, but there's another process server in the showroom. I told the man you were out, but he says he's going to wait on you. Since J. C.'s in a good mood, do you want me to ask him to talk to the man? If he can't put him off, maybe he'll pay him."

Buzz looked just a tad upset—nothing really monumental in a process server, he thought. Car people were pretty used to those people. As a group, car salesmen aren't exactly known for their good credit ratings. "No, but thanks," he said. "Hell, I might just as well add his to the pile. Thank God, J. C. doesn't care, though. I'll go see him now. At least it's in the family."

Buzz was right, too. It's one big family.

INSIDE THE FAMILY:
DEALERS, SALES MANAGERS,
AND SALESMEN

Like any business, the automobile business is its own little world, populated by folks who live and work in a rigid pecking order: first, the salesmen, who come and go just as quickly as a week of twelve-hour days; then the sales managers, guys who crack the emotional whip to keep the sellers working; and then general managers, who feed and tend to the crops of money that flow quickly in and out of parts departments, body shops, finance and insurance offices, and new, used, and wholesale car and truck sales. At the top of the whole pecking order is the dealer, usually a self-made man who grew up in the days when the automobile business made the Mafia pale in the depths of its dishonesty. If you're over fifty, you probably have your own memories of keys thrown on the roof at your friendly neighborhood car store—a nice technique to keep you there—or of new cars with no price stickers, or ads with prominently displayed "Caveat Emptor" notations, or a used-car lot filled with cars showing suspiciously low mileage.

During the late fifties and early sixties, many of those practices began to change. Federal law made it a crime to turn back speedometers, and mileage statements provided some measure of accountability for each car's mileage. The manufacturers finally succumbed to pressure and began placing "suggested retail price" stickers on most cars. And, more importantly, buyers began to revolt from the more offensive sales techniques of car stores. By the early seventies, horror stories were less frequent, and dealers and manufacturers crowed loudly over the new-found professional status of their business.

During all these years of change, however, one terribly important thing has not changed in the car business, and that is the absolute ignorance of the average car buyer. While improvements have made the selling of cars a more accountable process, the customer's knowledge of how dealerships function, of financing, of dollar value has remained back in the Dark Ages. Sure, car people want your mind back there and certainly aren't concerned with your proper education, but that's not the problem. The average customer either thinks the whole car-buying process is too difficult to master or else feels that perhaps too much knowledge will take the romance from what has always been regarded as a mystical process. Unfortunately, the only really mystical event is how quickly your money disappears. The automobile business is a magnificent money machine; it eats every cent you have, puts you in debt just long enough to require another chariot, and then eats again. And if you are going to have some chance of muzzling the beast, you will need to understand the opposition.

Who are you dealing with? On the salesman level, you are basically dealing with three types of people. Most stores have a few old-timers, the guys who were selling cars back in the days when list price was any figure the salesman wanted to create. These guys have dealt with every type of customer: the easy ones, the suspicious ones, and the crooked ones. They are professionals in the sense that years of selling have provided them a steady flow of repeat customers who have always dealt with them and always will.

Hanging around in the corners of every showroom and lot are the young eager beavers, the "floor whores," who pounce on the first person that walks in cold, just hoping the poor sucker really wants to buy and has the credit to do so. The next floor whore who waits on you could be a college kid passing his time waiting on a good job or an ex-con. One of the nicest things about the car business is its ability to forgive the past. If you want to be a salesman, your past doesn't matter; as a matter of fact, it really doesn't matter if you drink too much, or are hiding from the police, or have a couple of wives. All that matters is how efficiently you can sell cars. Most of the floor whores have slender roots, popping up at different stores every few months. To them the business is just a pit stop.

Many dealerships also have their share of former colonels and captains and noncoms, folks who have retired from the service and enjoy the freedom of being in business for themselves. Few dealerships employ women, though. In fact, until the early 1980s car dealerships were perhaps the most male-oriented businesses in America.

Regardless of the type of salesman who is waiting on you, he's probably not getting rich selling you or anyone else a car. Most dealerships pay their salesmen twenty to thirty percent of the "front-end gross," the actual profit on the sale of the new car. Or, rather, they pay them twenty or thirty percent of the profit above the "pack." Let's say the actual cost to the dealer of your average Expenso Gargantula is $12,000 dollars. But when the dealership's title clerk types up a stock card on that particular car, the invoice price is coded as $12,500 dollars. This "pack" is supposed to help the dealer pay his overhead. In reality it's just another way to keep from paying the salesman his due. Incidentally, many dealerships encourage their salesmen to show this pack figure to recalcitrant customers. "Here, Mr. Jones, that's the actual cost of the car. If you will pay me a $400-dollar profit over that figure, the car is yours." Presto, the house has just made $900 dollars. Most dealerships also pay their salesmen a small percentage of the profits from the sale of financing and life and accident and health insurance.

The average car salesman sells six or seven cars a month. He averages $125 dollars per car in commissions, if he's lucky. But on those six or seven cars, the house—the dealer—has grossed $5000 to $7000 dollars. But whoever said life was fair?

Another factor that tends to shorten the careers of salesmen is the tremendous pressure to succeed each hour of each day, a success measured on only one scale—selling. Because the average car salesman, especially the new-car salesman, is invariably on the downside of the income scale, this pressure to sell is not something solely manufactured by dealerships, either. If anyone other than the customer is "worked," milked of more than his fair share of money in the car business, it would be that fellow waiting on you. As a matter of fact, if anyone is more ignorant than the customer of the many ways people are taken in the car business, it's the salesman.

The house, the dealer, does its best to keep the boys working the front line from knowing about things like factory incentives: "write-downs"—used cars that have been lowered in value because of their condition or time on the lot; and "holdbacks"—extra profit built into each car invoice but not considered "cost" by the dealer. Dealers seem to think of their salesmen as cheap things to replace. They may smile at them, give them a bonus for Christmas, and occasionally visit a sales meeting, but most dealers hold the men who make them money in disdainful contempt.

Take Gary Oliver Davies, Killer's big boss. Sure, he started in the business as a lot boy, someone who serves as the dealership "gofer." Sure, he sold cars for a few years. But Mr. Davies doesn't think he has anything in common with the boys who work for him, managers included. "Hell, I'm smarter than those bastards—that's why I'm the boss," Davies likes to tell folks. If a psychiatrist were really to look into the head of Davies—probably many dealers—I would suspect that he would find lots of contempt piled up there. Contempt for the salesmen and other employees, contempt for the customers, and contempt for the whole messy world of cars. Maybe the money makes them that way.

Gary Oliver Davies was reviewing his monthly Dealer's Financial Statement, the total summary of his store's performance that must be sent to the factory each month. It's a complicated form, encompassing hundreds of figures and percentages on everything, from "selling gross, new and used"—the amount of the monthly gross from new and used departments left after paying variable expenses such as advertising, used cars, repairs, and commissions—to "service sales per service order." Davies was feeling pretty good. Though the year had been one of the worst in the history of the business, his store was showing in this ninth month a net profit just in excess of $270,000 dollars. The statement showed average new-car sales of one hundred fifty units per month, year-to-date, and average used-car sales of two hundred twenty-five units. His year-to-date profit also showed a tidy contribution from the parts department.

Parts was paying the majority of the fixed overhead on his whole store. His average new-car gross per unit was $650 dollars.

Davies paused at that figure. "Hell—$650—*that's* the real problem," he reflected. "You just can't make real money in years like this." Davies was thinking about the last really good year—the year his store had a net profit before write-downs of $850,000 dollars. Now *that* was nice. It was a time when the general population seemed to have a severe case of car fever. Once some customers came in and looked at an $8000-dollar car with a $1600-dollar profit margin. In slow times Davies would have happily had his managers accept a $200-dollar profit on that car. But in good times? Killer had been waiting on the couple. When the man had asked, "Well, what is the least you will take for that car?" Killer had looked the guy in the eye and said, "$8000 dollars." The guy had started to object, but his wife yelled, "Shut up, Henry, I want that car." Davies just loved that memory.

Davies' eyes continued down the statement. The service department looked like it was doing better. They were writing an average of two hundred and fifty R.O.s, repair orders, per week, at an average sale of $95 dollars. I guess my talk with the writers did some good, Davies thought; the average R.O. sale was up this month. But why did he have to keep kicking ass to make people work? Davies was sure—real sure—that no one worked around his place unless he kicked ass.

Then Davies looked at the used-car numbers. Grosses were really high—they always were when new cars weren't selling—but he saw a figure that drew his hand to the phone, something really bad. He paged Timothy Raxalt, the used-car manager.

Raxalt was in his office quickly. As a matter of fact, whenever the employees heard Davies paging, they always dropped whatever they were doing. He didn't page people often, and when he did, the reason was invariably unpleasant. There were no pleasantries during this meeting, either. Davies was talking before Raxalt had a chance to sit. "How many times do I have to tell you about ninety-day cars? I want you to look at every one of the used cars over ninety days and write them down again. Then, get some wholesalers in here, match up some of the lead with a few good cars, and get that junk out of here. I don't want any ninety-day cars on this lot next week." Davies was hot as he talked; his statement showed over $40,000 dollars tied up in cars that were over ninety days old. That money wasn't working for him. Idle money is dead money in the car business, and there would be no dead money at this dealership.

Raxalt didn't argue. It didn't matter that virtually every one of these cars was still on the lot because of Davies, that Davies had insisted on their high appraisals. It didn't matter that most of the cars were trade-ins of Davies' pals—sailing buddies and bankers and a couple of local pro football players. "Look," Davies continued, "I pay you to do your job. And *this*"—he pointed to the statement—"isn't doing your job."

Raxalt left without saying a word. He wasn't particularly upset, either. I mean, it's what you expect from the boss. He's smarter. Or at least that's what he says.

Gary Davies *is* a smart man, and there are many dealers out there like him who make money regardless of the temperament of the car-buying public. When new-car sales are down, they push service, parts, and used cars. When new-car sales are hot, they push their men to raise the gross.

These dealers will survive handsomely. They will weather any bad year the car business can bring. As a matter of fact, many will buy *more* stores during bad years. For instance, during the past three years, hundreds of dealerships with poor management have been purchased by management-oriented dealers such as Davies.

And that's the key: though Davies doesn't like to admit it, his best talent is hiring the best managers. Like J. C. Hollins. J. C. is really an odd type to be in the car business, especially as a general manager. He is college-educated, from a family of professionals, and much more sophisticated in his personal tastes than most managers. He is also a good man, the type of person who thinks nothing of lending his men money, even a guy he's fired for one thing or the other. J. C. is comfortable with people outside the car fraternity, mixing well with just about anyone. He belongs to Rotary, coaches his youngest son's Little League team, and goes to church, too. But in the car business, J. C. is known for one talent: he is a troubleshooter. That's why Davies hired him away from another dealership five years ago, in the midst of a recession.

J. C. was used to people like Davies calling him in the slow times. He'd also heard the same sob story over and over again: a small dealer who grew rich, started to play, and forgot to tend his store. Hell, J. C. had known the problems before he'd asked the questions, but he had asked them anyway.

"Well, Gary, you say there's water on your used-car lot. Just how much?"

"Hell, I don't know—I just know that we can't wholesale a damn one of our cars." Davies had approximately $300,000 dollars' worth of used cars at his store—the actual dollar amount his people figured the cars were worth when they traded for them. If those cars can be wholesaled for only $275,000 dollars, he's got $30,000 dollars in water. Water is an obsession with dealers—it's lost money just as surely as if someone took the same amount of money from their pockets. The problem develops when appraisers put more than wholesale in a trade—or when someone's hand is in the till.

"Well, what about your R.O.s? If you're losing a lot of money in the body shop, have you checked the R.O.s?"

No, Davies didn't have the time to have someone pull through old repair orders. "No one would be stealing in the body shop, anyway. The manager back there is an old friend of mine."

J. C. would want to know more about that later, but right then he wanted to know a little bit more about the used-car operation. "Gary, I know you say you've got water, but are your people wholesaling cars anyway? Are they even breaking out of any of them?"

"Hell no! Every used car we wholesale is at a loss. I think we sold three cars last month at what we had in them. The rest were all losses."

The phone conversation had lasted no more than twenty minutes, but J. C. smelled at least two rats. He was also very interested in the dealership's deposit procedure when new cars were sold. "Tell me, what type of receipts do you give your customers after the business office is closed?" Davies wasn't sure but believed that the night manager simply wrote them out a receipt. "Gary there's just one thing more. How did you hire your present general manager, did you know him, or what?"

"Listen, the guy is not a crook. He just doesn't seem to know what's going on around here," Davies retorted.

J. C. thanked the man for the call, and added, "Oh Gary,

I want to tell you one thing. I don't think your general manager is the only one who doesn't know what's going on. And if you hire me, you can be damn well sure I'm going to fire whoever needs firing—including your buddy in the body shop. Now, do you want to do business on that basis?"

His last comments are probably the reason that J. C. and Davies aren't friends but, rather, business associates. Davies really didn't have a choice in that conversation, however, for the waters at his store covered more than the used-car lot. Mr. Davies had made two classic mistakes as he climbed quickly up the dealer's ladder: he had hired friends and at the same time stepped away from the daily operations of his business.

When J. C. took over the Davies store, it took him less than a week to find three sets of sticky fingers. His first morning there, he'd invited the used-car manager out for a cup of coffee. The guy was too nervous in the beginning, and J. C. noticed that the nervousness increased considerably when he casually mentioned, "You know, I noticed that you wholesale a lot of cars to the same people pretty regularly. I sure would like to meet those people." The guy's nervousness turned quickly to physical shaking. J. C. just smiled at him. "And I also noticed that you sell a lot of trades to some of the salesmen every now and then. I didn't know Mr. Davies allowed any curbing here." Curbing refers to the practice of salesmen buying nice trade-ins from their own stores and then selling them privately. It's a nice way to make a few bucks.

The guy just sat there, his hand over the coffee cup and eyes anyplace but on J. C., who continued. "You know, I once had a guy working for me that you might be interested in. This S.O.B. would have a nice used car come on the lot, maybe a car that was worth $2000. Nine times out of ten it would be a real pretty car, too, one that makes a nice resale piece. But, no, this guy would call up some wholesaler—as a matter of fact, he would usually call up the *same* wholesaler, and he'd sell it to the man for $2000. But—damn, this was a funny thing—he would always tell the man to give him a check for $1800 and the rest in cash. I never could figure out where that $200 went to, either." J. C. paused just long enough for the words to press down on the guy a little more. "And, do you know what else he'd do?—I guess he did this just because he was generous or something—well, that same wholesaler would come by the used-car lot with some sled worth $1000 dollars. The hog would want to sell it to us for about a thousand, too, but my friend would pay him $1400 for it. Hell, we'd be stuck with that tub *and* $400 dollars in water. Well, anyway, one day I talked to the wholesaler myself, and do you know what? The bastard said *he* only got $1200 of that money— he'd given the rest to my friend."

J. C. didn't say anything after finishing that little story. Instead he just sat there drinking his coffee. In a couple of minutes, the man sitting across from him simply said, "Well, what do you want me to do now? I've already spent the money." He had, too. All $80,000 dollars.

The body-shop skim was just as easy to find. When a body-shop foreman needs parts to repair a car, he simply fills out a parts ticket and sends that ticket over to the parts department. Each part is "charged out" to the ticket. The part is also listed on the repair order attached to the windshield of whatever car is being repaired. In theory, the parts listed on the R.O. should always be on a parts ticket also. But Mr. Davies' old friend the body-shop foreman had a much better idea: he would contract for private repair work at his house, check the parts out from the dealership, list them on a legitimate repair order in the shop, and then have free parts for his home repair work. J. C. caught that quickly, just by comparing the new parts on a few repaired cars with the parts listed on the car's R.O. He readily found a car with an old windshield that should have had a new one.

Another nice way some folks try to make money on the sly is simply to tear up repair orders. J. C. had that problem at another store he'd managed. It was a real sweet operation. The service cashier would wait for some customer to pay cash for repair work, then put the cash in her pocket rather than the register and quickly destroy the repair order.

All of these little tricks are not too hard to catch in a tight store operation. But that had been the problem with Mr. Davies' store—nothing had been tight. J. C. was one of the best specialists in the business because he never trusted a soul and always watched the little things. "I'll tell you what," he was fond of saying, "if you watch the little things, the big things will take care of themselves."

Management in the car business is a "closed thing"—you won't find, for instance, the sales manager from an insurance company hired to be the sales manager of a car store, and for good reason. There are few businesses in the world as complicated as the car business. A good general manager or sales manager at a car store needs years of on-the-job training simply to understand what is happening at his store. And J. C. Hollins is a good example of a good general sales manager. He understands that a store is like a giant sieve: regardless of how much is poured into it, there are literally hundreds of little places where profits can be drained away. There's the salesman who promises a set of floor mats to close a deal and neglects to tell his manager. That's $30 dollars off the top. Or the lot boy neglects to check the coolant in a nice trade-in, and a $4000-dollar piece of merchandise quickly needs a $300-dollar engine overhaul. These all add up.

And then there's the cash flow problem. Even in the most profitable dealerships, cash flow is a daily challenge and headache. Like the Wade deal. The Wades paid $17,300 dollars for a hardtop that cost the dealership $16,000 dollars, a nice profit. But the Wades had a one-year-old trade-in that was worth $9000 dollars in real cash. After subtracting that $9000 from the dealership's selling price of $17,300, the dealership received a check from the Wades for $8300. The dealership then had to pay off the "floor plan" on the new car, $16,000 dollars. On paper, the store made a $1300 profit, sure. But in cash-flow terms, they had to pay out the difference between $8300 and the $16,000 owed on the car's floor plan. Until the Wades' trade-in is sold, the dealership will have a net cash *loss* of $7700 dollars. There's an old axiom in the car business that selling lots of cars with trade-ins can break a dealership.

And finally, there's the personnel problem. After the experience of running a staff of car salesmen most sales managers and general managers can relate really well to the den mother of a Cub Scout pack or, more appropriately, to the house mother at the Lotsa Whoopie Fraternity house, just down the road from Worldly Wise U. Most car salesmen end up working in car stores by happenstance rather than career planning. Because they sell under tremendous pressure and get the smallest cut of the profits, it's no wonder these stepchildren have a short tenure. This stepchild attitude also accounts partially for the rambunctious nature of salesmen as a group. J. C., for instance, has received more than one call from the local gendarmes to bail out a salesman. He's always firing guys for not selling or "skating," stealing another salesman's customer.

J. C. doesn't resent all these problems, either, because they are a given in his job. A general manager in most stores doesn't have the luxury of stepping back from his business as his boss does. He is on the front line each day, taking flack from the dealer, the customers, the guys in the service and parts departments, and the new- and used-car sales boys. He's dealing with the factory, trying to resist their rep's weekly cajoling to buy a few more of this or that slow-moving car, to order more tilt steering wheels, and to shape up things like the restrooms and the general condition of the used cars. He's worried about the "floor-planners," the guys who come by without notice to be sure each new car's "mortgage" is paid on the day the car is sold. Automobile lending institutions, the guys who loan dealers money to floor-plan their stock, don't like dealers who sell their collateral—the cars—but neglect to pay off their loans.

Each moment of his waking day, the general manager is also watching the sales board. Dealers don't want success every month or quarter; they demand success—selling—every hour. J. C. knows this and doesn't begin to smile inside himself until the customers' names start going up on that tote board each morning. If by noon the list isn't long, he begins to growl to the sales manager. If by two the list is still short, he'll call a special sales meeting. If by five the deals are still short, he'll call another meeting. "Now, God damn it, *no one* is leaving this place until I see some paper," he'll tell the guys.

It's the J. C.'s who make a car store tick. You may not see them much, may never meet one, but they are there, pulling the strings, orchestrating the four-wheeled ballet of buyers and sellers. And that's where you, the buyer, enter the picture.

First the Good News:
They Really Will Sell You
a Car for Less

In combativeness and in pure, raw competition, the automobile business makes the forces of Attila the Hun look like a group of butterfly collectors running through the fields in their safari shorts, squealing, "It bit me, it bit me!" Salesmen froth at the mouth each time some customer says, "Well, there's a car just like your car just down the road," and sales managers age quickly each time they see a customer's pocket filled with cards from dealerships selling the very same merchandise. Everyone in the store knows that the fickle nature of the customer rivals any teenybopper's loyalty to her latest beau. Some customers have actually bought cars at below cost thanks to this rivalry between brothers.

Car dealerships survive this siege mentality by adhering closely to the "bird-in-hand" theory: a definite $200-dollar profit, right now, today, is much better than some vague chance of selling the car to someone for a $500-dollar profit tomorrow. This theory is especially strong in today's environment of consumer disenchantment. Dealers are continually crying that people have been brainwashed into believing foreign cars are better than domestic ones, or that the government has begun to legislate dealers right out of the business, or that customers "come into dealerships expecting us to practically give away a new car, and we're not going to do that." These last sentiments, which belong to Joseph Ricci, president of a Grosse Pointe car store, are echoed by the vast majority of dealerships around the country, and the sentiment is a valid one. After years of believing that car stores are the closest thing to some shill game on Forty-second Street, the car-buying public has finally decided to fight back.

Unfortunately, the confrontation is not productive for either party. Dealerships lose sales every day simply because their customers are too paranoid and uninformed to accept legitimate buys-of-a-lifetime. And customers are taken every day because salesmen feel some desperate need to rip off easy marks for all they're worth, as some form of retribution against all the nonbelievers who won't believe the truth under any circumstances.

These realities may not be pleasant, but they do present the informed car buyer with the best opportunity to buy a new car at the lowest possible price. That fact in itself is not the answer you need, however. Dealerships do not survive, much less prosper, by selling new cars. The new car is simply one of the first steps in a multi-step transaction of churning money, and you will be lost from the moment you set foot on any lot in America unless you understand each step.

But let's not complicate the most important fact: Virtually every dealership in America will sell you a car for less. They will give you maximum dollar for your trade, if you want to trade. They will even sell you money to buy that car at a rate that may rival your bank's. All you have to do is ask. And know a few things in the process, like how to handle salesmen.

Take the Webbs. They could have purchased a car very cheaply—*if* they had managed their salesman correctly. The Webbs had been to three other stores, writing down carefully each discount and list price on the three cars that interested them. They really liked the one Forrest DeLong was showing them now, too.

"Forrest, if you'll sell me that car for $6500, we'll buy it,"

Carl Webb spouted out. "We're tired of looking and I'm tired of dickering. I am going to buy a car today."

Forrest looked at the price code on his stock card and figured the guy's offer as a $100-dollar deal. There was no trade to sweeten the deal. He didn't really like the couple; they were too sure of what they wanted and what they would pay. Why the hell should he sell a car and make $25 bucks, his share of the $100? "Carl, you may buy a car today, but you're not going to buy it for $6500, at least not this car."

Forrest just sat there, a bundle of frustration and impatience. The Webbs didn't know enough to insist their offer be submitted, and they left the showroom, walking past J. C. as they headed to their car. Oh God, Forrest thought, *that* was a mistake. I should have T.O.'d them. He was right. J. C. was at his desk in a second.

"Why the hell are those people leaving without talking to someone else!" J. C.'s tone wasn't that of a question, and Forrest backed up two steps. J. C.'s words betrayed a hotness all the guys knew too well.

"The guy wouldn't pay anything over a $100, and I knew you wouldn't take that, J. C."

"How did you know that? You don't know *what* I'll take. Did you hear what I said about letting people walk?" De-Long shifted his weight to his right leg, but said nothing. "Son, you're not long for this world if you keep that up," J. C. said as he walked away. He was right, too.

DeLong won't last long in the car business—he's too independent, likes to work his own deals, decide for himself when the profit is right. You may have met his type before, the guy who never has a boss. Car stores don't want this kind of person working for them for a simple reason. If your salesman is bossing his own deal, then he is your adversary, the person you must conquer in the battle for money. However, in the sixties, many dealerships refined a nice psychological ploy to remove this adversary relationship from salesman and customer. The technique involved large doses of the words "they" and "we." "They" represents the house, the bosses, the greedy people who must approve a salesman's deal. If Forrest DeLong had been using this system in dealing with the Webbs, he would have said, "Mr. Webb, I don't think *they* will accept $6500 dollars for the car, but why don't *we* write it up at $6500, and then I'll go in there and fight for *us*. Remember, I don't make any money if you don't buy a car."

The Webbs now have a friend, someone on their side against the house. It's a nice system, and while no dealership likes to sell cars for a $100-dollar profit, they will probably do that *if* the customer can't be raised. There is one small catch to this system, though: Would you know a small profit even if it bit you? Perhaps you could just ask your salesman, "Am I really getting the best price?" while at the same time gazing with trust into his eyes. That would probably be as safe as entrusting your goldfish to the cat.

Well, Just How Honest Are Car People?

The vast majority of them are just as honest as you are. And therein lies the problem. They will not lift bills from your wallet when you leave the room or take advantage of your pretty daughter if the opportunity arises. The majority of them will be honest with you—as long as that honesty serves their ultimate purpose: a sale with a nice fat profit attached. A car salesman's greatest sin is not the direct lie but the sin of omission. For instance, the salesman has no obligation to make less money just because you don't know any better. Can you imagine any businessman in his right mind saying, "Oh, that's a $1000-dollar profit—let's cut it back to $500"?

This sin of omission is involved in virtually every step of a car transaction. No salesman will tell you that a certain car line historically has maintenance problems, or that he is allowing you less for your trade-in than its usual wholesale value, or that an "easy payment" plan—one designed to stretch your payments years beyond the prime life of the vehicle—is a dangerous financial business for those of us that live from paycheck to paycheck.

This belief and acceptance of "convenient" truth by the nice fellow sitting across from you in the closing booth unfortunately limits, and perhaps precludes, any chance of helpful answers. A visit to an automobile dealership will probably be your closest opportunity to experience a great diplomat's negotiations with an adversary: lots of smiles and nice comments, but absolutely no credibility in anything anyone says. Let's not call your local dealership a den of thieves, because they're not that. Let's just say it's a house of one-sided truth.

The Salesman's Greatest Talent

Killer was back in the service department, standing next to the young kid who spent his days taking care of the used cars. The kid was removing a worn tire from the left rear wheel of a car Killer had sold the night before. Killer had taken the car to the state inspection station just an hour earlier; he'd promised his customer the car would pass inspection, and the damn thing had failed because of that tire. The kid slipped it off the car and jacked up the left front wheel of another used car, removing the tire and transferring it to Killer's car. It was a good tire, one that would pass inspection quickly. And it would just as quickly be replaced with the worn tire once it was time for Killer's delivery. Killer smiled. Those damned inspection people were just too picky, he thought. And not nearly as smart as they thought. He walked toward the showroom, stopping in the customer's lounge for a Coke, barely noticing the old man sitting right by the machine.

"Hey, DeMarco, what are you doing back here!" the man said enthusiastically. He was an old customer of Killer's, who had purchased his last new car over four years ago and was sitting in the lounge waiting for the guys to finish a quick tuneup.

Killer smiled again—the customer's lounge had always brought him luck. He grabbed the guy by the arm and said, "Hey, Loren, come with me. I want you to feel something sexy." The two of them walked back to the employees' parking lot, and Killer opened the door to his new demo.

"Loren, just rub your hand over this carpet and tell me what that reminds you of." Killer walked around to the other side of the car and sat in the front seat. Loren was already sitting in the driver's seat and took the keys without a second thought.

"Here, feel the padding over your head," Killer said, as both men pressed their hands hard against the ceiling. "And Loren, pull that lever by the door and lean back."

Loren stretched his body, pushing the seat like a lounger, his eyes closed, a relaxed "ahhh" exiting his mouth. "You know, Bob, all I need is a TV and a beer!"

Killer laughed. "Hell, Loren, you've got those at home! What you need is this car. Now, get up and let's take a drive." Killer sold Loren the demo in thirty minutes, traded in his car without once driving it, and waved as he drove off.

It is the car salesman's greatest talent: titillation. Any good car salesman is the master of tactile excitement, the mark of a good pimp. Even in an age when the public has supposedly ended its love affair with the automobile, cars are still sold by touch and smell, not by any sense of objectivity. You, for instance, may enjoy looking at *Playboy* or *Playgirl,* but would you have more fun if those pictures were replaced by real people? A smart pimp knows that. Sure, you like the pictures, but put you next to the real thing—let you smell the heavenly scents and touch that supple skin in person—and reason flies out the window, along with your pocketbook.

Smart car salesmen use tactile excitement in many ways. They want you to feel the padding under that $200 vinyl roof, caress the leather, slam the doors; they want you to do anything that will make you fall physically in love with one specific car. Privately, the salesmen and managers take a slightly less romantic view. Cars are referred to as hunks of meat, lead, potatoes. They serve only one purpose: as decoys for the ducks, the surest lure for monetary reward. And you've seldom met a more proficient marksman than a good car salesman, either.

The Salesman's Favorite Targets

The nice old lady drove up in a plain brown sedan. A widow who had never purchased a car before without her husband, the woman was nervous. She had a right to be, too. Women and older people are usually easy business for any car salesman.

Buzz was the first person to reach her. "Hello, ma'am, I'm Peter Kiever. People call me Buzz—short for Buzzard." He smiled. "Thanks for coming in to see us."

The woman was smiling by then and quickly fell under the spell of this "nice man," as she referred to him. Buzz was patient. He spent two hours with the lady, never pressuring, the "ma'ams" flowing from his mouth like honey from a bear's lips. He could afford to spend time with her. After all, Buzz knew that ladies, particularly old ladies, don't like to argue, want to believe that niceness is honesty, and invariably buy cars from people who *are* nice.

Women and older people are just two favorite types of customers. First-time buyers are really popular, too, especially the young first-time buyer, a person who breathes the heaviest when first sitting behind the wheel of a car. Innocence, enthusiasm, and a trusting nature make the selling process so simple. Many poor people, black and white, are also favorite targets—people who actually feel inferior the moment they walk on the lot. "What do these folks know about wheeling and dealing?" is the car salesman's attitude. And then there are the people who think their credit is marginal. It may not be, but if you're one of these types, keep thinking negatively, please. Your salesman will sense that your main concern is not getting a good deal but getting financed. Car salesmen make much more money on you, thanks to that.

But who's the best target? *Anyone who makes the assumption that nice people will sell you a car for less.* Next to a water moccasin, a nice friendly car salesman is probably the most dangerous thing in the world *because* it's so easy to trust him. And trusting just about anybody in the business of buying and selling cars will cost you money.

Profits, Not Profit

The actual negotiation for the sale or trade of an automobile is one of many ways dealerships have of fleecing you honestly, though many times it is the least profitable part of the transaction for the dealer. Killer knows that better than most salesmen, and therefore he likens an automobile dealership's need for other profit sources to a rapidly flowing river. The river is never filled by the random raindrops that fall every now and then, but rather by the small streams of water that pour into larger streams, each one adding to the massive flow of the river. So the dealership fills with money.

If you prefer, think of your friendly dealer as playing an enormous game of "Gotcha." Lurking around every corner, in each innocent statement of the smiling salesman, is something or service that will grab just a little more money for the dealership. Virtually all of these extra dealer profit sources are not presented to you until you've signed your name on that buyer's order—your salesman probably just asked you to "Okay these figures," which sounds much better than "sign the binding contract here, sir."

For instance, are you familiar with the miraculous new "sealers" that dealers offer? Most charge you over $100 dollars for this service; the product costs them less than $5. Or, would you prefer to purchase one of those factory "extended warranties"? Most of these warranties provide two or three years of extra protection for certain components. What they don't address is the damnability of the *need* for an extended warranty at all. You are spending $5000 to $10,000 dollars or more for something that needs protection from self-destruction after one year—does that make sense?

Extended warranties are usually a hundred-percent-profit item for dealers. Are you financing your purchase through the dealership? In certain instances, dealer financing is a smart way to purchase a car, and for a very few, dealer life and accident and health insurance are a good buy. But if you're not careful, you'll wind up paying hundreds of dollars more than the exact same terms or benefits from other sources.

Supply and Demand

This old bugbear of the economics student is the reason the identical car can vary in selling price from store to store. If a dealer has only one of the hottest-selling cars on his lot, you won't buy that car cheaply. If the same dealer has fifty slow-selling models, he'll give them away at cost, if need be. The law of supply and demand is probably the nemesis of the car business, because the lead time required for supply to follow demand is a long one, and invariably, the moment supply has been adjusted, demand will have changed again. Thank you, fickle ones.

The most dramatic example of just how fickle you really are began to take place in 1977. Then, large cars were still selling like nickel dollars, and manufacturers directed virtually all of their production to them. Within three months, the marketplace—that's you—completely changed its mind, and dealerships all over America began to burst at the seams with unloved biggies. Small cars, the cars most Americans had really hated for so many years, became gold. And because the manufacturers could not quickly change their building habits, they did the next best thing— for them. They began to raise the prices of small cars, thinking that perhaps a little blackmail would send you back to your former favorites. Self-destruction at work.

So, How Do You Win?

In order to win, you really need to understand what's ticking inside the head of every person at the dealership. You need to understand why they think and react as they do. This book takes you inside that world and exposes the way it works. But even so, it will still be up to you to act on that information. As you read, you would do well to remember that the moment you walk into a dealership, it's a war for your pocketbook. Make it a gentlemanly thing. Have a good time visiting with that nice young salesman. Drink lots of coffee, or let the guy buy you a Coke. But don't forget that it's going to be a war. To win, you will need to know what is happening in each and every part of the buying and selling transaction.

KILLER MONSOON'S
FAVORITE SELLING TECHNIQUES

It was Saturday night, the last night of the store's "Beat the Clock" sale, and Killer picked up one of the last cold chicken legs on the table at the end of the showroom floor. A few customers were still sitting in front of the big board that listed every single car on the lot. Each hour for the past twenty-four, one of the salesmen had been assigned the honor of "marking down" the cars $25 dollars. Many of the cars still listed on the board had bright red stars beside them, indicating "bonus cars"—"Beat the clock, and buy a bonus car, and we'll give you a free color TV!" the radio and television ads said.

People actually believe that crap, Killer thought, as he watched a man who had been sitting in front of the board hour after hour, finally jump up and yell, "I'll take that one, the one with the $300-dollar discount!" Killer burped. Chicken sales weren't his idea of selling cars. Sure, it was a good technique for the suckers, but anyone can sell a car to a sucker.

J. C. walked up to the board and taped a "sold" sign by stock number 224. Killer laughed to himself. Not one single customer in the room knew that the car wasn't sold—J. C. just didn't want to sell it at such a big discount. During the entire twenty-four hours, no one had received a TV, either. The salesmen would say, "I'm sorry, folks, but at *that* price, we just can't sell you a car and give you a TV." The line worked every time, for every "giveaway"—bicycles, toasters, vacations. During Killer's twenty years in the business, he took pride in having never given away a single premium yet. Screw the show biz, Killer thought, as he slipped out the service door and headed to the Dead End.

Have you ever driven by an automobile dealership and seen a giant "tent sale" in progress, balloons flying high in the air and clowns running around pinching all the nice customers' kids? All car stores like to create a carnival atmosphere, promising fun and prizes, and generally intoxicating the customers with an air of excitement. And why shouldn't they? Car people have learned from experience that the average customer doesn't want too serious an environment during car negotiations. Customers seem to revert to a childlike attitude when they think about cars—to suspend reason and judgment. You would do well to resist this urge to return to the crib, for while you are giggling away, smart car people are using very effective psychological techniques to lower your defenses even further. Have you ever been the victim of any of the following techniques?

"Will You Buy a Car Today at Some Price?"

It's a salesman's most important question: it tells him whether or not you are going to be an easy sale. If you say "yes," the guy will probably start salivating, especially if you're in heat over one particular car. If you say "maybe," he'll be extra nice and probably even volunteer to show you his "best deal" of the day. As he talks to you, the guy will be looking for your "button"—the one psychological element he can push that will turn you into a buyer today. If you say, "No, I'm not buying today at any price," the guy will in all likelihood put you out on a "ball," an impossibly low price, on the one car you've shown interest in. You would be surprised how many people come back in, too, and then let that same salesman raise them another $600 dollars for the same car.

Be honest when someone asks you this question, but couch your honesty in self-protective terms if you are dead set on buying a car, a specific car, that day. Try something like this: "Yes, I am going to buy a car today. But I am going to buy it from the dealership that meets my price and financing terms." If you really want to put the salesman off guard, add, "And from what I've heard of your prices, I don't think I'll be buying it here."

One of the most important defensive techniques you can learn to use with car people is the ability to be negative in a nice way. Don't let that thought make you uncomfortable, either. Would you be passive and mushy if someone were lifting your wallet? Of course not. Yet some customers actually seem to feel that any indication of disagreement with a salesman will bring immediate expulsion from the dealership, as if they're being banished from heaven. Don't forget that every dealership in America survives on all of us. Each and every one will not only sell you a car if you are strong and demanding—they will respect you for it, in their own convoluted way.

"If I Can, Will You . . . ?"

The Fillmores were walking around the new-car lot with Killer, past the large, plush, expensive models and the stingy little sedans, too. They had asked for Killer, because Mr. Fillmore worked with one of Killer's bird dogs.

"Mr. DeMarco, these are all pretty cars, and I'd be lying if I said I didn't want to own one, but all of these things are too rich for my blood. I'm a poor man, you understand."

Killer chuckled, looking straight into Fillmore's eyes. "Why, of course you are. And I appreciate your concern. It's ridiculous how much cars cost these days. But let me ask you something. If I can sell you this car right here [it was one of the most expensive sedans on the lot] for a price and payment that is reasonable to you—if I can give you more than you think would be fair on your trade—Mr. Fillmore, if I can do that, will you buy it today?"

How do you answer Killer's question? Of course, most of us would buy a car if the payment were reasonable and if we felt we were getting more than our trade was worth.

"If I can, will you . . . ?" however, is not a fair question, because normally if you will, they won't. The question is simply a nice way to confirm to any salesman that you will buy a car if you *think* you are getting more than your due. The question can also lead you into deep waters quickly. For instance, once a salesman has determined that you don't want to pay over $200 dollars a month for a car, and that you consider $175 dollars per month an easy payment to make, he automatically knows you are a buyer if he can find a car you like that will fit that payment. So why shouldn't you be happy if he can? Because you might be able to buy that same car for $125 dollars a month, if you bargain.

The Sincere Salesman-in-a-Contest Ploy

If every car salesman went on a winning trip each time he said, "Ma'am, this car will send me over the top," there would be no more car salesmen in America—they'd all be away on trips. Sure, there are contests, many of them. Dealerships place bonuses for salesmen on the most new or used cars sold, the largest gross (profit) per car, the most rustproofings sold, the highest number of financed cars. Dealerships and manufacturers also employ contests to sell slow-moving cars. But these contests and bonuses don't necessarily mean you're going to receive a better deal. Don't fall for the sympathy routine; negotiate even harder with these contest fellows. After all, if they are really going to win a trip or extra money, they can afford to make a little less on you.

The "I'm Salesman of the Month" Routine

Do you think that nice salesman with his picture on the wall was picked for his service to humanity? No, he probably was picked because he makes more *profit* for the dealer than the other guys. Sure, the nice salesman can afford to be relaxed, to laugh, smile, and act like St. Francis of Assisi—after all, would a saint take you? You bet he would. Do not forget that this is a business transaction, not evening prayers.

The "I'm a Trustworthy Salesman" Ploy

Because most customers are naturally suspicious of car salesmen, smart guys know that they *must* gain your respect if they're going to sell you a car. There are lots of techniques for doing this, too. If Killer is talking with a customer who seems determined not to buy a car that moment, he'll look the person straight in the eye and say, "You know, I'm really glad you're not buying today. Quite honestly, the house is holding out for too much profit today. I can save you a lot of money if you'll come back tomorrow."

Sometimes Killer will close a deal with a large front end (the profit on the new car) by telling the customer, "Folks, don't ever quote me on this or the boss will can me, but you *will* get a little better financing rate if you go directly to the bank down the street. I'll be happy to call the loan officer for you." Isn't that nice of Killer? What he doesn't tell the folks about is *his* relationship with the loan officer—Killer gets paid a fee for each person he refers.

And then, there's Killer's best line for used-car buyers. You're looking at a used Toyota when he walks up and says, "Sir, I wouldn't recommend that car to you. It really isn't a very good car. Let me show you something else." What do you think of Killer? Do you instinctively trust him? After all he *was* being honest with you. Perhaps. He may be telling the truth, but because he is so well trained in a favorite technique of used-car selling, he is usually simply gaining your confidence for the kill: that six-month-old clunker with a cracked head sitting in the back lot with a bonus on it.

"Setting You" on a Car:
The Demo Ride

A good salesman will always insist that you drive the car you like best. Remember, if there are a hundred hookers to choose from but you're only allowed to touch one, that's the one you'll probably take. That's the salesman's most important job, getting you behind the wheel of that car. He'll probably insist that the whole family go, too—kids and a spouse can quickly become a salesman's best friends. By all means, drive the car you like. Play with all the buttons, feel the nice seats, and enjoy the ride. But don't let your adrenaline take control: be cool, be objective. Don't fall prey to the guy's spiel, and for God's sake, don't let him "reinforce" you. That's a nice technique that goes something like this: "How does the ride compare to your present car, Mr. Smith? . . . It's a quiet car, isn't it? . . . How do the seats feel, aren't they comfortable, just like an armchair?" The salesman saw you drive in, the smoke belching from the rear of your tattered Hudson. He *knows* you've got to like the scent of new plush, and he *hopes* your reason will be smothered under all this beauty and comfort. A new car is never as nice after a week or two, especially if you've learned how much money you wasted. Don't forget that hookers, too, are never as pretty the morning after.

"We Can Allow You This Much With
a Difference of This Much and
a Deferred Payment of This Much.
Now, Just Sign Here"—The Old
Confuse-Them-and-Control-the-Sale Ploy

Confusion is the salesman's best friend. Most folks after a day's shopping at several different dealerships hardly remember their own name, much less understand the offers and counteroffers whisked before them. Salesmen use confusion to keep you from buying a car at another dealership. They *imply* that enormous savings are waiting for you on your return. They tell you about the customer who has been waiting for a trade-in just like yours, hoping you'll fall for that classic line.

Confusion is also used in more specific ways. For instance, if you are a "payment buyer," smart salesmen will continually quote you only payments, conveniently forgetting to mention the trade-in allowance or discount. If you are a "difference buyer" (if you care only how much difference you must pay between your old car and their new car), salesmen will try to convince you that "allowance" (how much they say they are actually giving you for your trade) is more important than difference.

Don't tell a salesman that you only care about your payment. Don't tell him you only care about the difference in price between your old car and that pretty new four-footed thing. Those are expensive ways to deal, since you'll be lost in the confusion. The only things that count are what your car is really worth in wholesale dollars, what their car actually costs, how much profit you are willing to pay, and which financing costs the least.

Justifying the Sale

These days, most of the major automobile manufac-turers have videotape presentations designed to teach sales-men how to overcome customer objections. One good series is called "Justifying the Sale," a nice euphemism for mak-ing nickels look like quarters. A new salesman at the deal-ership, a nice kid who enjoys talking with Killer, Robbie Miers, is sitting at the feet of the master, Coke in hand, listening to war stories. The topic is overcoming objections.

"I remember the time this smart-ass came into the deal-ership so set on exactly what he wanted on a car that the other salesmen gave up," Killer said with a smirk. "I bet four of them twenty each I could sell the guy, and I did."

Robbie sat there in anticipation. Killer just looked off in space. "Well, come on, what did you do?" the kid asked.

Killer started laughing, a belly laugh. "Hell, I did just the opposite of what I'd done with the customer before him! God, this business is fun. Well, anyway, the first guy had wanted a specific car, but with a vinyl roof. I convinced him that vinyl roofs allow moisture to build up and cause serious rust. He also didn't really like the car being red, so I just put him on the phone with the used-car department— the guys up there told him red is the most popular resale color and would bring him more money in trade. Then, this second jackass came in, the one none of the guys could sell, and he just wouldn't have a vinyl roof and definitely had to have some light-colored car. I showed him the used-car book—the place where you add on for vinyl roofs in figuring the value of a trade—told him how much quieter cars are with vinyl, and convinced him that the roof insulated the car so much he'd save a gallon a mile on air-conditioning!

Then I told him how much light colors rust, and that black cars had less rust than any, and he bought it all!" Robbie smiled. Killer was better than any videotaped spiel.

Killer was not lying to either one of those customers, just telling the selective truth. Bright colors are more popular at resale time. Some vinyl roofs do encourage rust but at the same time provide deadening and insulation. Black cars do rust less than light-colored cars. As a matter of fact, most of the techniques used by salesmen do have some ring of truth in them. For instance: "Do you think it's too expensive? Just think what you'll save on repair bills." "You don't want to finance for forty-eight months? Why not, you can pay the loan off earlier if you want to." "You want to think about it until tomorrow? Why? You said you liked the car and the payment. If you buy the car today, I'll even give you a free undercoating."

So how in God's name do you make any sound judgment with all these semblances of truth flying around? It's easy. If you need to justify what you are spending or what you are choosing, if you have doubts about what you are doing: STOP THE TRANSACTION. Go home and defuse. Don't try to think in the midst of confusion.

"Ah, This Is the Beauty of a Trade-In You Mentioned?"—The Ploy of Bringing You to Their Reality

Killer was standing by an up's trade-in. The man had ridden to the store that morning with a friend. It was a cool Saturday afternoon in October, one of those days that seem to draw every looker in the world to car stores, and the two men had planned to kill a few hours looking over all the new models sitting proudly in front of their temporary homes. Killer normally has little patience with these "bumble bees," the people who light at one store just long enough to draw a salesman from the showroom, waste fifteen minutes of his time, and then fly off to the next candy store. As a matter of fact, he never paid any attention to the type. But Gary Oliver Davies had been on the warpath that week and had passed down that damn edict from whatever particular cloud he was nesting on at that moment. "I want a salesman at every single up's car before the door is open," he'd yelled. "Hell," Killer mused, "I guess his damn boat needs a new set of sails." It was common knowledge at the store that Mr. Davies' fifty-foot sailboat was regularly maintained at dealership expense.

These two guys had been nice enough, though, and one of them even exhibited a reasonably serious case of car fever, enough to garner Killer's attention. It was this man, Tommy Hines, who had now returned to the store with his trade-in. But Mr. Hines' battle-worn car looked nothing like the glowing description presented to Killer that morning. "Mr. DeMarco, I want to tell you my car is one of the prettiest four-year-old Chevys this side of Detroit!" he had said with obvious enthusiasm. Killer was used to statements like that. Everybody who came in the store seemed to have no problem at all believing their trades were things of beauty, even if fenders were missing, seats were torn, and large pools of oil formed quickly on the pavement each time the junkers rolled to a stop. And, for sure, you couldn't tell people how bad their cars really were, since those old jalopies were just as much a part of the family as their bratty little kids who loved to run up and down the showroom floor. But over the years Killer had developed a really nice technique for handling this "blind love." And he was just about to unleash it on Mr. Tommy Hines.

"Tommy, this does look like a mighty nice car. You know, I remember when I had one pretty much like it. . . ." Killer continued to talk and started working his way slowly down one side of the car, something like two steps, before stopping to continue his story. Each time he stopped he'd look at the car again. If a small dent was within reach, Killer would simply rub his hand over it and continue walking, talking all the time. When he was standing by the hood, he pulled out a large handkerchief and vigorously rubbed the worst area of faded paint; then Killer ran his finger along the windshield molding, right to the large rust bubble in the corner. Tommy, of course, was seeing these little problems for the first time. Like most of us, he'd become used to the pimples. But Killer never once mentioned the little problems with the car as he stood by the driver's door.

"Hey, Tommy, you know, I may have a customer for your car. Why don't we take a spin around the block?" Tommy didn't really like the idea—the brakes weren't too good really, something he'd kept meaning to fix, and the worn-out shocks bounced the car up and down in a good imitation of a camel loping across the desert. But, how could he say no? After all, this was supposed to be a really "nice" car. They headed down the road, Killer jabbering away, seemingly not in the least aware of the lope or the brakes. He did run his hand over the torn armrest and do his best to push the ashtray in—the damn thing kept falling down, as if it were trying to talk—but words weren't really necessary. Tommy was getting the message by osmosis. The dreamboat just wasn't that great, after all.

Or that's at least what Killer wanted him to think. Smart car people will do their best to "educate" you about the value of your trade before they try to sell you a car. It's a smart move, one you can't refute very easily. If you don't know the real value of your trade *before* you drive on the lot, you will lower its value in your own mind every time a salesman points out its weaknesses.

The "Other Customer" Ploy

You're sitting in the salesman's office, and you want to think about his offer until tomorrow. "Sir," he says, "there *is* someone else interested in that car; the people are expected back here at five. If you really like that car, why don't you just give me a small deposit to hold it for you?" Don't do it, even if your spouse threatens to cut you off. Clear that glaze from your eyes and say no. You are spending thousands of dollars, and there are thousands of cars out there, too. You will invariably get a better deal and be more comfortable with your purchase if you wait a day.

But let's assume you follow this advice, only to return the next day and find your dreamboat gone. Don't be upset; car people know the disappointment you feel usually means you won't buy anything from them, and so they'll bend over backwards to make you an even better offer on another car. Some smart buyers use this technique deliberately; they pick out a car and wait for it to be sold to someone else, when they really wanted some other car on the lot.

The T.O. System

Let's say you've spent two hours at a dealership. You've found the car you like, one of those special-edition Expenso Gargantula Imperial Majesty Hardtops you have always yearned for. Your trade-in has been appraised, and though you are not really sure what they want to pay for it, you think their offer sounds pretty good. Or at least the salesman thinks it's pretty good, since you've noticed that he giggles every time the figure is mentioned.

The monthly payment they've quoted you doesn't seem that bad, either. Sure, it's twice what you pay now, but the finance manager, who came in the office with the salesman, showed you how much lower it is. "Yes, it's $6 dollars a day more, but that's only twenty-five cents an hour. And you'll probably save that on gas, once gas gets up to $3 dollars a gallon." You know, *that* type of logic.

However, you are tired and a bit confused, and you have been trying to leave for a little R & R. The salesman has even lowered the price to keep you there; he's also told you about his children and his sick mother. ("She's a real saint, I tell you.") But still you want to leave. The salesman excuses himself and returns with his sales manager, who wants to dicker some more. Still you resist. Pretty soon, he leaves, and now the general manager drops in. He wants to dicker a little more. You buy the car. After all, you had to, just to get out of there. You have been the victim of the T.O., the "fresh face can do miracles" theory. *Don't* put up with that. Don't feel guilty for leaving—it's really not a prison bust-out, though you may feel that way. Smile, shake hands, and say "good-bye" until tomorrow.

Getting a Deposit

Every car salesman lives for that moment when you pull out a roll of bills or your checkbook. The significance of paying a deposit is not what you think it is, though. To you, it is an agreement to buy at a certain price. To the salesman, it simply means he has something to hold you with, something to keep you from leaving when the raises begin.

Killer has two favorite ways to get you to transfer that money to his hot little palm. "Our manager requires a deposit before he will approve an offer this low," he says. Boy, you must really be driving a hard bargain. Or, if it really looks like you may leave without buying right then, Killer will probably say, "Why don't you give me a deposit to hold your car overnight while you think about it? I'll give you the money back tomorrow if you don't want the car."

What would you say to those statements? Tell him to get your offer approved without a deposit, if he wants you to buy from him. What's the guy going to do, refuse to sell you a car or call the cops? Then tell the guy you don't really care if the car is gone tomorrow. That may ruin his night, but it certainly won't ruin yours. Salesmen are there to control you. If you are going to win, *you* must control *them.*

The Raise

Has this ever happened to you? You sign an order, give the salesman your deposit, and sit there while he goes off to fight for you, to get the manager to approve your offer. This guy is really on your side, you think. In truth, however, your salesman is probably in the lounge with the other guys having a Coke. He's never seen the manager.

The guy comes back and says you're so close. If you can just help him a little—perhaps give them another $153.49—he's sure the offer will be approved. Well, by God, of course you'll do that—after all, they're down to pennies now. This is just what they hoped you would think. Experienced salesmen know that most people who would be suspicious of an even-figured raise will believe an odd-figured one.

There is an odd "Catch-22" in the whole "bumping" syndrome. Some customers actually want to be bumped. If the house should take their offer without arguing, they feel there must be too much profit in the deal. Conversely, many dealerships won't try to bump people who have agreed to very low grosses; a customer that close in his offer may leave if he's bumped. One thing is sure, though. Dealerships just love to bump people who are on *high* profit deals on the first offer. Why? Managers feel that anyone dumb enough to agree to a high profit will probably be dumb enough to be bumped.

Do not be patient with raises. Smart salesmen will try to raise you three or four times, until the well is dry. Managers are continually telling their guys, "Don't leave any money on the table." If you have determined what the new car costs, what your used car is worth, and what profit you intend to pay, don't go above that figure. The following chapters discuss each of these items in detail, telling you how to determine each one. Tell your salesman you won't budge when he goes to get your offer approved. Look him in the eye when you say it, and don't smile—even grimace a little. Threaten to leave if your deal's not approved; he will get the message.

Lowballing

Let's say that you have not been able to get your offer approved or that you simply don't want to make an offer on the Expenso today. As you're walking from the showroom, the salesman makes one last try. "If you will come back tomorrow, I'll try to get you that car for $500 less than the figure you mentioned." Or he says, "I think I can get you $500 more for your trade-in, if you come in tomorrow."

Don't go home and celebrate. You've just been low-balled, "put out" on a price they just know will bring you back tomorrow, you masochist. Most people who are "put out on a ball" will invariably spend hours arguing with salesmen at other dealerships, saying, "But the other guys have said they will give me $500 more." They exhaust themselves trying to buy a car from the ball figure, and finally return to the first dealer the next day only to be told, "Gosh, I'm sorry, but we had a customer on your trade-in that would have allowed us to give you $500 more, but he bought something else just before you got here." And would you believe that most people, from pure frustration, will actually pay the $500 simply to end it all?

Why not take the offensive with the salesman who makes you a ball offer? If what he proposed really would be a fantastic deal, grab him by the arm and drag him to his sales manager. Tell them both you'll buy the car right then and there for the figure, and if you can't, you'll never darken their door again. You will either buy a car very reasonably that day, or else your body will be found floating upward in some muddy river.

3
A Look in the Mirror: Know Yourself

The Allen Chases live north of town in one of those new subdivisions with big artificial security gates that are supposed to look imposing but in reality seem pretentious. The Chases are not wealthy, but they would like people to think that at least they're getting there. Their home, though small, has two large stone urns by the front door. The flowers that used to bloom well there have slowly withered from neglect. "Honey, I've just been *so* busy," Allie continually tells her husband. Allison Chase is very involved in the lesser social scene—you know the type.

"Well, damn it, what do you think I do? Whose work is it that lets you be that busy?" Allen invariably snaps back. The Chases fight quite a lot, usually over money. As a matter of fact, they seem to spend what little time they have together either fighting or silently watching their new giant, rear-projection-screen television. It's financed, too, like most things they "own." They drive two cars: one a three-year-old station wagon, the artificial-wood type predominant in the suburbs these days; the other a large, very clean, high-mileage luxury hardtop, one of those cars that seem to blink "we are rich" while passing lesser cars and people. Both cars are financed, but Al Chase has determined that, yes, he can trade in the hardtop for one of

those new down-sized Gargantulas, the type that are supposed to save so much on gas. They will buy that car and
receive an excellent deal in *anyone's* book. They will receive excellent financing rates, too. But that new down-
sized Gargantula will spell the end of the Chase's solvency
not too far down the road. They don't know that yet,
though; they won't, until it's too late.

Buck and Carolyn Allgood pulled back on the express-
way, one of those perimeter highways that ring large cities
and seem to sprout automobile dealerships on any unoc-
cupied parcels of land. Carolyn was writing on a note pad.

"You know, I really liked that fastback and think it was
just about the right list price. The seats were good, too,
high enough for me, and practical with the kids. And I like
the way that man didn't try to pressure us. His sales manager was nice, too."

Buck shook his head, biting on the end of his pipe in
some salute that seemed to signify yes more than the nod.
"Yeah, you're right," he added in mid-puff, "and I think the
fifteen percent discount was good. *Consumer Reports* said
those mid-sized ones have about an eighteen percent
markup. Three percent profit would seem fair to me." He
looked in the mirror twice, turned his head just to make
sure the lane was clear, and headed slowly up the ramp to
the next dealership on their list.

Buck and Carolyn Allgood are careful buyers. He is the
comptroller of a small company located just twenty miles
from the city. Carolyn teaches school, the second grade.
They are thoughtful, nonemotional buyers who trade cars
only when the repair bills come too quickly and irregularly
on their present car. They are not in the least in love with
automobiles. Their Saturday visits to four dealerships have
been preceded by several weeks of careful study. The make

and model car they hope to purchase is no casual choice. Their shopping method is good, too: find several specific cars, drive them, discuss price, and then go home for the night to think objectively over the individual deals. Neither of these people feels that any salesman or dealer can pull the wool over his or her eyes. Both are wrong.

The Estrums, the youngest of our couples, seem to possess qualities of both the Chases and the Allgoods. They are upwardly mobile, solvent, happy with each other, and in love with those physical possessions they honestly can afford to pay for. The Estrums usually trade cars every year, in the midst of new-car introduction time, or perhaps a month after that time. "I always wait until they've dropped their prices some," Phil tells his admiring neighbors as they inspect his latest purchase, "and, do you know what: our payments didn't go up *a nickel* the last time we traded!" The Estrums are proud of their car-trading ability and of the new car that reigns proudly in their driveway. "We never spend a dime on repairs, either. I tell you it pays to trade every year." This nice couple can afford to trade cars every year. In the course of their lifetime, however, they will throw away $40 dollars a month, year in and year out, because they buy when and as they do.

IN THE BUCKET AND DIPPING:
THE PROBLEM WITH THE CHASES

The guys were "pulling" for Cokes, four of them standing around the Coke machine, an old machine that still dispensed bottled pop, not cans. The object of the game was to pull the Coke bottle made furthest from them, and Killer came out on top again, or so he thought. "Oregon! Let me see you beat that!"

Ronnie Cheatum, the store's F and I man, financing and insurance, slipped his fingers down the row of Cokes and pulled one from the bottom. He looked at the bottom of the bottle and, in one slow motion, extended his hand, palm up, saying, "Pay me." The guys looked at the bottle. It said "Honolulu."

"You bastard," Killer said. It was a collective statement, as each handed Ronnie a ten.

"Hey, Ronnie, at least you owe me a favor, now," Killer said. "Get that Chase deal bought. I got no gross, but I know you'll take care of that, if you can get the guy financed." Everyone chuckled, a respectful laugh of sorts. All the guys liked Ronnie—they called him "Magic." He was a miracle worker who could get just about anybody financed, and he would put half of them on "the chart," a nice high interest with lots of insurance added on. But Ronnie had a problem with the Chase deal; the guy was in the bucket. He had a trade-in worth $6000 dollars, but he owed $8000 on it. Sure, his credit was okay, but the guy was a "hand-to-mouth"—every cent he made each month was already obligated to payments, like that big rear-screen television—and he didn't have a cent of the $2000-dollar "down stroke," the cash that would be needed to make up the difference between the $12,000 the finance company had agreed to finance on the new car, and the $14,000 Chase would owe on the new car.

"Killer," Ronnie said, "I tell you what, if I get him dipped today, you buy me a drink tonight."

Killer put his hand on Ronnie's shoulder. "You get him dipped today, and I'll buy you *two* drinks, my friend."

The dip will be the proverbial straw to Al Chase. When he comes into the store to pick up that shiny new car, Killer will have him sign the normal papers and contract obligating him to forty-eight payments at *$385*. He will then put him in that car and ride him to the local easy-loan store down the street. Mr. Chase will sign papers there for an additional $2000 dollars, pick up the check, and immediately sign it over to the dealership. He has been dipped. He now owes $12,000 dollars plus interest on one contract for a car that will be worth $9000 dollars tomorrow. He also owes $2000 plus interest on the few pieces of household goods that weren't already mortgaged. With interest, Mr. Chase owes over $18,000 dollars on that car. He is paying $65 dollars per month for double life and double accident and health insurance. In four months when the sap realizes he can't handle those payments, he will come back into the dealership and ask them to buy his car back.

Sure, they'll buy it back—for $9000. And since the payoff, the net amount owed on that car, will be virtually the same amount he financed, since the payoff on the dip is still the same amount, Mr. Chase won't be able to sell his car. Or rather, if he sells it, he'll have to pay the dealership the difference between its $9000-dollar value and the $12,000-dollar payoff. He'll still have the $2000-dollar loan, too.

But why would the payoff on both loans be the same if Chase has made four payments on each? Surprise: the first year or so of payments don't reduce the loan much—they reduce the *interest.* Except for credit unions, most financing institutions compute the repayment of interest by the "Rule of Seventy-eights." If you'll look on the back of the last contract you signed, you'll see some clause to that effect. Simply stated, the rule of seventy-eights, also called the Sum of the Digits Method, says that you pay virtually *all* the total interest *before* you reduce the principal substantially. For instance, take Mr. Chase. The total interest on the $12,000-dollar loan for the forty-eight months is $3800 dollars. If he made ten payments on his car at $385 dollars a month, he would *still* owe approximately $11,000 dollars on his car. That's why most institutions, banks included, that finance on a monthly basis just love for you to pay off your loans early—as long as you have paid for enough months to cover the interest due for the original length of the loan, not the period you actually paid. Aren't financing institutions nice?

Since financing institutions are going to rip your knickers anyway, don't fall for the dip routines, even though car salesmen have such wonderful ways to make them sound sensible. Listen to Killer as he sets up a nice old couple for the kill: "Mr. and Mrs. Carnes, as I told you, the payment on the car will be $225 dollars a month. But what I didn't tell you is that you will pay $225 for only two years. The remaining two years, you'll pay only $175 per month."

Killer smiles, and the couple smiles, too. "Mr. DeMarco, that sounds just fine, but how do you do that?"

Killer smiles again. What a helpful guy. "Folks, what we are going to do is borrow you $1500 dollars from one company for two years, and only finance $5000 through the other company. Then, if you get some extra money, you can pay off the small loan sooner. I like to do this for people because it means they owe less on their car. And it's no trouble, really. You'll just need two stamps each month, rather than one."

Are you laughing at these suckers? Are you saying to yourself, "Hell, I'm not in the bucket, no one will ever dip me?" Don't laugh until you check your payoff. If you are like the vast majority of people, you will probably find out you owe more on your car than the actual wholesale value of the car. Even if you owe a couple of hundred less, don't smile. Unless you owe at least five or six hundred less than your car's wholesale value, you, friend, are sitting in the bottom of that wet, slimy bucket.

Exactly how does a car store know how much to dip you? What determines the amount of money financed on any car, new or used? On a new car, it's simple. If you are reasonably strong, if you have a good credit record, virtually all financing institutions will loan you the invoice price of any new car. For instance, Al Chase did appear to be a good credit risk, since he had met all those payments on TV, furniture, and his other cars on time. The invoice price on the Expenso was $12,000 dollars, and the dealer's financing source agreed to loan that much. Mr. Chase was also trading his old car. That car had a real cash value of $6000 dollars. That $6000 is deducted from the $12,000-dollar invoice price, leaving $6000 dollars. But Mr. Chase owed $8000 on his old car. Add that figure to the $6000, and you now have the total amount that needs to be financed, $14,000. The dip is the difference between the invoice cost, $12,000, and the $14,000.

On a used car, financial institutions will normally lend you no more than the "loan value" of the particular car you want to purchase. In the used-car section, we discuss loan value in detail. But for now, whether you plan to purchase a new or used vehicle, remember that financing a car at invoice or loan value is the way everyone gets in the bucket in the first place. As we discuss later, you will always want to finance less on any car—less than the financing source will lend you. If you do that, you really will be able to laugh at all the other suckers.

SINGING THE BLUES:
THE TROUBLE WITH THE ALLGOODS

Just about the time that Killer delivered the Chases' car, Buck and Carolyn opened the door to their car and headed to the showroom. The Allgoods had made their decision: they would buy here, and they would buy today. Killer walked to them. "Hi, folks, can I help you?"

"Yes, we'd like to see Mr. DeLong. We told him we'd be back today." My God, Killer thought. Some "be-backs" that actually come back.

"Ma'am, I'm sorry, Forrest is off this afternoon. But I'd be glad to help you. Of course should you buy a car, the credit would go to Forrest." The Allgoods looked at each other. Well, at least they'd asked for the guy; it wasn't their fault he took the day off. Sure, Mr. DeMarco could wait on them.

You must remember that the Allgoods are the careful shoppers. The previous night, they had figured out to the penny the cost of the car sitting just outside the showroom door. This morning, before driving to the dealership, they had called their bank and checked on the latest financing rates. They had also asked the loan officer to check in the bank's blue book, again. "Now, you're sure that $2200 is the average wholesale on our car, aren't you?" Mr Allgood had said.

"Yes, sir, and this is the latest book, too."

"Good. Then you can expect to see us later in the afternoon. We'll be putting $2000 down and only want to finance the car for twenty-four months." Allgood placed the receiver down, feeling just fine. Their budget would be a little strained with the short payment period, but it would be worth it—think of the interest they would save.

Killer had the Allgoods in his office. He liked these people, and he talked at length to them about the careless types who bought so many cars. "Yes, let me tell you. It's refreshing to see people who are thoughtful buyers." Killer took the keys to their trade and excused himself. "Folks, I'll be back in just a few minutes."

He drove their car behind the used-car offices and yelled to Timothy Raxalt, the used-car manager. "Hey, Rax! Come take a look at this car, will you?"

The two of them looked over every inch of the car. Each part of it was clean, and the trunk was cleaner than most front seats. Sure, there were a lot of "nickels," small dents from rocks, but for a five-year-old car, this one was a cherry.

"Well, what do you think, Rax? It's a hell of a lot more than an average car." Killer was beginning to work the guy. Good salesmen also work the used-car department.

"Yeh. These things are real hot this month," Rax said. "I'll tell you what, see if you can trade for it for a quarter [$2500]. If you get close, call me, and maybe I can stretch it a little."

Killer looked shocked. "What do you mean a quarter? You couldn't buy a car like this at the sale for $2800 if you tried all day."

Rax walked around it again. Without saying a word, he walked inside and picked up the phone. Within a minute he was back outside. "Killer, if you can trade for the car at $2800, trade for it. Bobby says it's worth it." Bobby was a road hog, a traveling salesman, whose specialty was cars like this.

Mr. Allgood had his pad, filled with notations, lying out on the desk when Killer returned. "Mr. DeMarco, so that we won't waste your time or ours, let me review the figures that will be acceptable to my wife and me." Killer sat down and listened thoughtfully. "We have figured the cost of your new car at $6500 dollars. We think a three percent profit would be fair to both of us. And I know that my car is worth $2500 dollars. Can you sell us the car with those figures in mind?"

Killer's expression was solemn. "Mr. and Mrs. Allgood, I

believe the manager would agree to a three percent profit on this car, that may not be a problem. But I'm sorry, your trade-in is nice for its age but it's not worth $2500 dollars. We have been trading in cars like it for around $2000 dollars."

"Only $2000!" Allgood was angry. "I know my car's worth more than that. The bank said at least $2200."

That's what Killer wanted to hear—what the guy really thought he would get for the car. "Mr. and Mrs. Allgood, let me explain the problem. Your car is nearly five years old. Since you are familiar with financing, I'm sure you know that five-year-old cars cannot be financed at most institutions. Even if they can, twelve months would probably be the maximum months it could be financed. That makes it very hard for us to sell the car, since most folks don't pay cash when they buy." Allgood nodded. That made sense.

"Let me do this, Mr. Allgood. Let me take your car back up to the boys once more. Maybe they'll help us a little," Killer volunteered.

"Good, good, I appreciate your help," Allgood said. At least the guy seemed to be on their side.

Rax watched Killer driving up again. Hell, he needs more money, the used-car manager said to himself. And I'll be damned if I'll give him a cent.

"Hey, Rax, I am so close to a deal. Listen, if you'll give me two more, I'll do it. Man, we need this car, I've got someone that will buy it in a minute." Rax started to object. "Wait a minute! If you don't want to put the money in it, just let me take it around town a little. I know I can get $3000 for it. Rax, you can't put too much money in a car like this."

Killer was right, and the guy knew it. "Okay," Rax said.

"But I want you to dehorse the guy. Send him home in your demo tonight. Tell him we need to have the car right now." Rax didn't need to tell Killer that. He never lets people ride when the deal is sweet; they might decide to shop some more.

The Allgoods were still sitting there, and both of them watched Killer as he entered the office. He had a smile on his face. "Folks, we did it! I told that guy we needed help, and he finally agreed. I've got you $2100 for the car!" The couple shifted in their seats but said nothing. "I also called our general manager from there and have gotten him to agree to rustproof and undercoat your car for free. You know, we usually charge $150 dollars for that. So, you are really getting $2250 for your car!"

The Allgoods bought the car. They paid their three percent profit. Plus they gave away their $3000-dollar car for $2100. Killer's total gross on the deal was the three percent—$250 dollars—plus the $900 dollars in gross his deal gained by underallowing on their trade. The "$150-dollar rustproofing" cost $30.

What did these people do wrong? They believed in a book to determine the value of their car. The only way to really know the value of your trade is to shop it. Chapter 4, Know Your Present Car, tells you *how* to shop it.

THE NEWEST TOY:
THE PROBLEM WITH THE ESTRUMS

Many people just love to buy a new car at intro time. They rush to the closest car store on show day and invariably pay hundreds of dollars more for the honor of being the first kid on the block to own Detroit's latest version of the ultimate car.

Take Mr. Estrum, for instance. Phil Estrum barely graduated from high school, but he was smart and ambitious. He entered the insurance field when he was twenty-five; he studied, listened, polished that smooth tongue of his, and became a successful salesman in five years. He's proud of his profession, too, not something that many car salesmen will honestly say. Phil began trading cars every year his third year in the business, and the new one he bought this fall was his tenth.

And of course, Phil had dealt with Killer each of those previous years. After all, he knew from friends that Mr. DeMarco was the top salesman at the store, and Phil likes to deal with the top people in everything. The Estrums had an appointment with Killer one night, eight o'clock. Killer was coming in on his day off, something he made sure the Estrums knew. He even had a little present for Mrs. Estrum, one of those spray bottles of Chanel, which he planned to give to her before talking about the new car. Killer knows his psychology—he also knows that other salesmen are always very easy prey for car people, especially when they are "peacocks," the first-kid-on-the-block-with-the-new-toy type of folk. And the Chanel only cost Killer a buck, anyway—it pays to have friends in the "independent gift" business.

Their meeting evoked one of those reunions of long-lost brothers and sisters, Killer kissing Sue and grabbing Phil's hand in a double grasp. "Come on!" he yelled. "I've got the car over here." It was sitting by itself, away from the other cars and any other distractions that might lessen the moment of unveiling. The car was newly serviced, polished to mirror brightness. The engine was warm; Killer had personally let it stand at idle for five minutes. The interior lights were left on, too, spreading a nice friendly glow over the contours of velour and leather.

The Estrums drove off alone in that pretty thing. Killer told them to take a nice long cruise, even stop for a drink or two on the way back. He would have the papers together when they returned; he'd "even have all the figures filled in, that's okay, isn't it, Phil?"

Phil laughed, a repeat of last year's laugh, and the year before that. "Sure, Bob! Why don't we not argue this year!"

"Phil, don't be so rough on me this time! I nearly got fired last year when you finished with me!" Right. Instead of heading back into the dealership as they drove away, Killer quickly slipped into his demo and swung out toward the Dead End. After all, it was his day off. And it was going to be a day to celebrate, too.

Phil Estrum does negotiate each time he buys a car, and he got a good deal. He also received a fair price for his trade. Two things, however, were working against him, as always. Because he just must drive one of the first cars out each year, he's accepted the fact he'll pay some premium for that honor. Killer has reinforced that thought many times, too, reminding Phil that "these cars are impossible to get at intro time, you know that. And don't forget that you will be driving a current year model for twelve months, not just the seven or eight months you'll have if you wait. Your car will be worth more when you trade." The logic is fragile at best, but it works every time on people who want to be convinced. If Phil is determined to trade cars each year, it doesn't matter *when* he trades; it does matter that he trade at the same time each year. Phil could buy the same car in January and normally save $600 or $700 over an intro deal. His trade wouldn't be worth less the next time around, either, *if* he traded in January again.

Phil's other problem is his own ego, his sure-fire conviction that "any man who is good at dickering over life insurance is good at dickering over cars." Phil has forgotten that he always oversells insurance to car salesmen *because* of that same logic: car salesmen are just so sure of themselves as negotiators that they think *they* know how to wheel and deal with their local insurance salesmen. Maybe Killer and Phil deserve each other, after all.

FACING OUR FOIBLES:
THE PROBLEM WITH ALL CAR BUYERS

Maybe you've glimpsed yourself in some action of the Chases, Allgoods, or Estrums. Maybe not. Different personalities, they make different mistakes. But they share one failing: they don't know their own weaknesses. They haven't explored all the important questions. We will.

How Naïve Are You, Really?

A customer's false pride is a salesman's best friend. The Chases thought they could get a better, newer, smaller car for less but failed to understand their financial situation. The Allgoods were *sure* they knew how to get the best price for their trade-in. Phil Estrum just had to have a new car at showtime and really believed *any* good salesman could handle car hacks. My conscience is burdened at times with customers like these, who have dueled with me and lost. They were so sure, so confident, saying things like, "I *know* how much money you guys make, so let's cut out the crap. I'll give you $7000 dollars and not a dime more." Invariably, I could feign respect and say "yes" to these types. After all, what's the sense in my working if the customer is telling me I can make more at the customer's figure? You will be richer if you know your limitations in the automobile arena; caution is the operative word.

Impulse Buyers: You're a Favorite

Several years ago, a carrier truck was unloading a bright red $15,000-dollar sports car in front of the largest Gargantula dealership in town. A lady screeched to the curb in her equally elegant sedan. "I want it! I want it!" she screamed. The salesmen fought among themselves for five minutes, trying to decide who would "help" this lady. Finally a slightly bloodied young man made his way to her side and walked her into the office. The lady wanted a discount of $1000 dollars, and the salesman said no. She agreed on the spot to pay the full price. She then decided to trade in her car. It was appraised at a true value of $9000 dollars. The salesman offered her $7000, and she said no. The salesman left the office, supposedly to show the car to someone else, and the lady ran—*ran* after him. "I'll pay it!" she yelled.

It's a true story. The lady paid $4000 dollars more than she needed to for that car because she had given away her bargaining power. Now we all know you are not going to be that dumb. You never let your enthusiasm show, never say things like, "It's just what we've been looking for." You don't do that, do you?

WHAT SHOULD YOU BUY?

Need vs. Want

The people came into the store a little after six in the afternoon. They had just finished their shift at one of those local doughnut shops that make their fare from scratch, and the salesman didn't have to look too hard to see the light touches of flour on their clothes, the tired eyes, and the strained smiles of folks who work hard for a living. Two jobs, really. They both worked at the doughnut shop from ten a.m. to six p.m., and then worked as security guards from midnight to four a.m. Killer was off that day, and one of the new guys just happened to be walking on the lot as they drove up. Their car was old and as tired as they were. And they were nervous. It was a fortunate thing that an inexperienced salesman was waiting on them—at least it was a fortunate thing for Davies Motors—because these two very poor-looking folks wanted to look at the most expensive and sporty car on the lot. Any experienced sales-man would have asked them a few qualifying questions and quickly left them to walk along. After all, how many doughnut people can buy a car that costs twice their yearly income?

Ted, the new boy, hadn't learned to be that sophisticated in his questions, though, and he happily showed them the deep silver and burgundy coupe that stretched low and sleek by the showroom. The Nelsons had never owned a new car. They had four children of their own and a couple of kids no one else would adopt because of their color. They had a nice, very small house back in the woods. "It's not very fancy, but we're proud of it," they told Ted, the hesi-tant and defensive nature of their words betraying great discomfort merely at standing on a lot filled with $20,000-dollar cars.

Ted came into Don Burns' office quite casually. "Hey, Don, I've got a deal on these folks." For a new salesman he was a very thorough fellow, and he handed Don a neatly filled out buyer's order, showing a $2400-dollar profit and an equally neat credit application outlining the financial life of the couple. It all looked just too nice: the only people who let themselves be taken this badly were always people with bad credit. Don walked back into the closing booth with Ted and struck up a nice, friendly conversation with the Nelsons. "Mr. Nelson! I wanted to personally thank you for coming into the dealership today. And I compliment you on your taste in cars—I drive one just like it. By the way, don't you folks work at the doughnut place just down from the courthouse?" Of course they did, Mr. Nelson happily volunteered. "And I noticed on your credit application that your last car was financed with the Beach Bank. Do you by any chance know Sid Oliver, the chief loan officer?" Yes, they knew him well, Mr. Nelson volunteered with enthusiasm. That was a good sign. People with bad credit don't act enthusiastically when you talk about their loans.

"Well, Mr. Nelson, since this is a pretty expensive car, though it's worth every penny, I think it will help your loan application if we indicate that both of you would like life *and* accident and health insurance on the full amount of the loan. And I think we'd better call this to our *own* financing source. They're much more used to handling cars like this." Why, of course they wanted the insurance. And Don could finance the car wherever the dealership wanted.

The next morning Don personally called the Nelsons' deal into the house financing institution. By three that afternoon the manager called back, hesitating just slightly as he spoke. "Don, I know I should turn this deal down. These people have never had a payment this large in their life. But they pay everything like clockwork. And the bank does anything they want. I guess we'll go with the deal. By the way, do you really want to put all that insurance on them?" Why, of course. A $2400-dollar profit was nice on the deal, but the F and I profit would be nearly that large. "And besides," Don volunteered, "anyone that works that much might get sick. You need the protection, too." His source said yes to the insurance, too.

The Nelsons loved that car, caressed it daily, and drove it

proudly to work for seven months. But in the first week of that month, Mr. Nelson had appendicitis and missed his paycheck for two weeks. The insurance Don had so happily sold them didn't cover that gap in their income, either, since the insurance didn't begin to pay until the fifteenth day of any illness. Mrs. Nelson came down with ulcers the next week and had to miss work for two weeks, too. Ted, the salesman, brought them both to Don's office shortly after that. "Don, we really appreciate all you did for us. But finances are a little tight right now, and we were wondering if you could buy our car back. We'll buy something else from you, of course, that's a little bit more reasonable."

Don shifted in his chair. How could he buy it back? They owed $3500 more than it was worth. He found some quick way to hedge. "Luxury cars have really dropped in value, you know," and excused himself.

Within two weeks they were back again. "Don, please help us. We just can't make the payments. Please do something."

Don Burns was not totally devoid of heart. Behind the dealership, close to the garbage dump, was a six-year-old station wagon with a broken windshield. The car had been sitting on the lot for over three years, slowly dying. Besides the broken windshield, the block was cracked a little, and three of the tires were flat. The paint had turned one of those gray-brown colors that is the sign of many years of neglect, and dust had settled comfortably on the seats and dash. That car had been written down to nothing; each ninety days its economic worth lowered, until the moment the comptroller had walked into J. C.'s office and said, "Well, you've got one free now, J. C."

But the wagon did have some value to a small loan house. Those people will loan money on just about anything, so Don placed a call to the local office of a favorite dip house and quickly arranged a loan for $1000 dollars. He also called the loan manager at the Nelsons' bank and borrowed them another $1000 dollars on their signature. Banks are very lenient with their regular customers and seldom check credit bureaus or automobile lending institutions if a person pays them regularly. He called another dip house and borrowed the Nelsons $1500 dollars on their household goods. Most of those goods were already mortgaged, but dip houses don't really care about that, and they listed a couple of bicycles, the old furniture on the back of their porch, and their clothes as collateral.

Don and Ted also worked on that station wagon for the Nelsons—put tubes in the tires, replaced the windshield, and actually replaced the block. The car is still running now, and the Nelsons are maybe a little bit happier. Their payment is lower, too. That nice luxury coupe cost them $345 a month. They pay $225 on the five-year-old wagon—the total of their three payments.

We know about the Nelsons. But why did *you* trade cars the last time you walked into a dealership? Have you really always wanted to own a sports car? Does your spouse ever subtly hint that one of those nice new smaller station wagons would be a good thing to have? "Honey, we really do a lot of hauling—taking all the kids and their friends—and don't forget, the 'estate wagons' are on sale this month, or at least that's what I read in the paper."

Do you ever have some unexplained urge just to pull in to some car store and look over the new merchandise, thinking all the time that a new car "is really just more payments. And I make car payments anyway, so why not drive a new one?" In the last forty years—really during the lifetime of about any person who may be reading this book—the American automobile has been much more than an unemotional means of moving from one place to another. The car has been the most easily attainable symbol of family and individual affluence. The Wraithmores, for instance, may live in that big house on the hill and may measure their ancestry in centuries rather than decades. But in all likelihood they drive a car pretty much like one you can afford, too. They may even drive one that is just a little bit older and less luxurious than yours.

The majority of Americans have had access to this moving realization of our aspirations because of a nice thing that took place in 1915—the advent of installment buying. What we couldn't buy in a lump sum we could buy "on time." Now anyone would be a fool to say that our enchantment with the automobile is some fickle and wasteful thing. It's not. Sure, we may not "need" new cars every year or two, if you always define a need as something essential for life. But what's wrong with just craving something, with enjoying the touch and sound and feel of the machine and the envious looks of our friends as we drive by in the latest embodiment of Detroit's or Japan's idea of style and success? I would imagine that if our society were based on needs rather than wants, we wouldn't have much of a society or economy at all.

In the past decade, however, many of us began to break the inviolate rule of a credit society: taking longer to pay for products than they will last or than we will want to own them. Because of nicely worded and portrayed advertisements, and with no thanks to our convenient desire to believe easy lies that turn fantasy into truth, the American public signed up wholeheartedly for these long-term, easy-payment credit plans. It would be nice to blame this little problem on automobile manufacturers and dealers, who righteously say, "Well, if we didn't bring out forty-eight-month and fifty-four-month financing, people just wouldn't be able to buy cars." But that would be too easy, laying blame on the pusher who sells you the fix, rather than on our own weakness for needing the fix in the first place. No, we've done a fine job by ourselves. Car people like to tell you how the automobile recession of the late seventies was caused by basic problems with the economy and a drastic restructuring of our driving habits—"It's those damn Arabs who caused it all." But I would suspect that there's another reason. "Easy" financing terms became the most popular way for Americans to buy cars in the seventies. Who could resist that nice man's spiel that "forty-eight months will really keep your payments affordable, folks"? Sure, the payments were easier to make. But, as we've indicated, that nice, pleasant payment really accomplished only one thing: it increased the negative worth of your estate.

During the late seventies, literally hundreds of thousands of people who wanted to trade cars couldn't because of that negative worth. Many of these people hadn't returned to the car market by 1980; they were still in the bucket or were still smarting from the realization that new cars just are not as much fun to own as they used to be. Lots of them went broke, too. They fell prey to our most dangerous myth: if people will lend you money, then that must mean you can afford to pay it back.

I have too many memories of good people sitting in my office, some quiet panic pervading every movement, asking for help in releasing them from their monthly time bomb, the car payment. All of these people owed hundreds, and, at times, thousands of dollars more on their cars than any sane person would pay them. I had the unhappy duty of telling each of these people that we would be glad to take their car off their hands if they would hand over the car *and* $400 or $600 or a $1000 dollars.

Well, how in God's name are you going to correct that now? The new smaller cars cost more than you ever dreamed of paying for transportation, and you really don't like paying more for what appears to be less car, anyway. Would it be better to simply fall out of love with all four-wheeled beauties and drive some dull gray motorized wheelbarrow, or maybe look for something else as your shiny play toy—bowling ball, vinyl kite, model airplane?

There's no need to do that. You can still drive something that quickens the pulse a little, still take lots of pride in that thing that's just a little bit nicer than your neighbor's. But you're going to have to be smarter when you walk in the store. And you're going to have to modify somewhat your definition of what is really need and what is really want.

A smart person will define "need" as something that is worth some risk. You need food, for instance, and I imagine most of us would even steal if people we loved were really starving. "Wants" are things that should not deserve much risk. You want to go to the show, for instance, but you certainly wouldn't risk your financial well-being. You want new carpeting for the house, but would you risk not having the money to buy food just to have a new nap under your feet? Of course not.

Well, then, why are you risking your credit, muffled phone calls from impatient lending institutions, and checking accounts with two-digit balances just to drive a car? We all need to have wheels, to be able to make it comfortably from point A to point B. But the extent to which we fill that need must be determined by our ability to pay. If you can pay cash for that car and barely miss the bucks, you probably don't have many unfulfilled needs that money alone can meet. You buy the car that fits your fancy, then your cash. But if you're like most of us, who have to hire money, you can't afford the luxury of paying out too many dollar bills that automatically cost a buck fifty when you pay them back. Buy a new car, if you can afford it. Or buy a newer car. But don't obligate yourself to payments that never really lower your debt. And you never lower your debt if the thing you are buying is always worth less than the payments you've made.

Which brings us to a simple conclusion: if trading cars is something you don't *have* to do, don't do it, unless you know that you can always sell your car for more than you owe. If you can afford the nicest, smartest car on the block, by all means, buy it, if it gives you pleasure. Just make sure then that you're strong enough to pay for the damage up front, not down the road.

What Can You Really Afford?

If you are the type of person who just must have car payments to be happy, your most important decision before visiting showrooms is the amount of that payment. Can you afford a higher payment? In all honesty, would a lower payment, maybe just $30 or $40 dollars lower, support your habit? Car people will tell you "inflation" means you have to pay more, an American tradition, or something like that. Sure—just like high gas prices are all the Arabs' fault, and gas companies aren't making more profit.

You need to budget your car payment just as you do your food purchases. For instance, do you blow your whole week's food money on Kobe beef just because it's on sale this week for $22 dollars a pound? No, you control your spending on food, because you plan before you shop. Do that with your car purchase. If you follow the steps outlined in the rest of this book, you will have a lower payment than folks who don't buy cars carefully. And if you're really smart, you'll perhaps have a payment lower than your present one. Even though your method of buying is payments, you must consider every single part of your transaction as if you were paying cash.

New vs. Used

The Johnsons had come to the dealership planning to buy a $4000-dollar used car. They had always purchased cars that were a few years old, usually nice, simple, mid-sized sedans. Normally they paid $1000 dollars down, too. The Johnsons are in their sixties: sensible folks who seldom do rash or wasteful things. However, their rational thinking was disturbed that day because there was a sales contest in progress for the new-car guys, and Killer needed just one more new car to be on top again. This time the prize was a trip to Las Vegas.

Of course, Killer didn't get these folks by accident. Though he's primarily a new-car salesman, Killer considers just about anyone on the used-car lot a prospect for a new car. Good salesmen always believe to some degree what they say, however contorted the logic, and Mr. DeMarco felt very strongly that the Johnsons should be driving a new car. He met them at their car, parked just between the new-car storage lot and the used-car lot, and quietly started laying out his most effective new-car sales pitch.

"Mr. and Mrs. Johnson, we do have some mighty nice sedans up there on the used lot. But let me ask you something," he said, while walking slowly toward the new sedans. Killer knew the people would walk with him; they always did. After all, who wants to appear rude? "Would you consider buying a new car, one with a warranty, one that no one has abused and that will be much more economical to operate? Would you consider that, if you could drive the new car with no more debt than a used one and with a payment that's even lower than a used one?"

Both of the Johnsons had started to interrupt Killer the moment he mentioned a new car, but he just kept talking. By the time he'd presented his irresistible logic, they'd stopped walking and looked at each other. "Mr. DeMarco, just how are you going to do that?" Johnson had an amused smile on his face.

Killer laughed. "Now, Mr. Johnson, I can do it, but that wasn't the question. Would you consider a new car under those circumstances?"

"Well, if you're telling me I'll owe less on a new car than a used one, and that my payments will be less, I guess I'd be interested. I don't think you can do that, though." Mr. Johnson's tone was both skeptical and hopeful—who wouldn't rather drive a new car? He'd really wanted one all along.

Killer unlocked the driver's door of a baby-blue sedan—the Johnsons were driving a light-colored car, a good indication they didn't like dark ones—and sat down, reaching in one movement to the passenger door, pushing it open. "Mr. Johnson, sit down for a moment and let me show you a few things. Could you get the back door for the missus?"

The Johnsons without thinking got in the car—it's a nice psychological trick: don't ask people to do things, *assume* they'll do them—and Killer pumped the pedal twice, starting the air-conditioning at the same time, talking quietly as he sat there.

Mrs. Johnson made the first really positive statement. "My it smells so good. Why does it?" She was giving the first buying signal, and Killer looked at Mr. Johnson's shirt pocket—there were no cigarettes there.

"That's the smell of a car with no cigarette smoke, or spilled beer on the seats, Mrs. Johnson."

"Oh really, I like that; you know we never let people smoke in our cars."

"That's a mighty good thing, ma'am—you just wouldn't believe the things our used car people have to do to make some cars clean." Both the Johnsons nodded without knowing it. "Mr. Johnson, do you know a road around here that's really rutted and bumpy?" They were pulling out of the lot as Killer spoke. He hadn't asked them if they wanted to go for a ride; he'd just assumed they would.

"Well, there's that road that goes out to the mill—it's closed now, you know, but it surely is a bad one." Killer was conveniently already heading in that direction as Mr. Johnson opened the glove box, then ran his hand down the side of the seat.

Killer said, "You know, these new seats are orthopedically designed, and the rear seat has been angled differently this year—better support there, too. Mrs. Johnson, how does it feel?"

She laughed. "Well, I'll tell you one thing, it's more comfortable than *our* back seat!" This was another buying signal.

As Killer headed down the road, he suddenly steered the right wheels off the road, two wheels traveling on the pavement and two along a rutty embankment. The Johnsons were shocked for a second but then smiled. "How do you like *this* for a nice ride—I'll bet you couldn't do it in your car."

"That's really something. Do you do this with everyone?" Killer always does. It's not that a new car really rides better than an older one, however, but that normal people don't drive off the road too much. The Johnsons weren't thinking that of course; they were just impressed with the ride.

The sedan stopped before the Johnsons knew it, and Killer walked around to the passenger side and opened the door. "Mr. Johnson, I thought *I'd* ride a little, if you don't mind." The man probably didn't want to drive the car, but what was he going to do, tell Killer to walk back around? Getting Johnson into the driver's seat was the most important thing Killer needed to accomplish to sell that car—even more than money. Very few of us can resist the exhilarating pleasure of driving a new car, especially when quietly thinking in the back of your head, This car can be mine for less money than a used one. It's not a logical statement, is it? Read on.

Killer normally doesn't take people to his office when he's planning to show them a lot of figures; he takes them to the small conference room with the window overlooking the lot. The Johnsons were sitting on both sides of him facing that window, the new powder-blue sedan conveniently visible through the glass. "Before we talk figures, Mr. and Mrs. Johnson, I want to ask you just one thing. Do you really like that car? Do you like it better than any used car you've ever owned?"

"Yes, we like it very much, but there's the money problem," Mr. Johnson said.

"Well, then, let me ask you this: Will you buy it if it makes financial sense to buy it?" The technique is called an "early close"—a "yes" means the car is sold, and the Johnsons said "yes."

Killer drew a vertical line down a sheet of paper, putting the list price of the new car, $7800, in one column and the "asking price" of a three-year-old sedan in the other column. The asking price was a mythical figure—that three-year-old sedan was on the books at $3800 dollars, and the dealership would sell it for $4200. But Killer's asking price on paper was $5800 dollars. He then deducted $2000 dollars from both figures. "Let's just assume that your trade is worth this, folks; it's what cars like yours have been coming in for."

Killer paused for a minute for any reaction, but there was none. Good, he thought. We won't have to argue about their trade. It was a very safe way to find out what Mr. Johnson thought his car was worth. If he'd jumped, Killer would have said, "Now, Mr. Johnson, that's what the *average* car like yours has been bringing. I'm sure when we have it appraised, yours will be worth more."

"Now, just for comparison's sake, we're going to forget that you owe anything on your present car. I believe you said the payoff was $800, and since you are paying $1000 down, we don't really need to be concerned with your payoff." That sounded logical, Mr. Johnson thought.

"Now, we have a balance on the new car of $5800 dollars and on the used car of $3800 dollars. Used cars, as you know, especially when they're three years old, can only be financed for two years. *And* the law says they *have* to be financed at a higher interest rate, too. If you were to finance $3800 on the used car for two years, your payments would be . . ." Killer factored out their payment on the highest interest rate, the one that was really never used, then picked up an insurance book and tabulated their monthly insurance premium. " . . . about $225 dollars a month." The Johnsons, stunned, said nothing.

Killer continued talking. "As you know, there really are no inexpensive used cars any more. Now, on the new car, we have a balance of $5800 dollars. We usually finance new cars on forty-eight months, and of course, finance them at a lower rate. Let's see what your payment would be." This time Killer figured the payment on the "discount rate"— what the dealership actually paid for money. He seldom sold cars at that rate, but this time he was taking no chances. Killer conveniently neglected to add insurance to the payment. "There! Your payments on the new car will be only $155 dollars per month."

"Yes," Mr. Johnson said quickly, "but we're paying two more years than on the used car."

"That's right. But look at this for a moment. The twenty-four payments on the old car would total $5400 dollars. The forty-eight payments on the new car would total about $7400 dollars." Killer wrote both figures down, then pulled his used-car "blue book" from his pocket, flipping quickly to the middle of the book.

"Sure, you've paid $2000 more for the new car, but what is it going to be worth in four years?" His finger stopped on the line for sedans just like the new one outside the window, and he quickly wrote down the wholesale figure for "extra clean" models. It's a column in the blue book that is seldom used, since very few cars are extra clean. "Look here"—he pointed to the figure as he spoke—"a four-year-old one like this is going to be worth $3200 dollars. Sure, you will have paid $7400 in payments, but when you finish paying, you have an asset worth $3200. So let's deduct that $3200 from the $7400. If this book is right, and it's what all the banks use, you'll have a real investment in the new car of the difference, only $4200 dollars."

"Now, let's look at the used car. Twenty-four payments

is $5400 dollars. Now, in four years, that car will be seven years old. Let's look at the value of a seven-year-old sedan." Killer flipped the page and held the book up for them to see—there was no category for seven-year-old cars in the book. "Mr. and Mrs. Johnson, a seven-year-old car is really worth nothing. You might get a few hundred for it, but just for the sake of discussion let's say that you get $600 dollars for it. That would still mean, if you deduct the $600 from the $5400, that you have investment in the used car of $4800 dollars. You would have $600 more in it than the new one, and you would also have all those repair bills that older cars seem to incur."

The Johnsons took delivery on their new car in two days. The payment was just a little higher than the $155 figure that had been discussed, however. "Folks, I'm embarrassed to tell you this, but I completely forgot to figure your life and health insurance payment when we were talking. It's my fault, and I'll understand if you don't want to take the car." He wasn't worried, though—this little bit of reverse psychology always worked. The Johnsons argued not a whit at the $32-dollar-per-month addition to their payment. Killer gave Mrs. Johnson one of those bottles of Chanel, too. It was a nice exchange for the free trip to Vegas.

It would be easy for most of us to listen to the logic of Mr. DeMarco and drive off in a new car. And, quite honestly, the logic is correct. Killer didn't lie directly to the folks, either. But, if he had sold them the three-year-old car for *$4200* minus their $2000-dollar trade, if he'd quoted them a payment on a normal interest rate for thirty-six months—of course, you can finance three-year-old cars for thirty-six months, if you want to—the Johnsons could have bought that car for under $100 dollars a month. If he'd quoted them payments on the same amount of money for twenty-four months, the Johnsons would have paid less than $110.

What happened? First the Johnsons fell prey to the logic of numbers that lie too easily. Then they accepted Killer's figures on that nice used car without once questioning their accuracy. And then they believed the wrong columns in the used-car book. The Johnsons' new car is not going to be worth $3800 in four years. They'll be lucky if it's worth $2000. But don't think these folks are unhappy with their new powder-blue sedan, because they are not. Would it be too trite to say it? Ignorance is bliss, especially for these folks.

Unless you plan, and I mean are sure, to keep a car for a long time, a new car is probably one of the worst investments in the world. As a matter of fact, ninety-nine out of a hundred will drop *forty percent* in value the day they're driven home. For instance, let's say you buy a $10,000 Minutula, the cheapest car in the Expenso line. That car cost the dealer $7800 minus the "dealer holdback," the two or three percent of the profit Expenso Manufacturing Company "holds back" from the dealer. The dealer conveniently considers this a *cost,* since he actually pays the manufacturer this money. However, every three months or so, the Expenso Manufacturing Company sends the dealer a check for all those two and three percents. Let's say our $10,000-dollar Minutula had a holdback of $300 dollars. The $10,000-dollar car now costs the dealer $7500. Included in that figure, however, is "freight," what the dealer actually was charged for shipping the car. On our Minutula, the freight is $300. Now our value is down to $7200. Now, take from that figure the $50 dollars or so manufacturers charge dealers for "preparation"; the charge for gas, $10 to $29 dollars; the advertising allowance, $50 to $100 dollars. The remainder is the true cost of the car to the dealer: $7090 dollars, taking low figures.

But after a week, if you drive back into the lot to trade in your new Minutula, the dealer is not going to give you $7090 for it because he would then have to sell it for as much money as a new car, if he's going to make money. So, what will he give you? Try $6000 or less.

But there's another reason new cars drop so dramatically in value. Probably we owe most of the thanks to General Motors. In the early 1950s, the fellows there in the G.M. think-tank decided to "age" their new cars deliberately, change them each year rather than every four or five years. For several years it became hard to recognize a Chevrolet, the changes were so drastic. And since all of the nice customers out there liked this annual magic, pretty soon all manufacturers were following suit. It costs lots of money to make dramatic styling changes like this, so the manufacturers did what all business people do when faced with large expenditures—they decided to put most of their money in styling changes rather than product quality. It wasn't a decision to manufacture pure junk, either, but rather one to make cars whose working parts had an effective life of several years, rather than a decade, before needing major work. You've all known about planned obsolescence for quite some time; well, that planning is right at home, and evident, in your car.

But the manufacturers are not really at fault, are they? On the whole we don't want to keep cars for a decade or longer, and I doubt if we would pay for cars that would last like that, knowing they'll be leaving us in a few years anyway. Instead, people want cars that will entertain them for three or four years; they want the newer shape, sexy new color, the latest computer to titillate them.

But there is some *good news* in all this. There are actually people out there who are dumb enough to trade in brand-new cars, and if you can find one of those cars, it can be a very cheap buy. A car that is one month or nine months old can be as good as new and cost you thousands less.

We've said little here about how to appraise a used car should you decide to buy one, but the chapter on shopping will tell you how.

American vs. Foreign

Do you own an alligator? Perhaps an Izod sweater or shirt or pair of socks? Maybe even alligator underwear? If you do, why did you purchase it? Were you absolutely convinced the toothy little creature assured you of a better product and therefore justified the higher price? Or did you buy that Izod underwear simply to add a little status to your occasional desire to "open your raincoat," as they say?

Thanks to American car manufacturers, foreign cars seem to have firmly entrenched themselves as the alligators of the highways. For years Detroit either ignored the pesky little critters or blamed their popularity on the "Eastern intellectual elitists," who drove foreign cars purely as a status symbol. Real Americans wouldn't be caught dead in any of those snobby contraptions—Detroit was sure of that. American Motors, by investing in little beauties like the Metropolitan or Rambler, the big boys knew, was just jousting at windmills.

As usual, the boys who run General Motors and Chrysler and Ford were wrong. Most people weren't buying foreign cars for snob appeal; they were buying them because of quality. While the foreign automakers plodded along producing cars that never seemed to change in appearance but always improved in dependability, the bimbos in Detroit rode home in limousines while their plants continued to pursue superficial things such as flashy styling at the expense of economy. American manufacturers continued to instill in their workers that efficiency was more important than excellence of product, punishing workers who stopped an assembly line to correct a problem rather than rewarding them.

By 1978 the foreign-car share of the automobile market had grown to twenty-three percent. By 1980 that share had grown to nearly thirty percent. And, wonder of wonders, Detroit finally quit laughing. Of course, the boys didn't accept any blame for the changing market. They issued noble press releases describing the "new value systems" of buyers and redefined the "attitudinal perceptions" of buyers and actually began to produce cars which were equal in quality to any import, better in gas mileage than most, and lower priced than virtually all. Detroit then settled back in the smog that seems to envelop its corporate board rooms, poured itself a Gibson with two onions, and waited for the herds of true Americans to return to the fold.

But they didn't. After all the years of tinsel and baloney, sloppy workmanship, and general dissatisfaction with American cars, buyers simply kept buying foreign. The alligator continued to rule the road.

I don't have sympathy for the stupidity of Detroit, but I do believe that the myth of the alligator is just that now. The new generations of small American cars are every bit as well-made as their foreign counterparts. The individual concern for quality, from the designers to the assembly-line workers, is real and ever-present. The manufacturers don't hold this concern out of any deep desire to be patriotic or noble. They have espoused it to survive. Workers on the assembly line care about quality because their jobs depend on it. But the reason for their concern isn't important—the fact that they are concerned is.

Now that Detroit is actually producing something worth a damn for a change, it may be worth your time to try their products. But there's another reason that may appeal to those of you, like me, who believe in just deserts. During all those years when import cars were the only answer for many sensible people, the import manufacturers and dealers were ripping off your pocketbook on a scale greater than anything Detroit would ever attempt. Since these nice folks cornered the quality market, they saw no reason to ever, ever give the customer a price break. Virtually all foreign cars were sold at full list price. Many dealers who attempted to discount their wares were cut off by the factory. These dealers would receive a quiet phone call or letter stating, "Unfortunately, we will not be able to allocate you cars for the foreseeable future."

This foreign blackmail was very effective. It succeeded in taking millions of us. It made many foreign producers wealthy beyond Detroit's wildest imaginings. And it is still practiced by lots of manufacturers today. I have never respected people who sell bread for $10 dollars a loaf after a hurricane, and I'll be damned if I respect foreign-car manufacturers for that same reason. *That's* the second best reason to give dopey ole Detroit one more try. The first best reason? They *are* making better cars these days.

Trading Down

This does not mean buying a car from a dealer located on the wrong side of the tracks. "Trading down" is a term used when buyers want to trade their newer car for a less expensive and older one. It also refers to buyers trading very big cars for very little cars. Many people are doing the latter now, trading their full-size cars, the ones that used to be so fashionable, for one of the generation of new small cars. And, unfortunately, the process is always an expensive one.

If you are planning to trade down, you face two obstacles. First, larger, older cars as trade-ins are just about as popular as leprosy. The real dollar value of these cars, the wholesale value, is therefore very low. If your larger trade-in is financed, you will probably enter your buying transaction "in the bucket"—you will owe more on your car than it's worth. The second problem is the mark-up on new small cars. Even though the mark-up, or margin of profit, on small cars is now larger than it was several years ago, dealerships still make somewhat smaller gross profit per car on these units. Before you decide to trade down, read carefully the section on *selling your own car*. Your best chance in a trade-down situation is just that.

You should also consider selling your own car if you plan to buy an older and less expensive car than your present one. This type of trade-down situation usually requires a dealer to actually pay cash from his pocket when he deals with you—in essence to give you his car and change. Stores don't like to do this and will invariably offer you much less for your car than it is worth.

THINGS THAT IMPRESS
AND TERRIFY SALESMEN:
TRAITS YOU CAN CULTIVATE

Forrest DeLong was losing patience again. The lady he'd spent the past two hours walking around the lot was just too damned flighty: liking a small car and then a large car, in love one minute with four doors and then wanting to drive a coupe. And now she was trying to change her mind again, just as he laid the buyer's order in front of her. Bitch. This type of bird was even worse than the other one he'd had that morning—the one that didn't like anything, never once showed an ounce of enthusiasm for anything on the lot. At least *that* guy had bought a car from him. It wasn't much of a deal, less than $200 dollars, but, hell, Forrest didn't think the guy was even interested. And the guy had made it damn clear that he didn't really need to buy a car from here, anyway. "At least it was a sale"— Forrest kept repeating that.

It must have been the moon, for Killer was having trouble that day, too. His first customer, sent to him by a bird dog, was nice enough but just wouldn't fall for any line Killer threw out. "Now, Mr. DeMarco, let's just keep this sweet and simple. If you want to sell me a car, and I really do want to buy one from you, let's decide how much I'm going to pay for your car before talking about my trade." The guy really knew new car prices, too, and Killer finally agreed to a price that was just a tad above a $300-dollar deal.

"Now," the man had said, "let's get my car appraised. I have a pretty good idea what it's worth. I shopped it to three places yesterday, and I'm real interested in seeing how close your guys are." Killer normally can handle this type of guy; first he finds out what the man thinks his car is worth, and then he tries to talk him down. But the man would not tell Killer a thing; he wouldn't even say where he'd shopped the car. Killer nearly dropped his teeth when the guys on the used-car lot said they had already put a figure on the car the day before, a strong figure. I'll be damned, Killer thought. The guy has worked me in a hole. The man actually got the right price for his trade. And he'd already gotten the right price on the new one. Killer was on the phone to Allen, his bird dog, as soon as the guy drove out. "Hey Allen, do me a favor and send that type of guy to someone else, okay?"

Some people get good deals on cars by accident. Some get them by design. Forrest DeLong's lady customer did buy a car that day, a quick, easy deal, because she was the indecisive type. Killer's man got a good deal because he'd certainly done his ground work. You need to know the things that really impress and terrify car salesmen.

Indecision

If you are the indecisive type, you may be a lucky car shopper and a very lucky car buyer. Salesmen are not interested in long-term relationships; they need to sell you right then, when you're first on their lot. Always be indecisive, even after you sign a buyer's order, and you'll make those guys sweat every minute they work you.

Indecision to a salesman means you may not buy, or worse, may back out of the deal you've already agreed to. If you're lukewarm until the moment you drive out, your car will be polished to perfection, the service manager will probably have personally driven it, and virtually no hanky-panky will take place. They don't want to lose you.

Lack of Enthusiasm

You are standing by the one and only new car you think you love in the whole world. It's the perfect color, it has all the right options, including the digital ashtray, and your instinct is to kiss it right then and there. Don't. Don't even look at it, unless you frown. Tell your salesman how much better you like some other car down the road. Lack of enthusiasm is one of the easiest things you can do in a car negotiation. Put yourself in a salesman's place for a moment. There he is, spending his days talking to countless people who take up his time and then smile, shake hands, and say, "Thanks very much, we'll be back." These "be-backs" are the bane of car salesmen; they're perhaps the most frustrating aspect of the business. Why? Nine out of ten times a "be-back" won't ever be back: he'll end up buying a car from a dealership down the road. It's very important, then, for a salesman to sell you the first time you set foot on his lot. The larger dealerships have even developed procedures to make sure you don't walk away too quickly; they have people on the floor, "walkers," who do nothing but catch you as you head for the door and try once more to get you to buy right then. Some dealerships even fire salesmen who let customers walk out without bringing in someone else who might be able to close them.

So, how does a salesman feel if you're not enthusiastic, if you can't find one single car you really like, if you do nothing but talk about the *really* nice car you saw down the road, and the really nice price they gave you to boot? He is honestly going to be scared. He'll do anything to keep you there, including offering a price cut or two. One of the first quaint slogans every car salesman learns is, "be-backs won't make you any greenbacks." There is nothing stronger in your favor than that fear.

Knowledge

Car salesmen are so used to blind, deaf, and dumb customers that if you cannot be flustered by their tactics, cannot fall prey to their hypnotic spiels, you will save money and gain the respect of your salesman.

Nonromantic Attitudes

However hard you work, you know that you are going to lose money, so why should your eyelids flutter with the romance of it all? Let that salesman know you consider a car a necessary evil, not your paramour. Let him know you have better things to do with your time. Tell him straight out your romantic qualities concern your pocketbook only.

4

Know Your
Present Car

THE INSTRUCTIVE TALE
OF JIM WRIGHT

Jim Wright was a young person back in the fifties, when new cars were cheap, fancy colors and two-tone paint jobs were the rage, and the automobile business was in its "gold rush" days—owning an automobile store back then might have been even better than panning for those little nuggets and slivers tumbling through some mountain stream. It was a time when everyone was in love with cars, and few people had the vaguest idea of what mystical formulas constituted the buying and selling process. But, who cared? It was certainly a more informal business then. Cars didn't have "sticker prices," and one moment that pretty pink-and-cream Bel Aire Delux might have a list price of $2000 dollars, the next a price of $3000 dollars.

Financing was downright fun during those years, too. Virtually all stores were "recourse" operations: each dealer would have to guarantee payments to lending institutions on every car sold. If you lived in a small town and happened to know someone who worked at a dealership, credit applications just didn't exist. A quick call, saying "yes, these folks are good people," carried much more weight than any impersonal sheet of paper that bared your soul to the world.

The fifties were also a time when used cars were the step-children of the automobile business. Dealerships would take your car in trade if you insisted, but would just as quickly whisk that old thing off to some used-car lot down on the other side of the tracks. Or they'd sell it to a "road hog," one of the supposedly untrustworthy vagabonds who seemed to travel the countryside, peddling junky cars to "white trash" and the like. No self-respecting person would sell one of those things, much less *buy* one. Most folks put used cars in the same category as that old piece of furniture sitting on the back porch, the chair with the heart-shaped back, carved rose crown, and scalloped legs: who would want something like that when "modern" furniture was the rage, sleek things with toothpick legs and blue-knit backs your spouse had purchased. Proud chairs these that sat in front of your new ten-inch TV screen.

Jim Wright was twenty-two then, the year his father gave him a car. It was a regulation black English Ford, one of the few small cars sold in America, and it was not the type of car any self-respecting young man would claim as his own. During a time when cars were flashy, longer than high, and trimmed in "real double-dipped chrome mold-ings," when "fluid drive" automatic transmissions, and "Crown Royal Coupes" ruled the road, Jim Wright just didn't feel comfortable in something with turn signals that didn't blink, but rather two red little "wings" that unfolded themselves from the columns between the doors, pointing left or right like some dog's stunted leg stretched in the wind. Jim would keep that car far, far way from fire hydrants, for sure.

One day, not too long after meeting a young lady named

Gloria, Jim decided to get himself a proper car for courting. He didn't really have the money for a new car, or at least that's what he thought, but Jim got in that English Ford and drove down to the Chevrolet dealership, the one with the fancy new showroom overlooking the intersection of every important road leading to town. The new Chevys were lined up in front of that showroom like a chorus line of pretty girls all dressed up in pink and cream, and there wasn't a black car in sight, much less anything square with little wings. And dancing at the very center of that line was just about the most beautiful thing Jim had ever seen: a candy-apple red, two-door coupe trimmed completely in a thin stripe of white that seemed to follow each curve of metal and chrome. Now, here was the car for a young man.

Jim was surprised at how easily that car became his, too. The man who talked with him never once looked at or mentioned the Ford; he gave him $700 dollars "in trade," whatever that meant, told Jim his payments would be $50 dollars a month "with a balloon," and also talked him out of $400 dollars in cash—Jim's only savings.

That candy-apple red Chevrolet was the beginning of Jim Wright's education in the car business. About six weeks later, a young couple on Elm Street bought a Chevy just like it and just happened to mention to Jim's folks that "actually, $2800 dollars isn't much money for something like this." Mr. Wright looked at them for a second before speaking. "You say $2800? Well, it can't really be the same car as my son's—he paid $3500 for it." Not too many days later, Jim saw his old English Ford sitting outside Black's Pharmacy on the square. Some sixteen-year-old kid had bought it—for $100 dollars. How could the Chevy place do that, sell a $700-dollar car for $100? And then there was the "balloon." Jim's dad was the one who saw it on the contract. Twenty-four payments of $50 dollars. And one final payment of $1200 dollars.

He kept the car for exactly twenty-three months and then had to sell it to the dealership for a $600-dollar loss. He had no choice. Neither he nor his dad could afford the balloon payment. The salesman who had waited on him originally did offer him a piece of advice when he took the Chevy back, however. Maybe the guy was feeling guilty, or maybe he knew Wright was getting married that month to Gloria. For whatever reason, the salesman sent Jim to a road hog. "He will sell you something used," the guy had said. "We don't keep any of that used stuff here." Jim bought an old car from one of the hogs. He also spent a good deal of time with the guy, listening to every bit of knowledge, every funny story which seemed to spout automatically from the guy's head.

In four years, on his twenty-eighth birthday, Wright bought his second new car. He didn't trade his old car this time, either, but sold it to a road hog. He and Gloria spent two days driving to different dealerships in neighboring towns, asking each salesman the cash price on "real stripped-down Bel Aires." Regardless of what any previous dealership had said, Jim told them, one and all, "Your price is too high." The Wrights finally bought a car from a dealership two towns away from theirs. They didn't finance at that store, either, but took one more day from work to arrange financing at their local bank. This time the new Chevy would remain theirs. Their love of cars would stay the same too. Jim Wright had simply made a decision to understand the car-buying process. He used that knowledge on his second purchase. And he used it from then on, as we'll see.

All the previous sections of this book haven't exactly

added to the romance and mystique of car buying. As a matter of fact, I would hope that they have made you a little wary. But the intention of everything presented so far is not to take away any joy from those of you who look forward to your regular dickerings. I have not meant to portray car people as the only sales people who use ignorance and psychological warfare, either. Most of the same techniques and half-truths are used by anyone who sells, whether an insurance man or a furniture man.

It's really hard, however, for an insurance man to inflict great damage on your pocketbook, since most insurance companies' policies are reasonably competitive in their cost. Sure, some guy may sell you more insurance than you need, but for some reason our natural defense mechanisms protect us more from the overenthusiastic insurance man than from even a lukewarm car man. Have you ever turned to your spouse and said, "Honey, let's go driving this afternoon and visit a few insurance salesmen! I hear that there are some mighty ritzy new policies out this year!"?

Every illustration in this book is designed to help you do one thing: come out a little better the next time your natural urge compels a trip to the local car store. You can do that, if you follow carefully the information in the remaining chapters. After all, if the Wrights, now a middle-aged couple with two teenage kids, can learn the tricks of the car game, you can too. Hell, Gloria Wright can't even balance her checkbook, and Jim wouldn't know how to play a good hand of poker if he were holding a Royal Flush. He'd probably fold. But the Wrights do know how to buy cars. Just last week, they took delivery on a really nice Gargantula fastback and they were just as excited about driving into the store to pick up that shiny beauty as anyone in the world. What's even nicer is the Wrights' feeling about that car right now. They haven't had a moment of buyer's remorse. Not a second of doubt has plagued them, and I daresay none will. These people love cars in the most irrational way, but they have learned to keep that emotion far away from any decision-making process. The Wrights by lucky trial and error have learned just what *you* need to know.

Like the Wrights you must know the answer to the four most important questions if you're going to be a smart car buyer: what does their car cost, what is your car worth in actual wholesale dollars, what is a fair profit, and what is the cheapest and most advantageous financing. One thing is sure, however: your car will always be worth more than anyone will offer you. That value is not determined by any book, either. And the value should certainly not be determined by the dealer you are buying from. Instead, several things will determine the answer to this most important question—the value of your car: its overall condition, popularity, mileage, and the current local wholesale and retail market.

THE IMPORTANCE OF A
CLEAN, SOUND CAR

Love them though they may, the Wrights aren't exactly fastidious keepers of cars. Under the front seat, for instance, is a vintage collection of crumpled Big Mac containers, one coat hanger, a couple of pens, two unsmoked cigarettes, one sock, half of an AAA "Southeastern United States" road map, a toll receipt from the Florida turnpike, matches, and a very dirty dish rag used frequently to wipe condensation from the windshield. On the whole, a good imitation of the city dump. The dashboard is littered with the everyday needs of busy people, and the trunk contains enough forgotten merchandise to supply at least half of the Salvation Army's annual Christmas drive.

"Christ! Gloria will you look at this!" Jim had been pulling all the nice things from under the seat, when something soft and mushy stuck in the springs caught the attention of his hand. It was a baked potato. "I *knew* we'd ordered four potatoes! Now how in God's name did it get under there?"

"Who knows; I guess the seat was hungry, or something." Gloria was standing by the back door counting the change, over $3 dollars' worth of nickels, quarters, and pennies. "You know, I think money multiplies back there. We should pull this seat out more often."

The Wrights' cleaning exercise was not a frequent ritual, but it was a regular one. Every few years at car trading time, they would spend a day working on every inch of the car—a task they aptly referred to as "sending the car to the beauty parlor." Jim would remove the ashtrays and soak them, then he would use a brush on every single piece of chrome, including the ones most people don't look at too often, such as the ones around each wheel opening. He would also use up nearly a can of lighter fluid in removing the hundreds of little road tar specks that dotted the entire bottom third of the car.

They also used a brush on the grill. The damn thing was always a final resting place for careless bugs, many of them "love bugs," those little creatures that come to a crushing end in one final moment of ecstasy. Every single inch of the car's interior was scrubbed with a brush, too, including the headliner. Then all four doors were left open for hours. All in all, the Wrights' cleaning job would rival any scrub nurse's efforts at the local hospital. But was it worth it? After all, can a clean car really be worth more than a dirty one?

A good impression never hurts. More importantly, however, a clean car implies something much more important: car people, like most of us, assume that a person who really takes care of the way his car looks also takes care of it mechanically. That is a very dangerous assumption, but use it to your advantage. Whether you are planning to sell your car or trade it, spend hours polishing and scrubbing the thing, saying nice things to it as you work. Clean the door jambs and under the hood. Make the trunk spotless. If you have a little tear in the back seat, fix it yourself, or throw a pair of very dirty socks on it. Either technique seems to work well. Are there minor mechanical things wrong with it? Does the air-conditioning not work because the fuse is blown? Replace the fuse. Used-car appraisers can be very lazy, and they may assume your compressor is bad, regardless of what you tell them. A fifty-cent fuse can cost you $300 dollars at appraisal time.

Don't repaint your car if the paint is dull or scratched, though. Appraisers, and potential customers always believe freshly painted used cars have been in fender-benders. That new paint job could cost you $500 or $1000 dollars. Do touch up nicks if you've a properly matching paint. Do buff dull paint with oxidizing compound and wax—those few hours can earn you money.

IS IT A POPULAR CAR?

Do you own one of those twelve-cylinder sedans that automatically pulls into every service station along the road? Or a nice, big station wagon? Well, limousines are not too popular these days, and you should prepare yourself for some hard realities. But should you own a nice medium-sized economy car, you really own the most sought-after car in America. Most of us cannot afford new ones like that and will fight to buy yours. Whichever type car you own, its popularity will directly determine how much it's worth in hard cash.

But, how do you know if your current wheels are hot or cold? The most direct way would be to drive into your nearest used-car lot. If the boys clap, you're in luck. If they throw rocks, drive out quickly and minimize the damage. Beyond that, unless you are involved in the day-to-day business of trading cars, you have few guidelines to help you. Generally, the size of your car is the most important determinant of popularity. For instance, when small new cars are selling briskly, small used cars are too. Generally, two-door cars and fastbacks are more popular than sedans or station wagons, bright-colored cars more popular than dark ones.

A little later in this chapter we'll be showing you how to determine the true wholesale value of your car. This answer—the value of your particular car—is obviously what's important. For if you receive the *maximum* dollar for your particular car, regardless of its popularity, you will be faring better than most folks. Car people say it a little more succinctly: "There's an ass for every seat." For now, just remember to be realistic when looking at your car. Sure, you love it and have all those great memories about the trip to Niagara Falls. But it's just a commodity to other people.

WHAT'S THE MILEAGE?

Killer remembers fondly those years way back when there were no cars with high mileage. As a matter of fact, until the late sixties it was considered a downright honorable thing to "fix clocks." When some nice customer would present Killer with a car showing sixty or seventy thousand miles, he would quickly drive it back to the service department, singing all the way and yell out, "Hey, Harry! This damn thing has a broken clock!" Within the hour the car would reappear showing 12,841 miles. The guys would never make the clock show even miles, but rather some believable number. Such fun and games.

Used-car sellers will tell you the introduction of federal mileage statements brought an end to the friendly old clock-fixer's occupation. But, unfortunately, that is *not* the case. Most retail sellers no longer take the chance of incurring federal penalties directly, but many, many of them are constantly purchasing cars *that have been clocked* from auctions and individual wholesalers. As we discuss later, you can help stop the clocking and help catch the offenders by making sure that the correct mileage on your car is recorded on a mileage statement at trade-in time. Keep a copy of that statement. Should your trade-in's mileage be altered by a wholesaler or any subsequent owner, your copy of that statement can help trace the guilty party—as well as protect *you* from any future liability.

It's really unfortunate that mileage is such a determining factor in the value of a car. Since looking at the speedometer is such an easy thing to do, most people seem to place more importance in "average" miles or "below average" miles than in the things that really make a car valuable or worthless. Which car would you prefer, one with twelve thousand miles of city driving in a year or one with thirty thousand miles of highway driving in a year? In all likelihood the thirty-thousand-mile car will have a much newer transmission, since highway driving requires little or no shifting; that same car will probably have better brakes, too, and less wear and tear on its suspension system.

If you own a high-mileage car, you will have to expect it to be worth less. Don't run the speedometer back though; leave that to the people who don't mind courting jail. Just tell people you drove only on straight roads and never used your brakes.

COMPUTING YOUR CAR'S DOLLAR VALUE

Whether you plan to trade your present car, or sell it outright, *you will lose money* unless you really understand the term "wholesale" as it applies to the automobile business.

Automobile dealerships, all of them, know that the average customer has no earthly idea what his or her car is worth in actual wholesale dollars, and they constantly use that ignorance to the customer's disadvantage. If you were to have your car appraised by Killer, for example, invariably the following would take place: Killer would drive your car up to the used-car manager's office and work him for the highest appraisal possible. Let's say the manager placed a true wholesale value of $5000 dollars on your trade. Your car is at the moment a hot number, one that has quickly climbed in wholesale value during the past weeks. When Killer returns to his office, you casually pull out a copy of some wholesale book that indicates the value of your car is $4500 and inform Killer in no uncertain terms you'll not take a penny less. Of course, you've already lost— your big mouth has already made Killer $500 dollars richer. He takes the book from your hand and starts reading interesting footnotes to that particular edition: "Deduct for no power windows; deduct for body damage; deduct for A.M. radio." Within five minutes Killer has used your own sword to slice the throat a little deeper, and you accept $4100 dollars for your car.

Even if you are too smart to pull out some book figure or to show your hand, Killer will start by offering you much less than the appraised value of your car. This little exercise in self-destruction is called "underallowing" the sucker, uh, make that customer. It is continually practiced by every single salesman in the business, and you have absolutely *no* defense unless you read on carefully and learn how to shop your car before you sell or trade.

Your car's *wholesale* value (what the car is worth to someone who plans to resell it) will seldom change during any transaction. For instance, when a salesman tells you he will allow you more in trade, it does not mean the value of your car has changed; he is simply taking some of the profit built into the price of the car you are trying to buy and adding that to the wholesale value of your trade. As an example, let's say you are looking at a new car with a mark-up, gross profit, of $1000 dollars. You're trading a used car with a true wholesale value of $2000 dollars. If the salesman says, "Sir, I'll allow you $2400 dollars in trade," he has "overallowed" you $400 dollars, cutting his profit from $1000 dollars to $600 dollars. But the wholesale value of your car has never changed.

The wholesale value is the lowest dollar amount your car will be worth in any reasonable time period (two weeks or a month, usually). It is the amount you know you can get for your car at any time. The *retail* value of your used car is the wholesale value *plus* the profit a person hopefully will pay to buy the car. Remember, the retail value is what you *hope* to receive for the car. And you will never, never receive that figure unless you sell your car yourself.

DETERMINING WHOLESALE VALUE

All successful used-car operations, whether they are affiliated with a new-car store or not, are continuously looking for fresh meat, new pieces of merchandise for their lots. All of these operations purchase used cars outright from wholesalers, brokers—and individuals. *The only way you will know the value of your present car* is to take advantage of this continuing need for fresh meat. Jim Wright knows just how.

By two o'clock in the afternoon, Jim and Gloria were riding down the road in their shiny car. "Damn!" Jim's eyes took in the polished hood and spotless interior. "Honey, I don't even think we should trade it! The car looks better than the day we bought it." It was running nearly as well, too. Jim had put the car in the shop just a few days ago for some minor repairs. A couple of badly worn belts had been replaced, the timing had been adjusted, and a new solenoid put in—just about all the repairs needed, $60 dollars in all. The expense was worth it, though, because the Wrights planned to spend the afternoon trying to sell the car. Or, rather, that's what they wanted the car people to think.

The first lot they pulled into was one of the oldest used-car operations in the city. The lot also specialized in cars that were just a few years old, like their car. The moment the engine stopped, Gloria started acting nervous. After all, this was the first time she had been on one of Jim's "fishing" trips.

"Gloria, for God's sake, they're not going to shoot us or anything; now just calm down and I'll do all the talking," Jim said, as a young salesman walked to their car. He looked at the car more than the people in it. Jim liked that. He also seemed like a nice enough guy. That made Jim feel better, too, since he was just a tad nervous himself. Even after all the years of buying cars, Jim Wright never had become really comfortable when it came to talking about selling his car.

Jim told the guy what salesmen call the "basic truth"—just enough of the story to accomplish their objective. "Hello. My wife and I have been thinking about selling our car, and I was wondering if you guys ever bought cars from individuals." Why was he nervous, damn it? The guy looked at the car again for a few seconds and said, "Well, we do sometimes, but that's usually handled by another man. Can you hold on a minute?" The guy headed inside, and both of the Wrights breathed out slowly and deeply.

"Jim, is this really necessary? I mean, after all, we are going to trade it in on the new car."

Jim looked at her and shook his head. "Honey, we're going to trade it *only* if we can get as much money as one of these places will give us. And, anyway"—he looked at the two men heading toward them—"these people *may* end up with our car anyway. The dealership may sell it to them. That's okay with me, as long as we get real wholesale dollar for it. I just don't want the dealership to steal our car, and this is the only way to know its real value, shopping it. Now relax, okay?"

Jim nodded at the two guys. The other man was really nice, too. "Howdy!" The older man was talking now. "I understand you folks want to sell your car."

"Well, we're thinking about selling it if we get enough money. It is a pretty nice car," Jim said in a slightly defensive tone.

The Wrights walked around the lot as the older man took their car on a spin. He was back in a few minutes and yelled, "I'll be with you folks in just a minute," as he walked into the office. Good. He must be going in to figure what it's worth, Jim thought.

Within five minutes the man was back with them. "Folks, you do have a nice car, and I can tell it's really been taken care of. Would you sell it to me if I paid you $4500 dollars?" Jim thought the figure sounded pretty good but didn't say so. "Well, I'll be honest with you, we were thinking about more like $5000 for it."

The guy's face bundled up in a few wrinkles, and he just stood there for a minute. "Well, I'll tell you what, we might could stretch it to $4700 dollars, but that would really be the limit. Would you take $4700 for it?"

"We might. But, as I told your salesman, we are going to visit a couple of other places before deciding. Will you hold to that figure for the next few days?" The guy really didn't want to hear that—he needed the Wright's car on his lot; as a matter of fact, he needed all the nice cars he could find. "Yessir, I will hold to that price for a few days, maybe a week. As long as the car is in the same condition, you know."

They were on the road to a second dealership quickly, and now Jim's mood was just fine. "See! I told you this was worth doing! The guy at the bank told me it probably wasn't worth much over $4200! And did you hear me get that man to go up on his price? Now, let's see what the other places say."

The next used-car operation they visited wasn't quite as cooperative as the first one; they weren't buying cars from individuals right then and really didn't even seem to appreciate the question. The third place put the same figure of $4700 on the car. The fourth stop, at the used-car operation of one of the largest new-car stores in town, yielded a figure of $4300. And Jim couldn't raise them, either. On the whole, the fishing trip was definitely a success, though. The Wrights had learned the most important thing in any car transaction: what their car was actually worth in wholesale dollars, resale value. *You* must know the same thing.

Prepare your car for "showing." Clean it up and clean it out. Then drive it to three different car lots around the city. If you have a kid who drives, you can even let the kid go by himself, if you like. Just don't give him your power of attorney. Whoever is driving should go straight to the used-car department of a new-car store and also to a big independent used-car lot or two. Tell the boys you want to sell your car, that you are not interested in trading. Be firm with them; let them know that you really might sell if they give you enough money. Tell them you are going to decide where to sell it within a few days. Tell them you want a *definite, firm* offer.

Gather at least three bids in this way, and use the highest. Probably for the first time in your life, you will really know what your car is worth in *wholesale* dollars. It's probably worth even more than this, too. Car people always make conservative offers.

The vast majority of customers who receive bad deals in the automobile business do so because they don't know this simple figure. It doesn't matter whether you plan to trade your car for a new one or a used one; it doesn't matter if you plan to sell your car outright. You will never know how good or bad an offer is unless you have done your homework.

During times when new cars are selling slowly, all used-car operations are desperately in need of cars owned by individuals because of the simple mathematics of the used-car business in general. Normally, every new-car sale generates at least three trade-ins, and these trade-ins keep used lots in business. But when new cars aren't selling, there is a genuine shortage of nice used cars. Normally used-car operations grow in profitability during new-car recessions, for even though people may shrink from paying new-car prices, they continue to buy used cars.

But what if your car isn't a thing of beauty but a heap that has the ambiance of an abandoned tenament? You still need to shop it. Any car that runs is worth something. You'll find many used-car operations that specialize in cars worth hundreds instead of thousands, too.

WHAT ABOUT "BOOK VALUE"?

Believing in "black books" or "blue books" is another sign you're a sucker. A man drives into the lot with his own copy tucked away in his pocket and tells the salesman, "Now, son, when you have my car appraised, just be sure those fellows know I've got my *own* copy," patting his pocket in pride. Don't worry: the salesman will tell his appraiser, "Hey, Mac. We've got another sucker with a Bible."

These books are simply the average prices for which particular cars have been selling at various used-car sales around the country. The books are important to financing institutions because most of them lend money on this "book" value, usually eighty percent of the book value of any particular car. The problem with books is simple: *they can't write checks.* Just because a car is selling for $2000 dollars in March at a sale in Lakeland, Florida, does not mean the same car is worth $2000 at some sale in Michigan. It doesn't mean the car is worth $2000 *retail,* much less wholesale, at your local neighborhood lot.

The books also vary tremendously. They don't usually reflect the current "hot" cars. Do not believe books. Shop your car as we've discussed. Many times that's what car people are doing when they supposedly drive your car around the block.

SHOULD YOU SELL YOUR
CAR YOURSELF?

Killer would say no, and his arguments are persuasive—at least to the innocent. Take the Grays, the couple who were with Killer yesterday. The Grays had an average car, one that seemed nearly invisible on the highway. The paint was a dull beige, with very little chrome or other dressing to add sex appeal to the exterior, and the interior was stark and a little soiled. It was also a four-door. Until yesterday the Grays had liked the car; it had been a good statement of their lifestyle. Mr. Gray works in the accounting department of a large electronics company, and Mrs. Gray is a housewife. The extent of this couple's involvement in the business of buying and selling anything has been limited. Mrs. Gray was in charge of the cake sale at the church, but even that little foray into the business world was embarrassing to her. She would blush when someone asked her the price "of that nice chocolate layer cake" and apologize profusely as she took their money.

Mr. Gray's expertise is at about the same level. He loves to visit garage sales but has yet to bargain for anything, including the magnificent moose head now sitting in his garage. Mr. Gray didn't want the thing in the first place, but an enthusiastic neighbor—Robert DeMarco—had convinced him: "At this price, Albert, you can't afford *not* to buy it. These things are going up in value every year. And look at the points on it! Why, people will think you are the great white hunter! Now, do you want to take it with you, or can I drop it by the house later today?"

Gray was bagged as quickly as the moose, asking only one last question before loading the thing in his car. "Well, uh, Bob, it was the price that bothered me. Is that a fair price?" What do you think Killer said?

The Grays were sitting in the office with Mr. DeMarco. They had finally decided to trade in their car after at least two months of discussion and probably wouldn't be buying then, ". . . but, Bob, we know you. It's so important to know someone when you buy a car, don't you agree?" Killer just loves people like this. He is quite comfortable with their style of speaking. Virtually every sentence ended in a question of confirmation—Little Red Riding Hoods seeking comfort from granny wolf—and Killer happily told them just what they wanted to hear.

"Albert, you are more right than you know. You just wouldn't believe the horror stories in this business." Killer neglected to tell them most of the stories were about him. "Now, have you folks decided on any particular type of car this year?"

"Well, no, we just felt the time had come to trade. Bob, there are just so many new cars, many of them so small, what do you think would be a nice car for us?"

At that moment, Killer was sure he'd died and gone to heaven. "I'd like to show you a couple of cars. But before we do that, why don't I run your car up the hill and have it appraised? It'll just take a minute or two."

The Grays rustled in their chairs, and Albert started to speak, a slight stutter betraying his nervousness. After all, they didn't want to hurt Killer's feelings. "Uh, Bob, we think we're going to sell our car ourselves this time. We don't want to have to worry you with it. And you know, Mr. Merit, my supervisor at work, says it's actually much more profitable to sell one's trade-in directly. Is that right?"

Killer chuckled, a chuckle meant to imply "boy, have you people been misled," leaned forward, shook his head slightly, and spoke in a hushed tone of confidentiality: "I *wish* that were true, Albert . . ." He paused, as if the words were just too horrifying to be spoken in polite company. "But *that*—selling your own car—takes you out on very, very thin ice." The Grays probably had visions of pulling up "Jaws" while fishing through the ice with a light line, and they sat there, stunned and immobile, as Killer continued. "The used-car business is a very complicated business, filled with people—individuals, even—who like nothing better than finding nice folks like yourself. Just the other day I read about a couple who sold their car to some stranger, only to find that the man's check was worthless; and then there were the Smiths, customers of mine who sold their old car to friends. The car broke down within a couple of weeks, and since there was no warranty on the vehicle, the Smiths' friends decided to *sue* them. What makes that story even sadder is the fact that the Smiths received only $100 dollars more than I would have given them in trade."

Killer stopped just long enough for these heart-wrenching words to sink in, then continued: "And, of course, there are the practical problems. What price would you ask for your car? What if the person who wants to buy it has a payoff on his old car—how would you handle that? And who is going to make all those trips to the Department of Vehicle Registration and prepare the affidavits?" His description of the paperwork sounded more like a visit to the Gestapo than the title office.

"And, Albert, do you really want to put your phone number in the paper and have perfect *strangers* calling your home any time of night or day?"

Each of Killer's words chilled the Grays to the core. My God, how could they have been so stupid as to suggest this in the first place? Albert spoke with the conviction of the most rabid born-again type, fire and brimstone crackling in every word. "Bob, of course you are right. It was just a thought, anyway. And I'm sure you'll get us the maximum dollar in trade, won't you?" Uh-huh.

It would take one of the newer IBM computers to store all the lies and dealer-encouraged myths about selling your own car. Dealerships want you to think the process is difficult or dangerous to your health, the real cause of warts, the heartbreak of psoriasis, and stuttering, all wrapped into one. But why shouldn't they want that? The used-car business is more profitable than the new-car business. Many dealerships will sell you a new car at close to cost simply to own your trade. So, why give your car away? That's exactly what you do if you let them have your trade-in at wholesale: give them a car worth $2000 dollars wholesale, and they will give you $2000—at most. Wouldn't it be nicer to make a profit, perhaps get $2800 for your car? And still buy their car at close to cost?

That's exactly what Merit, Albert Gray's supervisor did— or nearly did. The man had done his homework. He had shopped his car at several lots, and one of them had been just a little higher than the others, offering $2000 in cash. It wasn't a nice car, either, but simply an adequate set of older wheels, a good second car for some family. After leaving the last lot, Merit had stopped into a local market in his neighborhood and picked up a copy of the community "swap and shop" paper, along with copies of every other newspaper on the rack. Merit wasn't ready to place an ad just yet; he simply wanted to see the prices other people were asking for a four-year-old Chevy like his.

Arriving home, Merit grabbed his oldest son and headed to his low, comfortable front porch with all the papers tucked under his right arm. Within twenty minutes, the two of them had circled every similar Chevy ad in each of the papers and written each asking price on a separate piece of paper. "Hey, Dad, here's a dealer that's asking $3200 dollars for one."

Merit looked at the ad. "Well, I'd say those people have the right idea for sure. They certainly aren't shy when it comes to asking for the moon." Most of the individual ads had asking prices below that figure, but the average price for all ten was right at $3000 dollars. "Okay, now; if most people are asking $3000, we'll just ask $3100 and write a better ad than theirs."

Merit just wanted to be in the ballpark—not too high or low, but in good dickering range. Since he knew the car could be sold to a used-car operation for $2,000, he would have $1100 dollars to play with. Even if he sold the car for $2400, he would be making money. Merit put that sheet of paper away and put the business of selling out of his mind for the day. Two answers were enough for the moment: he knew what his car was worth wholesale, and he knew the asking price he would build into his ad.

On Friday Merit placed several phone calls. The first one was to his bank. "Okay, you say the payoff on my car is $879.23?"

"Yessir, and that payoff is good for ten days. After that time it will go up slightly."

"Well, thanks very much. Now let me ask you some- thing. I'm planning to sell the car to an individual. Just what do I have to do to get you people to release the title on the car?"

"Just come to the bank with that individual. Please have him bring a certified check made out to you for the total sales price. We'll cash that, pay off the car, and give you the difference and the title while you're here."

That sounded simple enough. "But what about the sales tax? Don't we have to pay sales tax on this?"

"You don't have to worry about that. The buyer pays the tax, not the seller. The person buying your car simply takes your bill of sale to the tag office. He pays the tax when he has the car registered in his name."

"Good. Well, thank you again. I hope I'll be down there to see you right shortly."

Merit then placed the same ad in three newspapers. "Chevy Impala coupe. Low mileage. Clean, one-owner car. Serviced regularly. $3100, no trade. Call 5–9 weekdays, 10–6 weekends. Individual." The ad was simple, but it contained all the important information, including the fact that an individual was selling the car, not a dealer. Many people are convinced that cars can be bought less expensively from individuals, and Merit knew that.

Merit's first phone call came as he walked in the door Saturday afternoon. "Hello, I was calling about your ad in the paper—the Chevrolet."

"Yessir, what can I tell you about it?"

"Well, sir, my name is Robert DeMarco. I'm a salesman, a new-car salesman here in town. But I have a customer that's been looking for a car like the one you described in the paper."

"I'm sorry, I'm not interested in trading my car, thank you for calling, anyway."

"Sir, before you hang up, can I ask you what you'll be driving when you sell your car?"

"Well, I will be buying a new car."

"If I could give you more than $3100 in trade on a new car, would you consider talking to me? I really do have someone looking for a car like yours, and perhaps we could kill two birds with one stone, as they say." Smart car salesmen are always doing this. They simply sit down during slow times and call numbers listed in individual classified ads. And they invariably have some customer just panting to own your car. It's a very effective technique.

"I'm sorry, what did you say your name is?"

"DeMarco, Robert DeMarco."

"Well, Mr. DeMarco, I appreciate your call, but I'm really not interested right now. I will be happy to write your name down, though. Thanks very much for calling."

Scratch the first phone call. Hell, that call had really been more productive for Killer. He at least found out that the guy was going to buy a new car. Killer will call Merit back in a few days.

The next three phone calls were inconclusive. Each of the people asked guarded questions about the car and invariably asked, "Is that a firm price, or will you come down some?" Merit told them all he was a reasonable man. But none of the three made any attempt to set an appointment to look at the car. Maybe this car-selling idea wasn't so good an idea after all.

The fifth call—it didn't come until the next evening—sounded a little more promising. It was a lady. She asked a few questions, then made an appointment to see the car that night. She never showed up.

Finally, on the third day, a man actually appeared at the Merit residence. He was nice enough and didn't act nearly as nervous as Merit. After all, this was the first time Merit had ever done anything like this. Merit's hand would have passed for a cold fish as he grabbed the guy's palm. There was another man with him, too, or rather an eighteen- or nineteen-year-old kid, who walked around the car as Merit talked. The kid looked under the hood, opened the driver's door, and peered in without sitting.

"Why don't we take a drive?" Merit volunteered. He climbed in the back seat and sat there quietly as the older man pulled out the driveway. Merit didn't even recognize the buying signals the two of them were giving out.

"Hey, Dad, it's got a stereo radio." His father didn't seem to hear that. He was busy spreading himself out in the front seat, right arm resting comfortably on the seat back, left hand lightly holding the wheel. The man had a slight smile on his face.

As the car pulled back in the drive, Merit searched for some appropriate words. Hell, he didn't have the slightest idea what should be done next. "Well, Mr. Johnson, how do you like the way she drives?"

"I like it. It really seems like a pretty nice car. But I just don't know about that price. We looked at another car yesterday that was several hundred dollars less than yours."

Merit didn't have the presence of mind at the moment to ask the man if the car was the same year and model, much less if the car was as nice as his. But the guy had given him a clue. "Well, Mr. Johnson, I honestly don't want to sell the car for much less than $3100." Merit made a good statement without knowing it. He didn't say he *wouldn't* take much less; he simply said he didn't want to. "But, you said the other car you looked at was several hundred dollars less. Are you saying you would pay $2800 for this car?"

Johnson sat there behind the wheel for a few seconds and said, "Well, I might. But I would like to show it to my wife before saying yes. Would it be okay if my son and I drove it over to the house?"

Merit didn't like the sound of that. Regardless of how nice the people looked, he really didn't like the idea of strangers driving away in his $2000-dollar piece of merchandise. "Mr. Johnson, I would be happy to do that, but my insurance company just won't let me. Why don't I follow the two of you home; I'll be glad to do that."

"That'll be fine." Johnson's reaction made him much

more comfortable. Merit is a pretty good reader of people, and an indignant show of impugned honor would not have impressed him in this instance.

Mrs. Johnson liked the car and liked the price, too. They decided to buy it. "Okay, I guess we'll take it. Now what do we do?"

Merit had trouble thinking for a moment; all that he could visualize was the $800 bucks he was earning for perhaps twelve hours' work. Even after the cost of the ads and the gas it took to shop his car, he'd be netting over $700. "Well, Mr. Johnson, if you could give me a deposit tonight, I won't show the car to anyone else. And then tomorrow, if it's convenient, we can go to my bank to get the title. If possible, you do need to be with me, since those people will notarize the title for us."

"And how much money will I owe you, $2800 even?"

"Yes, you'll have to pay the tax yourself. And you'll need to bring a certified check with you. My bank says that is necessary."

"Well, I'm planning to finance the car. Maybe I'd better get the serial number tonight, and I'll call the credit union in the morning. I think they will make the check out to me, but if there are any problems, we can talk on the phone during the day."

Merit said his good-byes and headed home. He was excited, but also concerned about one little problem: what was he going to drive until he bought a new car? Merit was on the phone to Mr. Johnson the moment he entered the house and breathed a little easier when Johnson agreed to pick up the car in two days, not tomorrow. If worse came to worse, he would hitch a ride to work with Albert Gray for a few days after that. After all, Gray did have a pretty nice new car.

Merit was at the bank when Johnson arrived. He had typed up a simple bill of sale at the office and was prepared to hand it to Johnson on the spot.

Merit's venture into the car-selling business raises and answers several important questions about selling a car Since you'd like to do as well, let's review.

What Should You Sell
Your Used Car For?

Remember, you are now a horse-trader. You have determined the wholesale value. If you can objectively say you have an appealing and popular car, don't be afraid to put an asking price of $1500 dollars over the wholesale figure. The newspaper can give you a few guidelines for asking price: look in the classified ads. What are other people pricing similar cars for? What are the dealerships' asking prices? If everyone in your town is advertising Hirohito Fastbacks at $3500 dollars, you would do well not to price yours at $6000.

Regardless of the asking price, remember that you can always lower your price but never raise it. Dealerships are famous for putting comically high prices on some used cars, knowing that smart people will negotiate them down and dumb people will make them rich. Why not use the same technique?

What's the Best Way to
Hawk a Hirohito?

Once you have determined your car's wholesale value and decided on an asking price, call up your local community newspaper and your bigger city newspaper. Find one of those "trading" rags that will run your ad for free if the car doesn't sell. Place an ad in each of these papers.

Don't try to be Shakespeare when you write the ad, either. Use few words, but use words with real meaning to potential buyers. "One owner, low mileage, excellent gas mileage, very clean, service record available"—these words carry much more weight than "breathtaking and magnificent." Put your price in there, too, and then get a beer from the fridge and wait on the phone calls. You will get them. That is, if you remember to put in the best times to reach you.

Are You Afraid of the Dickering?

Don't be—it's easy and fun. Let's say that several people have called you and want to see the car. You've invited them at different times to come by your house. The first guy wants to trade: send him on his way and tell the fellow to sell his car and then come back. The second person wants to drive your car alone. Tell him your insurance is no good unless you are in the car. Ride with him.

This guy has good taste; he likes your car and offers you a $500-dollar profit over the wholesale value. Good grief! Don't take his offer, though. Come on P. T., negotiate. Tell him you need another $500 dollars, or even tell him you've been offered another $500 by someone who is coming back in the morning. (Isn't it nice doing this to other people for a change?) He will come up, believe it or not.

In all likelihood, you'll end up splitting the difference with him. But that's okay. Unless you are really enjoying the salesman bit, split the difference with him and be happy with that $750-dollar *profit*. Remember, if you had traded your car, the dealer would have given you wholesale; *he* would make that $750.

Your Payoff and His Financing

If you are selling your own car, you will be responsible for calling your financing institution and arranging a payoff once you have a buyer for the car. But call your financing institution for a payoff amount *before* you place your ad. Compare it to your selling price. If the payoff is higher than your final offer from an individual, you are in the bucket. Sorry. Read pages 164–67, *If You Are "In the Bucket."*

You will also be responsible for providing the new buyer with a title and a few other papers. None of these procedures are complicated. They do vary from state to state. Call your state Department of Motor Vehicle Registration or your local tag office for specifics.

The buyer of your car must be responsible for his own financing. You don't really care where or how he gets the money, unless the fellow looks like the type who recently made an unauthorized withdrawal from a bank. You are simply interested in cash or a certified check. Even if you know the person well, don't accept a personal check. You should provide the buyer with a bill of sale, too. This does not normally have to be a formal document. If you're neat, a simple handwritten statement like this will do: "Sold to_____for $_____, a 19–_____(make and model), serial number_____. Signed and Dated:_____." If your calligraphy skills leave something to be desired, use a typewriter or buy a pad of standard bills of sale at your local business supply office.

5

Dollars and Sense: Know Your Financing

It had been an easy deal for Buzz. The Crenshaws had dickered a little on the trading difference, but not much. They had also wanted to know how much their payments would be on the balance. At this particular store, J. C.'s store, customers are seldom worked for finance money until they come to pick up their car. J. C. likes it that way: the customers are excited, jumping in and out of their fantasy machine, champing at the bit to drive away. At a time like that, who wants to sit around and argue payments? Buzz knew that policy and had done it by the book. "Mr. and Mrs. Crenshaw," he'd said, "your payment is going to be in the $175-dollar range, give or take a few dollars. How does that sound to you?"

Well it had sounded just fine. The folks had left the dealership very satisfied customers, and Buzz had waved them away, walking straight from their car door to the finance office. Ronnie Cheatum was there as usual, busy as usual, calling in one of Killer's deals. He was talking to their own finance company: "Yeah, I tell you they are as strong as death. The guy has been on the same job for twenty years, their current payments are just about as high as the ones we want, he's got plenty of paid-out loans, *and* I've already called the credit bureau." The person on the other end of the line didn't seem to like that. What was Cheatum doing calling the credit bureau? "Now hold on," Ronnie said, "I want to spot-deliver these people. They're sitting in the lounge now and were trying to back out of the deal before Killer told them the car was theirs today. Killer's in the back getting it cleaned. Now before you start yelling again, damn it, listen. The guy has four paid-out loans, and they're all 'i-ones.' I called his office and he does work at the plant. We're into the car for $1000. And J. C. says to deliver them. So, I'll just take your yelling as an 'approved as called,' and say bye!"

Ronnie hung up, laughing, and turned to Buzz. "Hey, Buzz, what type of crap have you got this time?" Buzz didn't laugh. For the past week, every single one of his deals had been either conditioned or rejected. One of his customers had been a "skip" from another town, someone who thinks you can run from bad credit. Another guy was rejected for "overbuy"—he wanted to buy a car that would have given him a $300-dollar payment, and the guy's income was barely $300 a month. His *last* guy could probably have bought the car, but he had spooked the source, applied for loans on four other cars that week. But the Crenshaws were different.

"Screw you, Ronnie. These people are open with us now—they only owe eight payments on a car *I* sold them three years ago. And they showed me their payment book. They've paid ahead ten payments."

"Well, damn, that's nice of them," Ronnie injected. "If they've only got eight payments left, we've damn well got our interest. Hell, yeah, let them trade again! Here, let me look at that deal." Ronnie looked at the buyer's order and quickly figured their equity. "You say the car is appraised at $4000 and they owe $1400? Okay, it looks like they're into the car for at least $2600. I'll call on them right now, so just sit here." It looked like a very safe deal for the store since the new car cost around $7500. As Cheatum said, the people had about $2600 in equity in their trade. The financing source would be loaning only about $4900.

"Ronnie, I know the deal's okay. Now, just make me some money. I've got a hell of a deal on the front, $800 dollars, and I want to make as much on the back." Buzz didn't need to worry about that. Ronnie Cheatum was the best—"Magic," as the guys called him.

At four the next afternoon, Buzz brought the Crenshaws in. They had already seen their new car, loved it just as much as the day before, and had walked quickly to Cheatum's office, the bounce in their walk betraying both excitement and impatience. They were a nice couple, a bright couple who even knew their financing would be more at the store than a bank. Of course, they had justified that choice to themselves. "Well, we know we pay a little more here, but it's convenient to finance like this. Plus you people agreed to the payment we wanted anyway." Ronnie flinched at that. Buzz had quoted them a payment on the discount rate—what the store paid for money.

Ronnie nodded agreement. "Well, you know, our rates are regulated just like the banks. You really don't pay that much more here. And, as you said, a payment is a payment. Now, did Buzz tell you about the new services we have been offering since you financed your last car with us?"

"Oh, you mean the life insurance? Oh, yes, I want that. I mean, it's only a couple of dollars a month, right?"

Ronnie looked at them with his most effective expression and said, "Yes, of course, you want life insurance on you, Mr. Crenshaw. But we have two other services you might want to consider. We can put life insurance on your wife, first. When you think about it, insurance on her may be more important than insurance on you. For instance, Mrs. Crenshaw, you work, don't you? And I believe you folks also have a couple of teenage kids? God forbid, if something should happen to you"—he looked at Mrs. Crenshaw— "your family will need all the money they can get, like the rest of us." Both nodded agreement.

"Now, Mr. Crenshaw, I would also like to suggest that you let us place accident and health insurance on the loan. This will only cover you, but if, for any reason, you should become ill or disabled, this protection will automatically make each and every car payment for you." Ronnie was glossing over the details of the actual protection, but that didn't matter; he had touched the high points. Both of them nodded again.

"But, Mr. Cheatum, how much is all of this going to cost?" It was the question Ronnie was waiting for. Ronnie turned on his computer and began to punch in all the necessary information. The first factor was the interest rate. Buzz had quoted these people on the lowest interest rate, but that would be corrected right now—he entered the highest rate. Then he entered the total number of months, cash selling price, trade allowance, and payoff on their current car, and looked at the couple. "You're only going to be talking about $204 dollars a month." They both looked a little pale, but Ronnie just kept talking. "Now, I know that sounds like a pretty big jump from $175, but think about this for a minute: If something should happen to either of you, if you, Mr. Crenshaw, should become ill, that $29 dollars a month will pay for itself many times over. Don't you really think it's worth it? Is it honestly fair *not* to protect yourself?"

Mr. Crenshaw adjusted himself in the chair and thought for a minute. "Well, you know, I want the protection. But we honestly just did not want to spend over $200 a month for a car. I think we'd better pass on that other coverage. We'll just take life insurance on me."

Damn. With just the life insurance, there wasn't a way in hell Cheatum could raise the interest rate—the higher payment would be too obvious. "Mr. Crenshaw, since you are telling me you would like the coverage but want to keep your payment down, let me see if I can do something to help you." Ronnie punched a few more buttons on the machine, lowering the interest one half of one percent. The payment was lowered to $201 dollars. But he didn't tell that to the people; he simply sat there randomly pushing buttons. After a few minutes, he leaned back in the chair and started thinking out loud. "Well, I know you want the coverage. And I know you are concerned about the payment. But I just don't know how to get them any lower. I'll tell you what we could do, though. If you could pay about $200 dollars in cash, I think that would get your payment down to about $201 dollars a month. How does that sound to you?"

When he said that, Buzz quickly looked at the couple. Would they really fall for *that?* Ronnie was telling these people he would lower their payments $3 dollars a month for thirty-six months—a total of $108 dollars—and in the same breath telling them to pay him $200 dollars for the favor.

Mrs. Crenshaw spoke first. "Well, honey, I think we can afford the $200. And I think the insurance is a good idea, all of it." Without waiting for any more comments, Ronnie pushed the "print" button on his typewriter and discussed everything but payments as the contract slowly jumped from the machine. Within five minutes the papers were signed, and Buzz led them away.

It had been a nice half-hour's work. By raising the interest rate from the lowest to the highest, Ronnie had increased the financing department's profit by $285 dollars. The double life insurance premium netted him $241 dollars. The accident and health premium on Mr. Crenshaw netted him $275 dollars. The total "back end"—the pure profit from these three little "services"—was $801 dollars. Not bad. Not bad at all. And why should he feel bothered? The couple never asked any questions, much less the right questions. Ronnie billed the deal out on the spot, listing each of his nice profits in the F and I gross book, and headed to the lounge. He had twenty minutes before it would be time to help another customer.

Whether it's blind luck or astute thinking, many people do buy cars at very reasonable prices. Yet many of those same people just as quickly make very bad decisions on financing that car. Countless others include financing negotiations in their actual negotiations for the purchase of a car and quickly become lost in the murky valley of annual percentage rate versus difference in trade, allowance versus months financed, or life insurance versus payoff. If you are going to be a smart buyer, it's important to realize the two can't be mixed. First, negotiate the best possible deal on the car. And then apply the best method of financing.

So why read this section first? If you plan to finance, *you must know how much cash you can afford to buy and for how long before you know how much car you can buy.* You must know the best source and method of financing *before* you shop. To buy a car properly, you must first negotiate the sale, then apply the best method of financing. How can you apply what you don't know?

This section will help you determine the best financing source for your particular needs. It will provide you with a method of shopping your financing that will enable you to determine how much you really can afford each month.

Once you have determined what you can afford, this section will tell you how to determine the total "Available Cash" you will have to purchase a car. This section will recommend the number of months any car should be financed, give you the pros and cons of life and accident and health insurance. It will provide a little advice for those of you in the bucket. Finally, it will show you a simple method to determine payments for a particular amount of money. Because the financing business is one of the least understood businesses in America—up, or rather down, there with the car business—you will need to take particular care *not* to be influenced by any particular company's song and dance. Instead, selecting a company should be based solely on the cost and terms of their service. Automobile dealerships, for instance, sell their financing operations on the basis of convenience. Have you ever heard this? "Well, we will be happy to take care of the financing here for you. That will save you a lot of trouble, and, of course, our rates are regulated by the federal government, so they have to be reasonable." How much trouble is it to drive a few miles, if you save $500 or $600 dollars? And those federal regulations? They're about as useful as an Eskimo's electric fridge. Shopping for financing is just like shopping for a car: there are a lot of people out there who will take you with smiles on their faces. I hope this section will help you keep the smile where it belongs—on your face.

FINANCING SOURCES

You may find that only one of these sources is available to you, or you may find that all of them are. We'll give you some pointers on choosing and comparing later, but for now, here's a look at the options, from best to worst.

Cash Value in
Your Life Insurance

If you are one of those people who have spent years pumping money into life insurance, you can borrow that cash value for a charge less than half that of any other source. Your insurance will still be in effect, too. Call your agent and ask for a statement of cash value. If you choose to finance by this method, you would be wise to make arrangements to pay monthly sums back into your policy.

Credit Unions

The most straightforward and the cheapest people to finance with, credit unions have one great advantage over most banks and *all* other lending institutions: *They loan money on a simple interest basis*. They charge interest *monthly* on the *outstanding balance* of the loan. For instance, a credit union officer may tell you, "If you borrow $5000 dollars for thirty-six months at eight percent simple interest, your first payment will include one full month's interest on the $5000. Your second payment will include six-tenths of one percent on $4876 dollars, the balance of your loan. And so forth. Your last payment will include interest on only $200 dollars." In this particular example, your payments would look like this:

FIRST PAYMENT	$33.33	interest on $5000.00 for one month
	$123.35	applied to reducing the loan.
SECOND PAYMENT	$32.51	interest on $4876.00 for one month
	$124.17	applied to reducing the loan.
THIRD PAYMENT	$31.68	interest on $4752.00 for one month
	$125.00	applied to reducing the loan.

Now, isn't that a logical way to pay off a loan? You pay interest on only the *balance* of your loan each month.

Probably just *because* this method is logical and fair, the vast majority of banks and other financing sources *don't* use it. These sources have opted for an absolutely magnificent method of calculating interest, which should rank with the loading of dice in its fairness to the recipient. For instance, these sources would figure the interest on this same loan by computing interest on $5000 dollars *for the full thirty-six months.* Now, think about that for a moment. They charge you interest on $5000 even *after* the loan amount has been paid down to hundreds. Isn't that nice? Borrow the same amount of money as you would from your credit union, and pay $560 dollars *more* in interest.

But that's not the worst of it. As we mentioned earlier, these sources take each of your payments and apply a much larger part of that payment to interest *before* they reduce the loan. This dandy repayment scheme is called the "Rule of Seventy-eights," and works like this:

FIRST PAYMENT	$60.62	applied to interest (nearly twice the interest the credit union would collect)
	$111.60	applied to reducing the loan.
SECOND PAYMENT	$59.27	applied to interest (as compared to $32.51 at the credit union)
	$112.95	applied to reducing the loan.
THIRD PAYMENT	$57.90	applied to interest (compared to $31.68 at the credit union)
	$114.32	applied to reducing the loan.

And so on and so on. How convenient. These people collect most of the interest that would be due if you kept the loan for the total amount of months *before* they reduce the loan appreciably. That's why people borrow $5000 for three years, pay twelve payments, and *still* owe nearly $3600 dollars—after making $2100 dollars in payments.

So, what does this mean to you? If like most of us, you trade cars before your present car is paid for, you will have already paid the lending institution interest for all those months *you won't have your old loan.*

Doesn't all this make you want to open a loan company?

Other financing sources, such as most banks, GMAC, Chrysler Credit, and Ford Motor Credit, try to justify this insanity by telling credit union customers that, "You can borrow the money there, but if you do, you won't be building any credit. You know, credit unions do not report information to credit bureaus." Years ago that was a true statement. But today most established credit unions *do* use and report to credit bureaus. But even if yours doesn't report, are you concerned about building your credit badly enough to be a victim of add-on interest or the "Rule of Seventy-eights"?

Banks

Normally their rates are lower than the "captive houses," such as GMAC. Their particular lending rates for automobile loans are usually determined by your credit rating and the number of months the car will be financed. Many banks also give lower rates to customers who already have checking or savings accounts with them. Some will even give you trips to East Padooka and other places of interest. Unfortunately, banks are beginning to sound like automobile dealerships in their gimmickry. In a couple of pages, we'll talk about how to look past the hoopla.

Dealership Financing Sources

Yes, it's convenient. Yes, companies such as GMAC, Chrysler Credit, and Ford Motor Credit are usually more lenient in their lending policies. And, yes, these companies will normally finance a car for longer than other sources. But, what is the price of convenience? If you are a responsible person, why do you need lenient lending policies? And is it in your best interest to finance a car for forty-eight months, much less sixty?

Captive sources can be a good financing source in a few circumstances. If you are buying a "leftover" new car, let's say a new '81 in the '82 model year, these companies will finance more of the purchase price. If you don't mind dickering, individual finance men at car stores *will* lower their financing rates, too. Ask a bank to do that, and your checking account will probably be repossessed. Captive sources also have occasional "rate sales" during the year, offering financing money at rates equal to or lower than banks. To qualify for these rates, though, you'll need top-notch credit and a hefty down payment.

If you know for a fact that your credit is minimal in quantity, or marginal in quality, captive sources can probably be of help to you. But, don't just assume this; apply for a loan first at some bank. If your loan is turned down or "conditioned" (for instance, if you apply for $5000 and the bank only approves $4000), then talk to the finance man at the dealership. Many dealerships can influence their financing source, and all of them will do their best to arrange your financing. After all, if they can't get you financed, they won't make that nice profit on the sale of the new car, your trade, *and* the financing, will they? If dealership financing is really your only sound choice, thank them, but don't let them take you. Many dealerships will imply that folks with marginal credit must be placed on the highest interest rate. At some banks this may be true, but it is *not* true for captive sources: if one of these approves your application, you automatically qualify for the same rate financing anyone else would receive.

Finance Companies

If you must darken one of these doors, you would do better to walk rather than drive. Finance companies, "dip" houses, "small loan" companies—whatever the name, the result is always the same. You will be charged two or three times more for the same loan and normally will be required to place your household goods, furnishings, maybe even your soul on their contracts as collateral.

These companies just love to tell us what wonderful service they provide poor people with no credit or people with bad credit. Well, in my book their service ranks down there with your local loan shark.

Most of the people who do business with places like this have better credit than they think. The vast majority deal with these bloodsuckers because they are uncomfortable in more formal banking situations and prefer the down-home atmosphere of Friendly Fred and others of his ilk. As a matter of fact, testifying in a 1979 Illinois court case, an official of Citibank estimated that fifty percent of the customers of their subsidiary, Nationwide Finance, could qualify for bank loans. Other banking officials agree that this is the general case. If you are currently supporting your local dip shop, though, what can you do? Before submitting to another rape, apply for a loan at a dealership or bank. If you have paid your dip shop loans on time, you will most likely qualify for credit. And don't be self-conscious. Lots of folks have experienced credit problems and survived.

WHY SHOP YOUR MONEY
BEFORE YOU SHOP YOUR CAR?

Car people lump the millions of people who buy cars each year into four categories: difference buyers, allowance buyers, payment buyers, and cash buyers. Since all of us usually do fit into one or more of these categories, it's important that you understand each of these terms. If you are an allowance, difference, or payment buyer, you need to understand the terms in order to *avoid* that particular type of buying. Invariably it is when you see yourself as a type buyer that you will be taken most often.

Why? Any method of buying that confuses the total cash price of the car is dangerous. For instance, difference buyers are concerned only with the difference between the cost of their present car and the new car. These types of customers will say, "Son, your car lists for $8000 dollars. And I'll be damned if I'll buy it for more than $5000 plus my car." This man's thinking is logical, but flawed.

"Well, sir, how did you arrive at that figure?"

"Well, my car is two years old, and I expect to spend $2500 a year for each year I drive. *That's* why I'll pay you $5000!" Or, he'll say, "My car cost $6000 new two years ago. I figure it depreciated thirty percent the first year and twenty percent the second. *That's* why I'll pay you $5000!"

The man will barely feel the shiv. Both of his arguments are based on his *own* definitions, and neither definition is based on such a minor fact as the current value of his car. A salesman working this guy can: (1) Ignore the value of the man's trade-in. In all likelihood, the trade may be worth more than $3000. (2) Tell the man that people are now trading for $2800 a year rather than $2500. After all, inflation is really bad these days. If the man agrees, he's just raised himself $600. *Magic formulas and percentages just don't work.*

And then there's the allowance buyer. This customer isn't concerned with the *value* of his trade, but the amount of money he is *allowed in trade.* He will in all likelihood say, "Give me $4000 for my car, and you have a deal." A smart salesman can handle this type easily. He'll invariably say, "Well, folks, we can't give you $4000 on an Expenso Minutula. But let's take a look at these Expenso Gargantulas." And of course the Gargantulas have a larger margin of profit. Switching these people from a less expensive car to a more expensive one always increases profit to the dealer *if* the allowance stays the same. *Allowance buyers never know the real value of their trade or the actual discount on a new car.*

And payment buyers? You are the easiest prey. Invariably a payment buyer has only one simple request: "I don't care about anything else, as long as my payments are low."

"Well, what would be a satisfactory payment?"

"Just as low as you can get!"

Both the salesman and the customer laugh a little, and then the salesman goes to work. If you don't have a specific payment in mind, he will pick some impossibly high figure out of the air. The payment will be designed to shock you. The salesman will then lower the payment slowly until you're breathing again. If you have a payment in mind, the salesman will try to set you on a car that could be financed for lots less than your figure. The company of course will finance at your higher figure.

Where is the flaw in the payment approach? The entire

negotiation never was based on the value of your trade or the cost of their car, but *on some figure pulled out of the air.*

The horror stories generated by these methods of buying are endless. One poor sap, an allowance buyer, argued for three hours and finally received his allowance. The moment it was agreed to, he slammed his fist on the desk and said, "Now about the financing! I won't pay you a dime over $200 a month for the car!" The idiot. At the allowance figure he spent hours negotiating, payments would not have run over $165 dollars a month. But the man raised himself $35 dollars a month for forty-eight months—he increased the store's profit by *$1680 dollars.*

And then there's the couple who insisted on receiving $2500 dollars for their car. The salesman agreed to give them $2500 on a $6000-dollar tin can, one of the small cars. He then switched them to a $9000-dollar mid-sized car, allowed them the same $2500 dollars in trade, and increased his profit by $600 dollars.

Need I say more? Buying a car based on allowance, difference, or payments will only draw your attention from the questions that really matter: "What is my car worth in actual wholesale dollars? What is the total cash I can afford to spend? What is the cost of the car I'm buying?" If you know the answers to these questions, you will always be able to get maximum dollar for your trade, and you will always be able to buy their car for the least profit. If you have accomplished these three things, you will naturally have the lowest payment possible. *All car transactions are based on these questions.*

You've already learned how to shop your present car to determine its wholesale value, and you'll learn how to figure the cost of the car you're buying in Chapter 8. For the rest of this chapter, we'll focus on how to shop for money, and how to determine the total "Available Cash" you will have to buy a car.

NEW OR USED, HOW MUCH CAR?

Most finance buyers find a particular car, one that sets the pulse racing, and then breathlessly wait for a salesman or finance manager to tell them the damage: what the car will cost them each month. Invariably the customer is shocked at the payment. Invariably the payment is adjusted by some mysterious process; or worse, the payment is "justified"—a favorite sales term that simply means convincing the customer that castor oil really is a delightful and tasty thing.

There *is* a better way. It requires a restructuring of car-buying ground rules. But, if you follow this approach, you will probably really enjoy the entire car-buying process for the first time—because you will finally understand what you are doing. Here's the approach in capsule form.

First: Shop financing sources. Obviously a bank and credit union, for instance, will have different terms, but the cost of money can vary even between two different branches of the same bank. Some sources provide services free that cost hundreds of dollars at others.

Second: Decide how much money you can comfortably afford to pay each month for a car. Don't think about new or used or specific models; just think honestly about the payment check you will be writing every month. Deciding what payment is comfortable for you is your *most important decision.* It will determine how much car you can afford to buy regardless of the value of your trade-in. Once you've decided this figure, *stick to it.*

Third: Decide how many months you will make that payment. Don't automatically plan to stretch your payments over the longest period of time, either. "Easy-payment" plans that stretch your payments over four years are dangerous; many times you will be paying for a car long after its usefulness has departed. Even worse, extended-payment plans buy you less car for each dollar of payment. For instance, if you buy a car and finance it at an average rate of interest for two years, eighty-six cents of each payment dollar will actually pay for the car; the rest is interest. If you finance the car at the same rate for forty-two months, seventy-eight cents of each payment dollar will be applied to the car; the rest is interest. If you finance the same car at the same interest rate for sixty months, only seventy-one cents of each payment dollar is applied to the car; the rest is interest.

Fourth: Determine your "Loan Cash." An installment loan simply *buys you a lump sum of cash*. Once you have decided on the monthly payment and the number of months, once you have found the best financing source, use this information to compute the total cash dollars your payment will generate. You will learn a simple three-step method shortly.

Fifth: Let your "Loan Cash" determine your purchase. You may want to purchase a new car but decide to purchase a used one, or vice versa. You may be able to buy more car than you thought, or you may need to buy less. This chapter will show you how to derive and use your total "Available Cash" from your "Loan Cash" and the value of your trade.

Now, before going on to the detailed discussion of these steps, read the capsule description again. Understand the approach. If you will become familiar with each step and apply that knowledge, you'll have no surprises once the actual buying process begins. Incidentally, all the information and decisions can be determined while you're relaxing at home.

Shopping for Rates and Terms

Is it really worth the time to shop for your money? After all, what's a percent or two, here or there? It's a lot of money, that's what. On a $6000-dollar loan for forty-eighty months, the interest charge can vary more than *$1000 dollars!* Can you think of any good uses for $1000 dollars? Shopping the money market will make you lots of money. It is also easier to shop for money and terms than it is to shop for your car. But you will need to understand a little of the industry jargon.

Simple Interest. If you were to borrow $1000 dollars from me and agree to pay it back in one year at eight percent interest, you would owe me at that time $1080 dollars. You would have the use of the full $1000 dollars for a year. You would pay me eight percent and use all of my money for a year. That's the concept of simple interest.

Add-on Interest. If you were to borrow $1000 dollars from me at eight percent and agree to pay me back *monthly* over twelve months, you would not have the use of the full $1000 dollars for a year, would you? The interest would still total $80 dollars, but you would have the full use of the $1000 for only a month. At the end of the first month, you would pay me $90 dollars. That month you would have the use of only $910 dollars. At the end of the second month you would have the use of only $820 dollars.

Because you are still paying the interest on a full $1000 dollars, but having the use of less and less of that money, your *true* interest rate for this loan isn't eight percent, even though lending institutions used to tell you "this loan is only costing you eight percent."

In the early seventies the federal government was prodded by consumer protection groups to correct this definition of interest. The government made it illegal to quote installment-loan interest as simple interest. The government only made a partial improvement, though. They allowed lending institutions to call this method of calculating interest the "add-on" method. Lending institutions went happily about their business, casually saying, "Oh, this loan is at eight percent add-on." The institutions would say the last part of that statement very quietly, and most folks continued to believe they were paying simple interest for installment loans.

Finally, in the mid-seventies, the government began to reguire lending institutions to quote installment-loan interest in a way that would actually tell borrowers the true cost of their loans. The feds required all lending institutions to quote interest as an annualized percentage of the monthly loan balance. This method of quoting interest adjusts the actual rate to reflect the fact that *you have less of the lender's money each month.* For instance, an eight percent add-on loan for thirty-six months has a true annual interest rate of 14.54 percent. The *same* eight percent loan for forty-two months has a true annual interest rate of 14.45 percent.

Annualized Percentage Rate. The real advantage of quoting interest as an annualized percentage rate, or APR, is the convenience it provides you when comparing rates at different loan sources. APRs also remind you of how much money you are really spending in interest. Remember: the APR tells you how much interest you *really* pay *each year.*

If you have an eight percent add-on auto loan for three years, you actually pay a total of *43 percent interest*. The same eight percent loan for four years would cost you *over 60 percent*.

The actual calculation of APRs is very complicated, but don't let that bother you. Use APRs to shop for money. But remember that APRs are simply another method of quoting simple or "add-on" interest.

Finance Charge. The finance charge is the *total cost of the loan*. The charge includes the interest, any charges for insurance, state fees, credit checks, and the like. The finance charge tells you *how much more it costs you to finance rather than pay cash*.

Now, reread each of these definitions. Especially pay attention to the preceding paragraph on finance charges. Many loan institutions will quote you a low annual percentage rate and then add charges for things you don't really need, such as the insurance we mentioned. That's how they stick you, folks. They will say, "Our loans have an APR of fourteen percent." They will then promptly stick you with other charges that make their loan vastly more expensive.

Simple Money Shopping, Step by Step. Don't assume that any one source will necessarily be your best bet. Some credit unions and banks won't give you extended terms, for example. Others may have reached their loan limits and may want to charge you more. You would be smart to call at least three different sources, gathering the same information from each. If you have a credit union, call them and two other sources. Call the bank you deal with most often. Perhaps call the dealership you are most likely to purchase a car from. Tell each source what you are doing, too; in all likelihood they will work a little harder to get your business. And, for Pete's sake, don't be shy. No lending source, including credit unions, is doing you a favor—you are the reason they exist.

Gathering Information. Take a pad and put down a few basic assumptions. Are you going to buy a new car or a used car? Used cars are financed with rates that vary with the year of the car. For comparison purposes, the exact year is not too important; just if you plan to buy a one-year-old car or a five-year-old car.

Next, how many months do you plan to finance your car? Are you determined to hold the number of months down? If you are, you will save money. If you are buying a used car, the number of months will again be affected by the year of the car. But for comparison purposes, simply decide how many months you would *like* to be making payments, and write that number down.

Now, take your pad, and list each of the sources you plan to call by name across the top of the paper. Draw vertical columns under each source. Then, down the left margin, list the following questions:

1. What is your APR for new/used car loans for ____ months?
2. What is your add-on rate on the same loan?
3. Do you require life or accident and health insurance on your loans? (You will need a simple yes or no answer)
4. Do you have any other charges for making a loan, such as credit checks? (If yes, write down what it is and how much it costs)

Now, give your loan prospects a call. If you're calling your credit union or bank, simply ask for an installment loan officer. If you are calling a dealership, ask for their "F and I" department. Keep in mind that many people will try to confuse you with different financing "specials" or repayment methods. Stick to your questions. If one source has several rate plans, tell them you would like their "average" plan, not those requiring special conditions. Fill your answers out carefully, note the name of the person you have talked with at each source, and relax.

Now, take a look at your chart. If any of the sources require both life and accident and health insurance before giving you a loan, scratch them from your list. Life and accident and health insurance purchased like this is very expensive *and* very profitable to the sellers. If a source requires only life insurance, don't scratch them off the list yet. Now, compare the APRs. The source with the lowest will be your best bet, *if* they do not charge for credit checks and the like.

An Aside on Applying for a Loan. Unless you plan to finance your car at a dealership, apply for your loan at least a week before your plan to purchase the car. Make an appointment with the source and go to that meeting well prepared. Take your social security number, credit cards, and the institution names and account numbers of both checking and savings accounts, plus any current installment loans you have paid off in the past two years. If you have already determined the exact car you are going to buy, take that information, too. If you have not decided on a specific car, be prepared to tell them the approximate price range of the car you intend to buy. Most lending institutions will be happy to approve your financing without knowing the specific car.

How Much Can You Afford to Pay Each Month? How Long Will You Pay It?

As we have mentioned, payment buyers are the most easily taken customers in any dealership. The reason is twofold: most customers do not know how to relate a payment to the cost of a particular car transaction, and they do not understand that a payment represents a *lump sum of money*. Now, please reread. Put another way, you will not know how much money you can *spend* on a car if you do not know how much money your payment will *buy*. You know, for instance, that you can buy more car if you can afford to spend $200 dollars a month rather than $100 dollars a month, but tell me the answer to this: if you have a trade-in worth $4000 dollars but owe $3000 dollars on that trade, how much car can you buy for $200 dollars a month for thirty-six months?

Many sales managers have trouble figuring that one out easily—it's called "backing up" a deal—but it is very important to understand how to deal with all of these variables: How much money will a payment buy? How do you compute the effect of your trade on that money? How do you compute the effect of the payoff on your present car?

It's not really hard to do this. Grab your pad again and follow my thinking. If you will spend some time learning these few steps, you will know more about the mysteries of financing a car than your salesman. More than most dealers remember. More than many finance managers. Hell, you'll be the smartest kid on the block.

How Much Money Any Payment Will Buy. Do you remember the ways people refer to the cost of money? *Simple interest* is always computed on the balance of the loan. *Add-on* interest rates look the same as simple—for instance, both rates could be eight percent or nine percent—but add-on interest is more expensive because you don't have the use of the entire amount of the loan for the entire term of the loan. *APRs,* or annualized percentage rates, express the true cost of borrowing money.

In order to compute how much money any payment will buy, we are going to use the add-on method of quoting interest. We are going to take add-on rates and develop a *factor*. Factors are mathematical devices that enable you to figure what lump sum of money a payment will buy.

Incidentally, because we're using add-on rates, our answers won't be accurate if you plan to finance at your credit union—credit unions, as we discussed, make simple-interest loans. If you plan to finance at your credit union, you can *still* use the factors, though. The factor method will simply keep you under your budget. For instance, a factored payment of $172 would cost you only $156 at your credit union. If you prefer, call your credit union and simply tell them you want to know how much money your payment will buy. They'll be happy to provide you the figure.

Factors will also tell you how much of each payment is interest and how much is actually applied to the "principal." The interest isn't ours but belongs to the nice people who are loaning us money. The principal is ours to spend on a car. The principal is also our Loan Cash.

The Concept of Loan Cash. You won't find the term "Loan Cash" in the dictionary, and you certainly won't hear the words used in a dealership; car stores want you to remain confused. But understanding the concept of Loan Cash is one of the most important things you must do—if you plan to finance a car.

The concept is simple: cars are not bought for "$199 per month," or for "only $500 down and $100 dollars a month." Cars are bought for *cash*. Every time. The payment you make each month is buying a *lump sum of cash*. Your factor tells you how much.

How Do You Develop a Factor? Just pick any add-on

interest rate and multiply it by the number of years you plan to finance. And then add "1" to the front of your number. Here are some examples:

A loan of 8 percent for 3 years:	$8 \times 3 = 24$
The factor is:	1.24
A loan of 10 percent for 4 years:	$10 \times 4 = 40$
The factor is:	1.40
A loan of 9 percent for 3½ years:	$9 \times 3.5 = 31$
The factor is:	1.31
A loan of 10½ percent for 3½ years:	$10.5 \times 3.5 = 37$
The factor is:	1.37

Isn't that easy? Now, take your pad and develop factors for each of these examples. When you multiply, you can round off to the nearest whole number, as I did, or, if you're using a calculator, you can keep the fraction.

    (a) a loan of 10 percent for 3 years
    (b) a loan of 8½ percent for 3½ years
    (c) a loan of 11 percent for 42 months
    (d) a loan of 7½ percent for 30 months

Answers are provided below. Remember to convert months to years. For instance, fifty-four months would be 4.5 years. Once you're comfortable doing this, take some time and think carefully about how much money you really would be comfortable with as a monthly car payment. Think also about the number of months you would realistically like to pay. Talk this over with your spouse, if you have one. The time to decide how much you want to pay each month is long before you enter the showroom. You should think about it before you even begin to think

---

(d) 1.19 (rounded off).

ANSWERS: (a) 1.30; (b) 1.30 (rounded off); (c) 1.39 (rounded off);

about which car you would really like to own. Let the *payment* determine what you will buy. Don't be like most people and let the *car* determine what you will pay each month.

Determining Your Loan Cash

If you have decided on a payment and number of months, then look back over the different financing sources on your financing shopping list and develop a factor based on one of those rates. Choose the add-on interest rate of your most likely financing source, the one with the lowest APR. If the source would not quote the add-on rate to you, the chart on pages 353–54 in the Appendix will help you convert the APR to add-on interest.

As an example, let's say the rate will be eight percent add-on. You plan to spend no more than $200 dollars a month for thirty-six months.

> STEP ONE: DEVELOP THE FACTOR
>
> (8 × 3 = 24. The factor is 1.24)
>
> STEP TWO: DIVIDE YOUR PAYMENT BY THE FACTOR
>
> (200 divided by 1.24 = 161.29)
> The answer to step two is *the amount of money you get in each $200 payment.* The rest is interest.
>
> STEP THREE: MULTIPLY YOUR ANSWER BY THE NUMBER OF MONTHS YOU WILL BE REPAYING YOUR LOAN
>
> (161.29 × 36 months = 5806)
>
> STEP THREE tells you *how much cash you are buying, i.e., your "Loan Cash"*

Now, watch all three steps in these examples, or try them yourself.

1. You want to pay $100 per month for 36 months. The loan will cost you 7 percent.

2. You want to pay $150 per month for 48 months. The interest rate is 9 percent.
3. You want to pay $80 per month for 24 months. The loan will cost you 10 percent per year.

1. *$100 per month for 36 months at 7 percent*

   STEP ONE: $3 \times 7 = 21$
   the factor is 1.21

   STEP TWO: $100 \div 1.21 = \$82.64$

   STEP THREE: $\$82.64 \times 36 = \$2975.00$ *in Loan Cash*

2. *$150 per month for 48 months at 9 percent*

   STEP ONE: $4 \times 9 = 36$
   the factor is 1.36

   STEP TWO: $150 \div 1.36 = \$110.29$

   STEP THREE: $\$110.29 \times 48 = \$5293.00$ *in Loan Cash*

3. *$80 per month for 24 months at 10 percent*

   STEP ONE: $2 \times 10 = 20$
   the factor is 1.20

   STEP TWO: $80 \div 1.20 = \$66.66$

   STEP THREE: $\$66.66 \times 24 = \$1599.00$ *in Loan Cash*

What the Three Steps Tell You. By using the steps, you will know how much car you can buy in *cash.* It won't be necessary to rely on a salesman or finance manager to translate figures for you vaguely.

There are a couple of other things you'll need to know before walking into the dealership. But before going on, would you be kind enough to do a little homework? The answers are at the bottom of the page.

MORE WORK EXAMPLES
(a) you want to pay $225 per month for 36 months at 9 percent
(b) you want to pay $175 per month for 42 months at 8 percent

   (c) you want to pay $110 per month for 30 months at 11 percent

   (d) you want to pay $85 per month for 24 months at 7 percent

Using Your Loan Cash to
Determine Your Available Cash

A Preliminary Note: How Much Down? Before we talk further about Loan Cash, you need to consider down payments. If you listen to lending institutions, down payments are an easy thing to compute. On new cars, they'll loan the actual cost of the car; on used cars, the loan value of that particular car.

Well, thanks to this friendly advice, there are millions of folks out there who don't drive cars—they drive enormous metal hunks of liability. These people owe more on their cars than any reasonable person would be willing to pay them; they literally cannot sell or trade their cars without *paying* someone to take them. For many the down payment was a small amount of cash; for others, simply the equity in their trades. Some actually allowed the seller to arrange *two* loans—to "dip" them—to make even this minimum down payment.

Financing a car like this with a minimum down payment is dangerous. It means you will always owe more on your car than it's worth. Don't put yourself in that position. If you plan to buy a used car with a true wholesale value of $4000 dollars, for instance, don't finance $4000. If you plan to buy a new car, don't finance the cost of the car. If you will use the following guidelines, your car will never be a true liability—it will almost always be worth more than you owe.

———

ANSWERS: (a) 4212; (b) 5742.24; (c) 2578.20; (d) 1789.44

On a New Car. In Chapter 8, the section What Do Those Pretty New Cars Cost the Dealer? shows you how to compute the cost of a new car. Be sure that the amount you plan to finance is twenty percent *below* the true cost figure.

On a Used Car. Be sure the amount you plan to finance is twenty percent *below* the specific loan value.

If you plan to trade your car and have enough equity (the amount of its wholesale value over and above your payoff) you may not need cash. But if it still takes money from your pocket to be twenty percent below, *pay it.* It isn't easy to part with your hard-earned cash like this. But it is the only safe way to buy a car. If you will follow these suggestions, you'll normally be in a position to sell your car at any time and receive cash back.

If you simply cannot afford these suggestions, you will have to pay down a sum equal to the following:

Minimum Down Payments on a New Car. The sum of the profit you are paying on the new car plus the tax and miscellaneous charges. Since you don't know at this stage what the final profit figure or tax figure will be, be safe. Assume the profit will be $400 dollars on any car you buy; assume that tax will be computed on your Loan Cash figure. For example, let's assume that your Loan Cash figure is $5400 dollars and that you live in a state with four percent tax. Your down payment would need to be:

Tax on $5400.00	$216.00
Profit of $400.00	400.00
Charges for title and other fees	100.00
TOTAL DOWN PAYMENT	716.00

Minimum Down Payments on a Used Car. The difference in the actual loan value of the car and the total amount of money you will owe on the car, including taxes and other charges. Since you don't know any of these items yet, assume that tax will be paid on your total Loan Cash figure and that you will pay at least $500 dollars over loan value for any car. For instance, if your Loan Cash figure is $4000 dollars, you would need to pay the following down:

Tax on $4000.00	$160.00
(we assume 4 percent;	
use the rate for your state)	
Amount you are paying	
over loan value	500.00
Charges for title and other fees	
(to be safe, always assume $100.00)	100.00
TOTAL DOWN PAYMENT	760.00

Determining Total Available Cash. Telling you how to put this step into action is the subject of chapters to come. But right now, you need to know how to arrive at an Available Cash figure for specific buyer situations. Perhaps you are merely thinking about buying a car now; in that case, just read through this information and go on. But if you are seriously planning to buy a car, read this section carefully, stop and think, then actually work out a tentative Available Cash figure for several situations that might fit you as a buyer. For instance, you might be considering buying a new car and trading or simply buying a used car straight out. You should work out an Available Cash figure for both situations. After you've done so, note these figures and save them. You'll need them later.

If You Plan to Buy a New or Used Car and Have No Trade. If you plan to buy a car without trading, the Loan Cash figure tells you how much your payment will buy. This figure plus your down payment is the total amount of car you can buy—your Available Cash. For example, if you wish to buy a car and have decided to spend $150 per month for forty-eight months at nine percent add-on, your

Loan Cash would be $5293. If you plan to pay $1000 down, you'll have $6293 in Available Cash. Your Available Cash must pay for everything in the transaction: the car, tax, tag, and all other extras.

If You Plan to Buy a New or Used Car and Have a Debt-Free Trade. In this situation, your Loan Cash and the wholesale value of your trade will determine your Available Cash.

Once you have carefully decided how much you want to spend each month and for how many months, use the interest rate from your shopping list and develop your Loan Cash figure. Let's say you have decided to pay $200 a month for thirty-six months. The interest rate is nine percent add-on. Your Loan Cash figure will be $5669.

You have also shopped your trade and know it has a true wholesale value of $2000. Since you own the car outright, the trade will contribute its full $2000 value to the transaction.

How much can you buy and still keep your payments at $200 for 36 months? Loan Cash of $5669 plus wholesale value of $2000 equals $7669, your Available Cash. You can buy $7669 worth of car, including tax, tag, and other charges. In all likelihood, you will not have to make any other down payment than your trade, too. Just always be sure you are twenty percent under, as we mentioned.

If You Plan to Buy a New or Used Car and Owe Money on Your Trade. This section applies to most of us. Your Available Cash will be determined by the Loan Cash you can afford plus any equity you have in your trade. *Remember, equity equals wholesale value minus payoff.* Your car has more value to you than debt only if the wholesale value is higher than the payoff. For instance, if your car is worth $4000 and your payoff is $3000, your equity is $1000—its real value is $1000 more than you owe. If you owe more on your car than its wholesale value, you have no equity. You're in the bucket.

Since you owe money on your car, you need to know which situation applies to you. Call your financing institution and ask them for a "net payoff." The net payoff is simply the total amount you owe the lending institution minus any rebates for unused insurance and, at times, prepaid interest. Now compute your equity. Subtract your net payoff from your true wholesale value. If the answer is a "plus" figure, if your wholesale value is higher, breathe easier. If the payoff is higher, go buy a bottle of hundred proof before reading further. Then turn to page 164, *If You Are "In the Bucket."*

If You Have Equity. Now, sit down and determine how much you want to spend on a car payment for each month and for how many months. Look at your financing shopping list, and choose the rate from the source you are most likely to finance with. Now, develop your Loan Cash figure for that payment and write the amount down by your equity figure. For instance, if you have decided to spend $150 per month for forty-eight months at nine percent add-on, you know your Loan Cash in $5293. If your trade is worth $4000 and you owe $3000, you also have $1000 in equity. *Your equity and Loan Cash combined determine what you can buy: your Available Cash.*

In this instance, you can buy a car that has a total selling price of $6293. But, don't combine the figures together just yet. Remember that you will only have $1000 in equity *if* your car has a wholesale value of $4000 dollars. And since you are trading your car, the dealer is obviously going to try to give you *less* than $4000. For now, just be sure that you have four figures together somewhere in your pad: (1)

The amount of your Loan Cash. (2) The wholesale value of your trade. (3) The amount of your equity. (4) Your Available Cash, the sum of one and three. Then skip to page 168, for the step-by-step process of using factors to determine payments.

If You Are "In the Bucket." If you have a car that is worth $4000, but owe $5000 on it, you unfortunately don't have any equity. You have what is called negative equity, a nice way of saying that you are in the bucket. Negative equity simply means that you owe more on your car than it is worth. You probably will not be able to trade cars without paying cash down.

Now, before looking at an easy way to determine how much cash you will need to pay down in this situation, please listen to one piece of advice. If you are in the bucket and don't have the cash on hand necessary to trade cars, *don't* trade cars. Keep your car for a while. Small loan companies—"dip houses"—survive on people who borrow money to bail themselves out of their present car. Each one of these people is simply digging a deeper financial grave in preparation for the inevitable. Thousands of people have had their cars repossessed each year because some nice salesman has told them, "Don't worry about the money, sir. We can borrow that extra down payment for you." You don't need friends like that.

At times dealerships will bury you deeper in the bucket *without* dipping you. For instance, let's say that you are in the bucket, but still want to trade for a newer used car. You want to buy a Chrysler Newport for $4500. You have a car worth $2000 and owe $2500 on it. You're in the bucket for $500. And Killer is waiting on you.

"Mr. Jones," Killer explains carefully, "you have agreed to buy the Chrysler for $4500 dollars, and I am going to give you $2000 dollars for your old car. If you don't mind, however, I'd like to write this sale up a little differently, so that we can have you riding tomorrow *without one penny down.*" You quickly slip your tongue over your lips in anticipation. Sure he can do that. "What we are going to do is raise the price of the Chrysler to *$5500* dollars, and raise the amount I'm giving you for your old car to *$3000* dollars. Now, it will look like your old car is worth more than the $2500 you owe on it. That's important to the bank, Mr. Jones—they just won't approve any deal if you owe more on your car than it's worth, unless you put some cash down, too."

Killer quickly begins to scribble down a small column of numbers. "This is how we'll write up the order. We will deduct the $3000 dollars I'm allowing you from the $5500, and that leaves $2500. Since you owe $2500 on the old one, the amount remaining to be financed will then be $5000 dollars. And *that* just happens to be the loan value of that Chrysler!"

It's one of the oldest tricks. If you'll think about it, you'll realize that Mr. Jones may be getting a car with no money down. But he is also getting himself even deeper in the bucket on the Chrysler. Mr. Jones didn't really win any battle in this transaction; he simply postponed the time of his defeat. Every time that you buy a car, new or used, you are simply postponing the pain by not paying lots of money down—and that's why most people's cars are liabilities on their financial statements, not assets.

Depending upon the amount of your negative equity, you may be able to retail your car, sell it yourself, and at least come out even. For instance, if your car has a whole-sale value of $3000 but your payoff is $3500, you are in the bucket only $500. If you'll read the section on selling your own car, you should be able to receive at least that for your car.

If You Still Plan to Trade Cars, and You Are in the Bucket. Here's a good way to know how much cash you will need to pay down. This is extra cash, cash from your pocket. It has nothing to do with Loan Cash.

IF YOU ARE BUYING A NEW CAR, the total amount of down payment that will normally be required will be the total of the following:

1. The amount of your negative equity
2. The amount of profit you plan to pay on the new car
3. The charges for taxes, tag, title, and other things such as rustproofing

IF YOU ARE BUYING A USED CAR, the total amount of down payment that will normally be required will be the total of the following.

1. The amount of your negative equity
2. The difference in the car's total price (excluding your trade) and that specific car's loan value (you can call your bank, and they will provide you the loan value figure)

If you find that you are only $500 dollars in the bucket, don't think you will only need $500 dollars in cash, either. Let's take an example. You are planning to buy a car that has a true cost of $6000 dollars. You have agreed to pay the dealer a profit of $400 dollars. And your payoff on your trade-in is $500 dollars higher than its wholesale value. According to the formula above you will need:

1. $500 dollars in cash (the amount of your negative equity)
2. $400 dollars in cash (the profit you are paying the seller)

3. $240 in cash (tax, if you are paying four percent)
4. $100 dollars in cash (your tax, title, and other fees)
TOTAL: $1240

You will need at least *$1240 dollars* in cash *from your pocket* to trade cars. And you won't be twenty percent under, as we recommend; you'll be financing the maximum amount. Do you know what that means? You will be in the bucket in this car, too, from Day One.

Do You Still Want to Trade Cars? Okay, dope. Sit down and determine how much you want to pay each month on your next "bucketmobile." Don't forget you will also be paying out lots of cash from your pocket when you determine that monthly payment. Then, look at your financing shopping list, and choose the add-on rate from your lowest source. Now, develop your Loan Cash figure for that payment. Forget your trade—you would be much better off if you didn't have one.

If you are in the bucket, you will need to find a car that *fits your Loan Cash figure,* a car whose total price including tax, tag, title, and other fees, is no higher than your Loan Cash figure. For instance, if you have decided to spend $150 per month for forty-eight months at nine percent add-on, you know your Loan Cash is $5293. That's all the car you can buy. But that's not all the money you are spending. Once you have decided on a specific car, determine how much actual cash from your pocket you'll need to pay down just to keep your payment at your desired level. But *don't* think that cash is buying you more car, it's not. It is simply bailing you out of the bucket enough to give some lending institution the privilege of putting you in the bucket again.

USING FACTORS TO DETERMINE
PAYMENTS WHEN YOU KNOW
THE LUMP SUM

We've been using factors to determine Loan Cash, but they can also be used to tell you what the *payments* will be on a lump sum of money. This formula is a simple one and uses the information already at your fingertips: the number of months you plan to finance and the add-on interest rate.

Why do you need to know this? If you are lucky, you may negotiate a final price on a car that is *less* than your Loan Cash. If you do, this formula will provide you a quick way to compute your new payment. It will also allow you to check the other guy's figures—handy. The payment formula will also give you flexibility. For instance, if you decided to spend $6000 dollars on a car but then find a real dreamboat for $6600, the payment formula will let you quickly determine your new payment. And finally, it can bring you to your senses should you accidentally fall in love with some beauty $3000 over budget. In Chapter 9, Negotiating the Sale, we'll show you *when* to use this formula. Right now, let's learn how.

TO DETERMINE A PAYMENT FOR
A LUMP SUM OF MONEY

1. Multiply the lump sum by the factor, the same factor you used earlier
2. Divide the answer by the number of months

EXAMPLES:

$3000 for 3 years at 8 percent add-on
1. $3000 × 1.24 = $3720
2. $3720 ÷ 36 = $103.33 *per month*

$3500 for 24 months at 7 percent add-on
1. $3500 × 1.14 = $3990
2. $3990 ÷ 24 = $166.25 *per month*

NOW, YOU TRY IT. Answers are at the bottom of the page.
    (a) $3600 for 3 years at 9 percent add-on
    (b) $2669 for 4 years at 10 percent add-on
    (c) $7546 for 3½ years at 7.5 percent add-on

If you know your factoring, this is easy for you. But practice some more. Decide the lump sum, number of months, and interest rate yourself. Incidentally, the factor method of determining payments will be accurate to the nearest penny. If your state adds charges for documentary stamps to finance contracts, the factor method will develop a payment within a dollar of the actual payment. Factors *do not* include any extra charges for insurance.

SHOULD YOU BUY LIFE OR ACCIDENT AND HEALTH INSURANCE?

Virtually every automobile financing source in America offers credit life and accident and health insurance as a "service" to its customers. The cost for each is conveniently included in your payments. Just pennies a day, as they say. Should you take advantage of these services? Definitely yes—*if* your horoscope indicates imminent death or severe bodily injury within the very near future. (And *if* you believe in horoscopes.)

It's not that protection itself is a bad idea. Many of us do need to insure the payment of debt. But, we just don't have to make insurance companies and their "agents" rich in the process. And, regardless of the need, you are making those folks richer, indeed.

The premium is the first rip-off. It's a very high premium because of the high payout associated with each sale. In many states each dollar of premium contains forty cents for commissions and other kinds of compensation. In many other states the figure is higher. For instance, most southern states allow automobile dealerships to retain forty-five to fifty percent of each premium dollar as some type of "thank you." This income source is the purest profit any dealer can make. It doesn't require a stock of cars or dozens of salesmen. It simply requires a smiling man in the finance office. Wouldn't you be smiling?

Many dealerships make more than forty-five or fifty percent. These stores have formed their own umbrella insurance companies and enjoy total insurance profits exceeding sixty percent of each premium dollar. Many of these stores also enjoy finance profits exceeding $20,000 dollars a month.

But lending sources, whether banks or dealerships, make money or more than the premium on your loan. They conveniently add the premium to your loan, which obviously increases the amount you are financing and the total amount of interest on the loan. Then *they actually insure the insurance.* Nice. If you, for instance, decide to buy only life insurance on a $6000-dollar loan for forty-eight months, look what happens:

Loan principal	$6000.00
Interest on the loan	1725.60
Credit life premium	241.08
Interest *on the premium*	69.33
TOTAL	8036.01

Your lending institution is not going to insure this loan for $6000 dollars—they are going to insure it for *$8000 dol-*

lars. At their very silly premium rates. On the loan we've just mentioned, you will pay $6.47 a month for forty-eight months. That doesn't sound like much money, does it? But look what the same amount of money would buy you from about any life insurance man in town: If you are thirty-five years old, $6.47 would buy you over $12,000 dollars' worth of *level* term insurance for *five* years, fifty percent more insurance for a year longer. If you are fifty years old, $6.47 would buy you $8000 dollars' worth of *level* term insurance for *five* years.

The key word here is *level:* the amount of insurance stays the same. If you die during the last month of the fifth year, you would still receive the full amount of the insurance. If you purchased your life insurance from a lending institution, only the *balance* of your loan would be covered. Die just before the forty-eighth payment, and your $8000-dollar insurance policy will pay the last payment. Period.

But What About Accident and Health Insurance? A&H, as it's referred to, is theoretically designed to make your payments if you are disabled or ill. The concept is very nice, but the prices are much, much higher than life insurance, and the coverage is conveniently designed to make sure most illnesses and accidents are not covered. Virtually all A&H plans tell you in very small print that:

1. Coverage does not begin until you have been disabled and *under a doctor's care* for at least fourteen days. It's called the "elimination period," and I can't think of a more appropriate description. How many times in the past five years have you been totally disabled and under the doctor's care for fourteen continuous days? Some A&H policies have elimination periods of seven days. How many times have you been disabled and under the doctor's care for

seven days? *Some* policies even have an elimination period of thirty days.

2. Preexisting conditions are not covered. If you've had a little bout with something during the six or twelve months *prior* to buying A&H insurance, you won't be covered for that specific problem. Many A&H plans also require that you sign a "statement of health." This statement makes it perfectly clear that only robust folks should expect payment from their A&H insurance.

Unfortunately, A&H policies are not easy to purchase directly from your insurance man. Many insurance companies do offer "income protection" plans, but they, too, are expensive. You'll have to make your decision on A&H with a crystal ball. In all likelihood, if you are in good health, it's a very large waste of money. Perhaps you can turn to the horoscopes again.

Are either of these types of insurance ever a good buy? If you're in generally but not specifically poor health and cannot qualify for other types of insurance, yes. If you're much older, yes. Since both credit life and accident and health insurance are essentially "group" plans, usually no physicals are required, and persons in their late sixties pay the same rate as thirty-year-olds. But, if you fit into any of the following categories, save your money. It will enable you to buy more car.

DON'T BUY IT IF . . .

. . . you are under fifty and in good health. Other insurance sources will be cheaper.

. . . you are single. Insurance should protect survivors. If you die with no survivors, your insurance will be protecting the *lenders*. Let them worry about their own problems.

. . . you have enough existing insurance to cover your debts. You may already be insurance-poor.

... you really want to beef up your insurance in general. Take the money and buy some really worthwhile insurance.

Can They Make You Take It? An enormous amount of credit insurance is sold because customers feel they must take the insurance in order to receive a loan. Banks are probably more guilty of this technique than dealerships. But don't fall prey to this subtle blackmail. In most states it is against the law to approve credit on this basis. Banks may require you to have your loan covered with insurance, but they cannot require you to purchase that insurance from them or from any particular source recommended by them. In most states you can fulfill this requirement by "assigning" an existing insurance policy to cover your loan. If you have sufficient amounts of life insurance, an assignment of proceeds is obviously the best way to provide coverage, since you are already paying for that coverage. Your insurance agent will provide you with the form.

6

Big Town, Small Town: How the Boys Play the Game

In the car business, a small town is defined as an area or territory, the franchise area, in which only one Ford or Chrysler or G. M. dealer is located. If you want to compare your deal at a local store, you have to do a little driving. A big town has lots of franchise areas for each one of those small-town areas—maybe three Ford or Chevy dealerships within ten miles of each other. And, big town or small, each dealership has a nice line of logic telling you why it's better to buy in its own area. In theory, each franchise area is "protected" from the others—the local dealership in Clemville isn't supposed to advertise or proselytize in neighboring communities. In heavily populated areas, dealerships are allowed to advertise throughout the common metropolitan area, but they're not supposed to seek business actively more than X miles from their store.

Of course, the theory is just that—no one pays any attention to those fine lines of franchise agreements. And when you see a TV advertisement for Clemville's Friendly Ford dealership on the biggest TV station in town, they're certainly not making their pitch just to all those homes along the tranquil streets and country roads of that fine community. "Yessir, folks, drive a little bit further and save hundreds of dollars! We don't have high overhead, fast-talking salesmen, or fancy showrooms! What we've got is down-home prices, down-home looking, and down-home service! Why, even the cows like to get milked at Clemville's only friendly Ford dealership, located at the corner of State Road Three and the big oak tree!"

And what do the big dealerships do? They tell you how much money you save with their "Fantastic volume! World's largest selection! Lowest price in the state! Yes, ladies and gentlemen, shop every dealership in the world and then come to Stroker Ford! We'll outwheel, we'll out-deal even God himself at the pearly gates."

The cons may have a different ring, but the advertising messages are the same. The cost of new cars is the same, too, regardless of selling volume. What is different about the big-town and small-town boys is their approach to the customers. If you live in a small town—one of those places where everyone knows the dealer and his salesmen, along with the latest gossip about the young couple that just moved into the house with a bidet, for pity's sake—you're not going to be a victim of "system" selling if you trade with your neighborhood dealer. In all likelihood you'll deal with a single individual, who may even appraise your car, work you, and act as his own finance manager. And because of the "know-it-all" nature of small towns and their dealerships, you're also not likely to be taken in by some overly egregious manager. But don't think that the boys are really going to give you any break. Yes, their overhead is less than the big boys', but a small-town dealership may have a good month when it sells twenty cars, not two hundred. Those small stores have to make a pretty good profit on every car they sell, and small dealers like money just as much as the big boys. Many of the small-town stores are also blessed with the less competitive nature of their markets. If the nearest dealership of the same make car is forty miles away down some rutted road, customers are obviously less likely to shop a small store's deal than those people who live within a forty-mile radius of ten dealerships of the same car line.

There is one thing, too, that you will see in the smaller stores but never in the larger ones: the owner. It's not unusual at all for a store with six salesmen to have a dealer who doubles as a sales manager. But name me one time in your entire car-buying life when you have ever seen or talked to the dealer in a big-city store. As a matter of fact, name me one big dealership where the *salesmen* are even recognized by their own dealer. Gary Davies, Killer's dealer, once ran up to his general manager and said, "Damn it, why isn't someone waiting on that customer!" J. C. twitched his mouth, much like a guy getting ready to let loose his chew, and said, "Gary, that 'customer' has been selling cars for you for two years."

The big boys like Davies are no longer in the business of working with people; they're in the business of talking with their business managers and stockbrokers. They play golf with their banker friends and have homes right next to the old-monied folks who never dirtied their hands with a wrench or rolled a dead used car down the street to get it started. And maybe that's why they are so detached from the little folks that make the store run. Most dealers over fifty started in the business as nothings, and they have run uphill to the point where they really don't want to be reminded of the nothings. Many of these guys have their own private entrance to the store and never see the light of day of the showroom or the used-car lot. They wouldn't know if the place burned down until the daily "doc" sheet, the report card of the previous day's sales, failed to pass quietly through the door.

This "big boy" attitude, plus the sheer numbers of customers and salesmen that interact in the larger stores, is probably the underlying cause of "system" selling.

It was about six in the afternoon when J. C. walked into the control room, the sales manager's office overlooking most of the showroom and parts of the new-car lot. Without saying a word, he sat himself by the night manager, picked up the gross book, and stared silently at the rows of names and figures. Each line contained the history of each sale, detailing the customer's name, trade, new-car stock number, total gross on the new car, wholesale value of the used car, financing income, and financing source—the dealership's own finance company or one of the outside sources, such as a bank or credit union. The night manager just watched him. J. C. could be the friendliest boss in the world, but when he was this quiet, no one liked to be near him, much less sit by him. J. C. started talking, not to anyone in particular, but more a general venting of the things running through his mind. He always did this, talking around things out loud before drilling the matter dead center, and the night guy knew very quickly that the bit was going to come down on him.

"It's the damnedest thing. All day long our grosses are running odd—$351, $419, $125, $881. But then each night every single one of them runs even—$400 or $200 or $600. Hell, you'd think the boys look at the invoices or something like that." He continued looking at the book, then finally turned to address Crowley Miller, the night man. "Crow, look here. Here's a God-damned deal for $100 dollars. And another one. And another one. What are you guys *doing* around here at night, son?" J. C. had a way of saying that last word as if he *were* your father, a very mad one.

"J. C."—Crow paused a second before continuing, some shoring up of nerves—"it's just been too busy around here at night for us to go in on every deal, and our grosses are good, anyway, so what does it matter if we're letting the guys work from tissue?" His words were definitely not what J. C. wanted to hear, but Crow was unprepared for the violence of J. C.'s reaction.

"Too busy! Why you little bastard, I don't pay you to sit here and be a God-damned secretary! I pay you to work deals for me, not put names in this book!" J. C.'s finger was now jabbing Crow's chest in cadence with every word. "Eve-ry-bo-dy-works-deals-from-list! The boys don't *need* to see an invoice! *You* are leaving money on the table and it's *my* money."

J. C. left the office as he had entered, without saying another word, and Crow quickly picked up the intercom, paging all the salesmen to his office. Leaving Killer and one of the other guys on the floor, he led the rest of them back to the conference room, closing the door behind him. Crow was really a good guy. All the salesmen liked him because he was real easy on them, seldom sending anyone back for a raise and never taking a turn with a customer himself. When a salesman would come into his office, and say, "Crow, I've got this guy settled on a car, what type of deal do you want me to work him on?" Crow would simply look up the cost on that particular car and give the salesman a figure: "Tell the guy he can buy the car for $4700 and his. And don't go below $4400 without coming back to me." Sometimes Crow would just tell the guys the cost on a particular unit. Sure he was well-liked. But the salesmen working under him each night were making consistently less gross per unit than the day guys. All the salesmen on day shifts were made to work the system, whether they liked it or not. "The system" was now the subject of Mr. Crowley's special sales meeting.

"Boys, as you can probably tell by the large hole chewed in my ass, J. C. isn't too happy with how we've been running things around here at night." Everybody grunted in frustration. "So from now on, this is the way we're going to work deals. And *everybody* is going to work this way, too. Now, when you get someone set on one particular car, get them settled in your office and get their car appraised. On the way back from the used-car lot, pick up the stock card from that particular car. If that card says a car lists for $8000 dollars, you are to work your deal from $8000 dollars, *no* discounts in the beginning." "Shits" and "damns" flew around the room quietly, seeming to pop from one mouth into another.

"If a customer has a trade that's worth $2500 dollars, you are to tell him, 'Sir, we've been *taking in* cars like yours for $2000 dollars'—*do not* tell them their car is *worth* $2000 dollars. You are then to take the $2000 from the $8000. Now, I know everybody is going to jump, but that's the way we are going to do it. If your customer won't bite at that figure, you are to ask him, 'How much *will* I have to give you for your car?' Whatever that figure is, I want you to write it, to fill out a completed buyer's order, and get a deposit and bring it to me. Whatever the man says, even if he lets you write him on a list deal, I want you to tell the guy you will *try* to get his deal approved, but that only management can approve a sale.

"Once you have written up your customer at some figure, I want you to show me the deal, and then I want you to go back for more. Even if you have a list deal. Even if you lowballed the buy on his trade and have an overlist deal. And when you can't go back any more, I'll go in there with you. I want every single cent of profit we can make. We are not going to leave a damned cent on the table. And one thing else—nobody is to walk. If your guy jerks on you, hold him by the arms until I can get to him. If I'm not around, grab one of the other salesmen. And if there's no one else around, *deck him!"*

It was a good way to end the meeting, and most of the guys filed out in pretty good humor. Of course, they didn't really like the system; it could be embarrassing at times. But they all knew it *would* make them more money.

In strong system stores, salesmen very seldom know much more about the individual transaction than customers do. From long experience, dealerships have learned that salesmen who know the cost of cars will always work from that figure rather than from the list price. And, while most stores know that few people pay sticker price for new cars, *all* people bargain on a relative scale. For instance, if a car actually costs $6000 dollars and a salesman simply adds an additional $600 dollars to that figure, offering to sell you the car for $6600 dollars, in all likelihood you will negotiate downward in even increments until you buy the car for $6200 or $6300 dollars. If the salesman had been working the system, he would have looked you straight in the eye and said, "The price on this car is $7600 dollars." Sure, you would bring him down some, but probably not to $6600, much less $6200. Dealers who force their salesmen to use a high first asking price always have higher average grosses than dealers who don't. System stores also know that there are still a few people out there who will pay list price for a car. And, as one of my favorite sales managers says, "If the sticker price says $10,000 dollars, then we are entitled to every single dime of that profit."

The T.O. system is also an important part of system selling. Every dealer in America believes money is left on the table after the sale of each car. The amount left lying there may not be great by itself, but in the aggregate, it can be a really tidy sum. If J. C.'s store, for instance, could raise each of its customers just $25 dollars—not hundreds—Mr. Gary Oliver Davies' net profit for the year would increase by $100,000 dollars. If your salesman brings in some smiling face and says something like, "Folks, I'd like for you to meet my manager," don't think you're being accorded a great honor. You're just being T.O.'d for a little more profit.

Once you become a knowledgeable customer, system stores can be nice places for you to do business. Since most people in these stores will really know less than you do about the value of your car, the real value, and since most of them won't really know what a new car costs or the way to determine payments for a particular sum of money, you will be in a better position to handle pressure tactics than the salesman and his cohorts. They will be under the gun, not you. As a matter of fact, they are already facing the barrel of the biggest gun: a large store's "nut."

The pressure—the unrelenting moment-by-moment reality of meeting a big store's nut, the amount of gross profit that must be generated every day—causes an inward time bomb in system stores that burns out most sales managers in five years and drives away many salesmen in ninety days. If you live in a metropolitan area encompassing more than a half million people, you have several of these system stores like Killer's, and at least one mega-store. A mega-store must sell seven hundred cars, new and used, each month just to pay the bills: the floor-plan interest that may run $3000 dollars *a day,* the fixed payroll that may run $3000 dollars a day, and an advertising budget that requires $2000 or $3000 dollars a day. No business eating this much money can be run like your neighborhood country store. Killer used to work at one of these places, but he didn't like the pace. He does stay in contact with Lanny Maxwell, maybe the sharpest salesman at that store. You see, that mega-store is just six miles from Killer's store—and the Dead End.

Lanny and Killer were sitting in their usual back booth, right by the ice machine and the entrance to the rest rooms—no one really liked to sit there, and the booth seemed to have some unhung "reserved" sign on the corner of the seat closest to the john. Lanny was expansive, legs sprawled far apart, his diamond tie tack hanging loosely, not at all connected to the mauve silk shirt with the short-cut collar. "One of these days I'm going to retire and work at a store like yours," Lanny said. A typical toot of the successful salesman's horn, Killer thought. Lanny must have had a really rich day.

"Bob, I want to tell you, it was madness! It was the last day of our 'Invoice Plus a Dollar' sale, and the damn people staked out the car they wanted like it was a great big pot of gold just waiting to be mined; hell, I wrote five deals before the second session." At the mega-stores, sales meetings aren't held twice a week or once a day—they're held two or three times a day, and the hot car in the morning, the car with the bonus on it, is long forgotten by the two o'clock meeting. On this particular day, though, the hot cars were all "old maids," the Plain Janes that seem to adopt a dealership and spend months there collecting dust and rent.

"Perry [the sales manager or, rather, one of the nine sales managers who report to the new-car sales manager, who reports to the general sales manager, who reports to the general manager], Perry was frothing at the mouth to get all the old maids off the lot. Joey, the new-car sales manager, got the word from God himself that the cars were gone or he was gone—I'm telling you, we sold some cars for *nothing."* God to people at this store is Anthony B. Scarri. His three stores sell more cars than thirty dealerships like Killer's. Mr. Scarri is one of twenty mega-dealers in America. He has several large homes, a large turboprop plane, and a sixty-seven-foot Burger yacht.

Lanny Maxwell's average commission per car sold is a little less than Killer's and the commissions of the boys who sell in the country. And Lanny wastes no time before telling prospective customers that. Sometimes, he'll even pull out a sales slip from some deal and show it to every customer who walks in. "Folks, see for yourself. I made $25 dollars on that car, and the dealership only made $75. That's why I have to sell lots of cars just to make a living. And that's why you'll be glad you bought a car from me." His average commission isn't *that* much less than the country stores', however. Lanny may sell some cars for $100-dollar profit, but he also sells a lot for $700- and $800-dollar profits—to all the suckers who automatically think big stores sell for less.

Lanny is a tall, slender man. He's a little flashy, too: thick, gray hair swept back, seemingly carved in rock, the result of five or six sprayings of VO5 each day; his shoes are patent leathers or genuine alligator, and his tie is always just a bit too busy. Lanny's selling techniques are just as flashy. He's one of the few salesmen at the mega-store who greets his own customers—most of the other guys talk to ups after the "greeters," the full-time glad-handers, have led one and all to the registration book. At system stores, every up puts his or her name and phone number in that book before meeting a salesman.

Lanny's way is a little more direct. "Howdy, folks! Are you going to buy a car today?" Before the ups can speak, he answers the question for them. "Of course you are, and what a stroke of luck that I'm your salesman!" Lanny turns his back on these people, his right hand swinging in the air in a pulling motion as if he's hauling some high-flying kite behind him, and utters his most famous line: "Come on! Follow me, and you'll die rich!" All the time he's walking away from the people without once looking back. Nine times out of ten, everyone follows him, as if drawn by that magical string. Who can resist the open con? The other boys at the store do get a laugh every few weeks when this line doesn't work. They'll see Lanny marching across the lot, mouth moving faster than any seasoned auctioneer's, hands waving in the air—as the customers who should be following him quietly open the door to their car and slink off the lot. Lanny always seems to look back just as they drive off. He quickly turns in a circle in mock bewilderment, lifts out his right lapel, peers into the pocket to make sure the ups haven't crawled in, and breaks out in a grin from ear to ear.

He's one of the few refreshing things in this particular store. A mega-store is like those large, fast-moving assembly lines. Each employee has a specific task to perform over and over again; the line is always moving, and there's not a moment when the line workers can relax. First there's the greeter, who turns you over to some younger salesman. The young guy's chore is to qualify you—ask enough questions to know for sure that you have a reasonably good job and some type of credit experience. If you sound like the type of up that can buy, the young guy will normally turn you over to a lot walker, another nice young man who will help you find the car you like and then take you for a drive— usually in a demonstrator of the same make and model, not in the specific car you like. City people don't seem to want any miles on their "new" car, so the mega-stores use salesmen's demos for that first ride. Then when you return from your drive, the lot walker T.O.s you to a "closer," a man who does nothing but turn all the emotional screws, tightly. Closers are usually the best salesmen in the place, and their knowledge of the psychology of selling techniques is enormous. Closers also work in teams. If one guy can't close you, a sales manager or team captain will quickly appear.

It sounds like a lot of people to deal with, doesn't it? But you're not finished yet. Once you agree to buy, you've then got to see the "business manager"—that's a less offensive term than finance manager. In his own particular field, the finance manager is selling constantly, too. And don't think you can shorten your conversation with this guy just because you plan to pay cash for your car or finance it through a credit union. What would be your answer to a conversation like this: "Mr. Speck, I know that you want to pay cash for that pretty new car. But look at these figures for just a moment. You owe us $8000 dollars, the balance due on the hardtop. If you leave that $8000 in money market certificates, you'll continue to earn a minimum of twelve percent per year. That's $960 dollars a year. Now, let's assume that you finance the car with us for thirty-six months. As you know, we have a special financing rate now, nine percent add-on. Your interest each year on the loan will only be *$675* dollars. And, since your savings is making you $960 dollars per year, you're in essence financing the car for free. Plus, your $8000 in savings is there when you need it. And the interest on the loan is deductible from your taxes. And, Mr. Speck, let's say you get life insurance in your contract. If something unfortunate should happen to you the day you drive out in that car, your wife will owe nothing on it—it will be hers free and clear. *And* that $8000 in savings will still be working for her."

"Now, wait a minute," Speck says, "if my savings are

earning twelve percent, and if your loan is for nine percent, how can the savings be earning $960 dollars per year and the loan be costing only $675 per year?"

The guy laughs a little—he thought Speck was more sophisticated. Obviously, he's not. "Mr. Speck, savings are compounded on an annual basis or less. Money market certificates, for instance, are usually for ninety days, renewable at that time. Installment-loan interest is computed on an annualized percentage basis. The effective annualized yields of savings and loans is, of course, different."

The F and I man is garbling his facts on purpose; by this time, Speck has developed a mild headache and redirects his thinking to more familiar waters. "Well, if financing that car is going to make me so rich, I'll do it. But I'll do it through my credit union. I want them to check over the deal, anyway." And that's just what the F and I man doesn't want anyone to do—credit unions are another pain in the neck for salesmen. They have an unfortunate habit of telling people, "Boy, that's a high price!" Credit unions, like banks or any other outside financing sources, also remove control of the sale from the dealership.

"Mr. Speck, if you need to check with the credit union before buying this car, why did you sign the buyer's order? Didn't you agree this was a fair price?"

Speck stutters; he's vaguely aware that logic seems to be defeating him again. "Well, yes, I think it's a fair price."

"And don't you agree with me that it makes sense to finance: after all, you *did* say you would finance with your credit union."

Poor Speck. He's going down for the third time, small bubbles of frustrated air rising to the surface. "Well, yes, I did say that, but won't your financing cost me a little more?" The man is pleading for an honest answer, and he'll get it. Of a sort.

"Yes, it will cost you a little more—maybe fifty cents a day, probably what you'd spend on a Coke. But why would you want to tie up that credit source for a car? What if you want to buy something else in a few months? If your credit is tied up at the credit union on this car, you'll probably go to some other financing source. Mr. Speck, we finance nothing but cars. That's definitely to your advantage."

"But I'll have to *buy* life insurance if I deal with you—the credit union puts it on loans for free."

"Mr. Speck"—the finance man's voice has that slight tone of contempt again—"you know as well as I do that nothing is free. The credit unions simply build the cost of life insurance into their loan rates. Now, when do you prefer your payments to begin, on the first or the fifteenth?"

Unless money is your profession, don't duel with finance men at any store until you have studied carefully the sections in this book on financing.

After looking at the fun and games that rule in the megastores, are you still brave enough to enter there? After all, if these places must sell thousands of cars each year, wouldn't it be logical that high volume means low profits? Yes. These people will sell cars very cheaply. But, of course, they'll never do that without some work on your part. A sucker will fare just as badly here as he would at any store. And, in all likelihood, a mega-store's system selling will confuse and frustrate you much more than Killer's method of operation.

Okay, you're thinking, I'll just bypass the whole system, and get on the phone to some dealership, find some nice salesman who believes in phone selling, and do the whole thing by long distance.

No, you will really be in trouble if you do that. If you call a dealership and ask for a salesman, some nice voice will come on the phone and say something like, "Ma'am, you caught me in the break room. Give me your number and I'll call you right back from my office. That's where my stock cards are." Without thinking, you give him your number, at the same time giving away your anonymity. It's a great phone technique. Salesmen are instructed always to be in "the break room," or the shop, when they first talk to a phone up—this little white lie always works. When the guy calls back, you could ask him if he has a seven-door, five-wheeled, nuclear-powered tank in stock, and his answer would either be "yes, ma'am," or "no, but we've got one coming in sometime today. But lots of people have been waiting on that tank. If you think you might be interested in it, you should come down right away." Well, you don't want to go down there without agreeing firmly on some price on the phone. "Ma'am, I can't appraise your car over the phone, and I assure you our prices are as competitive as anyone's in town."

Regardless of the store size, all salesmen believe strongly in this wish-fulfillment—whatever you say you want, new or used, they will say they have it or can get it for you. Many people rushing down to a store supposedly to see some mythical car will be easily switched to something actually sitting on the lot. The telephone just isn't a friend of the car-buying public.

Lanny Maxwell and Killer had one last drink before leaving the Dead End, walked out the side door, and drove in one car to the lodge. It was a weekly ritual: seed-planting time. Within an hour each of them will have given out small packets of their business cards to eight or ten members of the noble order, asking the brothers to "put your name on the back of each one, give 'em to your friends, and tell them to bring the card in when they need a car. Everyone I sell is worth $25 bucks to you." And many of these guys take their bird-dogging seriously, working just as hard on this part-time job as they do on their regular jobs.

Lanny and Killer were back in their booth at the Dead End by nine, and Killer ignored the barmaid's message from J. C. at the store. "Honey, tell him to go stick it in his ear. I've done my work for the night." His next drink was a double tequila, straight up. A good start for "cocktail hour."

The Dead End is located perhaps halfway down from either end of "automobile row," the twenty-mile stretch of new- and used-car dealerships that skirts the city. Or at least all the salesmen who frequent the place believe it's downhill, since their cars seem to roll in that direction automatically each night at closing. By the time Killer's tequila was rumbling around in his belly, the lot had filled up with new cars of every description—demos—and used cars with dealer tags either stuck in the back window or fastened on the trunks with a magnet. Most of these guys didn't mix, except Killer, but hung out with their own, reviewing the day's war stories between sips of bourbon-and-Coke or Scotch-and-Seven-Up. And few of the new-car guys ever mixed with the "lot boys," those who worked at the anonymous little used-car operations that seem to sprout and die daily along the row. It's a matter of prestige: new-car salesmen consider themselves more "professional" than the strictly used-car boys. Salesmen from Cadillac stores are higher up the ladder than Chevy salesmen. And down there at the very bottom are the "paper" men, the guys who advertise: "Bankrupt? On the lam? Bouncing checks all over town? Nobody walks at Friendly Sam's."

"Hey, Sam, have you got that Chevy back on your lot?

Damn, I bet you've popped that piece of junk six times this year." Killer smiled. He was yelling to the best paper man in town, or the worst, if you will, and he waved the guy over to the booth. Sam didn't see that comment as anything bad, and he grabbed Killer's hand. "Well, hell, Killer, I thought it'd popped eight. I must be slipping."

The car in question was a ten-year-old Chevrolet. Killer had traded the thing in perhaps a year ago, a "giveaway" car. The damn thing was so bad the dealership had given its owner nothing for it. That hadn't bothered Killer; he simply raised the asking price on the car the guy was interested in by $300 and wrote another $300 on the "trade" line of the buyer's order. The junker had quickly been sold to Sam for a "buck fifty," $150. Sam had then put the car to work for him. When some poor sucker came in with the worst credit in the world, Sam would just tell him, "The Chevy's $800 dollars. You pay me $150 down, and $20 dollars a week, and it's yours." There were no credit checks, either. Why should Sam go to the trouble, since he had every penny of his investment back from Day One? Invariably the customer would pay on the car for two or three months, then fall just a little behind on his weekly payments. Sam would repossess the car immediately and sell it to someone else for a buck fifty down and $20 a week. This particular car had made Sam over $1400 dollars in the past seven months. But that was business, "and besides, who else is going to help these suckers if I don't?"

Convenient logic: Sam is helping people, that's why he's in this end of the business. Like most car people, he can make anything, any technique a just act. But compared to Killer, Sam is an amateur at the game of convenient logic. A little friendly one-upmanship is as much a part of an evening at the Dead End as the drinks.

Killer wet his throat with another swig, grinned at

Lanny and Sam, and launched into the Merit saga. "Hey! Let me tell you about a switch!"

Merit, Albert Gray's boss, was the guy who did do something right—he sold his trade-in straight out. He was pretty cocky after that, especially after talking to the loan officer at the bank. The officer had given him real "inside" tips on buying a new car, and the man obviously knew what he was talking about. "Mr. Merit," he'd said, "the smartest thing you could have done is sell your car. You see, there really is no way any of those guys can take you since you don't have a trade. For, Mr. Merit, we *know* what those new cars cost. The simple work comes next!"

Merit liked the tone of the guy, for sure. How could he go wrong now? The bank would tell what any car cost; all he would have to do is add a little profit on top of that and drive out with the best buy of his life.

As these nice thoughts were floating through Merit's mind, Killer was dialing the number of the phone sitting on the table right by Merit's head. The first ring seemed to push itself into the center of his mind, and he picked up the receiver, speaking quickly, as if he wasn't quite composed in his thoughts. "Yes?"

"Mr. Merit, this is Robert DeMarco, I called you a few nights ago concerning the car you had for sale."

"Yes, I'm sorry, but the car is already sold."

"Really? Well, I hope you received a good price for it. I bet you did." Killer knows the value of a well-placed compliment.

"Well, yes, actually I came out pretty well on the car." Merit resisted the temptation to say how well he did but continued to talk, a small bell finally pulling from his memory the name DeMarco. "Aren't you the person who works at a dealership someplace?"

"Yes, sir, that's me. And if you don't mind me asking,

have you had a chance to find yourself a new car yet?"

Merit thought fate was on his side again. Here was a man who not only sold cars but seemed to be nice, to boot. Probably not too smart, though. "No, I haven't. I have been to the bank to arrange the financing, and incidentally, also arrange to learn the cost figures on the new ones. You know, I'm a pretty tight man when it comes to cars. They're really nothing but transportation to me." Merit started saying several more things like this. He was certain it was a good way to let Killer know he wasn't any pushover.

And Killer was loving every minute of it. This guy sounded real sure of himself, and, nine times out of ten, people this sure could be tripped with their eyes open on a well-lit parking lot. Killer responded in a tone of subdued respect. "Mr. Merit, I like the way you talk. What are the chances of setting an appointment to meet down here for a look at our cars? I'm certain there is a car that fits your particular needs. And I'm equally certain that you will buy that car at a very, very low price." Both of them laughed. Merit's laugh was one of satisfaction. Killer's laugh? He was feeling pretty satisfied, too.

Sitting on the back of Killer's lot was a two-door hardtop much like the one Merit had just sold. It was not a fancy car, and though it was new, it was old and wrecked. The guys referred to cars like these as lepers. Most of the salesmen walked around them daily, never acknowledging their dusty presence much less taking customers to them.

The car had been damaged the week it arrived while sitting on the lot. One of the lot boys had backed squarely into the left door and the rear quarter panel with the parts truck, hitting the car with such force the rear quarter panel had finally been replaced. The door had been "drilled" in the body shop; small holes were placed at strategic points to help the body men pop the metal to its original shape, and then both damaged sections were painted. The paint never really matched either—it was one of those metal fleck numbers that are a dream to look at but hell to repair. The car wasn't hot merchandise after this little episode, for sure, and it continued to gather dust for nine months, each month collecting a little of the salt spray that seemed to settle regularly on most of the cars there.

Killer walked back to the clean-up department and struck up a light conversation with Leon, the black man who had spent fifteen years at this one store making the cars shine, applying a little makeup when necessary. He was a good man, probably one of the hardest-working men at the store, and he liked Killer. After all, Killer was the only guy who would slip him a few extra dollars for doing a really bang-up job on special cars. "Hey, Leon, I've got an emergency job for you, major surgery! As a matter of fact, the damn thing may already be dead!"

Leon put down his buffer and smiled. "Bob, what are you talking about? I've got five cars sitting back here that the man says have got to be ready to roll tomorrow. How can I put one in front of that? Are you trying to start a race riot or something?"

"Okay, smart-ass. If you'll put the little white palms of your hands to work on this one, I'll buy dinner for you and Lora at the pizza place this weekend. I'll even buy the beer."

"So, what's the car?" Killer just smiled. "Oh, damn it, you don't mean the tan one. You're the second guy today that has asked me to fix it. What have you got, a spiff riding on it?" Leon was right about that. J. C. had put a $200-dollar cash bonus on the car that morning—a good enough reason for Killer to sell it to Merit.

By six that afternoon the car looked like a new one. Leon

had buffed the repainted areas twice, and the slightly off-color paint appeared to match perfectly, until the light hit it at an angle. The small sores of rust that had slowly begun to push their way up through the metal had been sanded down carefully by hand and touched up lightly with a brush. Leon had even carefully used a razor blade to lift off the paint overspray that had been visible on several pieces of molding. The half-vinyl roof had been dressed, the tires coated with gloss, and each piece of rubber molding sprayed with silicone.

Killer was really satisfied. "Leon, I'm telling you, this is the best face lift you've ever done! I mean to tell you, *I* would buy this car."

Leon looked pretty satisfied too, making one last sweep with his cloth over the painted areas. "Yeah. But, let me tell you something, don't park the damn thing with the sun on this side. I did all I could, but the door really looks like it came off some other car."

"That's okay. The jerk that is going to buy it won't even notice. Now, do one final thing for me. Set the radio on a couple of those easy-listening stations and pull the car back where it was. I want the guy to discover it. And, Leon . . . can you smudge the bottom of the sticker just a little?"

Leon didn't really like the sound of that request. He'd heard it before. "Bob, I can't alter that sticker. I mean that's really against the law."

"Leon, I didn't say *alter* it. I just said scrape the bottom price a little, like you were cleaning the window."

"Well, I do need to clean inside again, I guess."

"Yeah, we want a clean deal," Killer said. He headed back to the showroom, stopping by the rest room as he entered. He looked in the mirror, pulled his tie a little askew, and tossed his hair just enough to give it the careless look. He wanted to appear appropriately humble when Mr. Merit arrived. After all, the guy was some big deal.

Merit drove up just on time and walked briskly from the car. Killer just grinned when he drove up—hell, the guy was driving the Grays' car. "Mr. Merit, I didn't know that you knew the Grays."

Merit looked surprised. "Albert works for me. Did you sell them this car?"

"I sure did. It's a small world, isn't it?" The two men shook hands, walking slowly from the parking lot toward the new cars.

"You know, Mr. DeMarco, I have very simple tastes when it comes to a car. I want something that is reasonably sporty-looking but isn't loaded down with a lot of crap. I don't want to spend money on things that are going to break down anyway, you know what I mean."

"I sure do. It's really ridiculous how much money people spend on useless options these days. I'm always telling the man who orders our cars to simplify! Simplify! But, no, he won't order cars like that, because most people don't buy cars like that." Merit shook his head in agreement.

After a few minutes of casual talk, Killer decided to start sinking the man with his logic. "You know, Mr. Merit, you mentioned your bank when we talked the other night, the fact that those people would tell you how much any of our cars cost?"

Merit liked the tone of Killer's voice. The man nearly sounded uneasy. "Yes, they will do that for me. Quite honestly, I think it's a much better way for a person to buy a car."

"Well, I just wanted to tell you that I agree. I would like to know just one thing. Assuming that we have a car here you like, what profit are you willing to pay? You see, Mr.

Merit, I make a living by getting a percentage of that profit, and I don't mind telling you I would like to make at least $30 dollars when I sell *you* a car."

Merit felt really smug when Killer said that. Hell, who would bust their collective ass like these guys for $30 dollars? "Mr. DeMarco, just what is your percentage of the profit, if you can tell me that?" Merit had always wanted to know how these guys got paid and his smugness grew as Killer appeared to agonize over the question.

"Mr. Merit, I would get fired if anyone ever knew I told you this. But I get twenty percent of our profit. Is that too much?"

"No, no, if you are saying you need to make a $150-dollar profit, of course I'll pay that."

Killer looked grateful from head to toe. "Well, then, I'll tell you what. And again, this must be private, you understand. Mr. Merit, I'll bring you the invoice on whatever car you select. You can study it all you want to. I want to sell you a car tonight, if I can, and if you need to see the invoice to buy, you'll see it. Just, for God's sake, don't tell *anyone,* including the Grays. I didn't let them see the invoice."

Merit was really beginning to enjoy this. In his entire car-buying life, he'd never seen that little secret piece of paper, and he enthusiastically said that of course, of course he could do business that way. Killer thanked him and directed their walk toward the back of the lot. He deliberately walked by two-door hardtops that were loaded to the hilt with options and carefully pointed those cars out to Merit. "My God, I didn't know there was this much money in the world!" was about the only comment Merit would make. Most of the cars were not only expensive but were coated in a thin coat of dust and looked nude without their hubcaps or wire wheels. All of the cars, that is, but the shiny hardtop sitting perhaps forty feet from the others. "Hey! What is that car? It looks like a nice one." The two of them walked toward it quickly, and Merit went straight to the sticker. "Damn! The bottom of the thing is smudged off. But the list of equipment is a lot less. I think we should take a drive in this one."

But DeMarco had a better idea. "Mr. Merit, why don't you drive me to the showroom, and I'll get you a tag. You can drive it by yourself while I get some information on the car." Of course, he didn't object, and the two of them drove to the showroom.

Killer jumped out of the car as it stopped and pulled a pad from his pocket. "Mr. Merit, since I don't see a stock number on this car, why don't you read me off each item on the sticker. I'll just copy it down and identify the car from that."

As Mr. Merit was driving the car, Killer walked to the manager's office and said, "Hey, Crow. You know that tan metallic coupe we've got in the get-ready, the one that came in yesterday? If you'll let me borrow the invoice on that car for a few minutes, I'll make you a good deal."

Crowley frowned. "Killer, you mean the one like the *other* one? Hell, man, why don't you sell the bonus car? I mean, we don't need two of those bastards, but at least sell the leper."

"Damn it, I'm *going* to sell that one. Now, just give me the tissue."

"Killer, you know that meeting yesterday? J. C. will kick my ass if I give you the invoice. He said sell from *list.*"

"Hey, Crow, I am going to make a hell of a gross and sell the leper. J. C. can't kick ass for that. Now give me the invoice for the leper's twin, okay?"

Crowley didn't even look up but reached into the drawer

of his desk and pulled out one of the first invoices in the folder. He held it up in his hand and started talking again, without looking. "You know, Bob"—it was very unusual for anyone to call him Bob—"I hope you know what you are doing."

"Look. I'm going to sell the man a tan metallic car and give him every option he thinks he's getting. Is there anything wrong with that?" Crowley said nothing but started entering a deal in the gross book as Killer walked out of the office with the invoice. Merit was back from his solo drive in perhaps ten minutes.

"Hey, Bob"—hell, even the customer was doing it—"I really like that car. And I turned on the damn radio and heard one of my favorite stations." Merit realized that his enthusiasm was showing a little too much, and he pulled the giddiness back in. "Now, what did you find out about that car?"

"Mr. Merit, the car was prepared for delivery by one of the other salesmen. Some man said that he was taking it for sure but never came in to take delivery. That's why it's so clean, and that's why the stock number had been removed. The boss said that we should really hold the car, in case the man comes in, but I went ahead and just 'borrowed' the invoice anyway." There was lots of laughter from both men.

"Now, I want you to take a look. Here, let me explain all the different figures to you. Here are the costs on the base car and all the options. Let's check it with the list you read off to me." They read over each option carefully. "Now, this figure is the cost of dealer advertising that's built into every invoice. And this figure is the dealer holdback, I'm sure you're familiar with that." Merit didn't want to sound dumb at this point, and he was enjoying this tour through the invoice; his answer was a clipped "sure."

Within a few minutes Merit had agreed to buy the car. He even read the list of optional equipment off to Killer again, as each item was listed on the buyer's order. The order also listed the color of the car and its interior and the actual cost of the car. Plus $150 dollars. Killer neglected to place a stock number on the buyer's order, however. But that was of no consequence to Mr. Merit. The buyer's order was signed on the spot, and Merit also handed Killer a $200-dollar cash deposit.

"Now, Mr. Merit, I can't promise you at all that the boss is going to take this deal. But I'll give it my best shot, okay?"

"Bob, you just tell your boss that he will take the deal or I won't buy."

Killer walked off, taking a slight detour by the small table that held the store's stock cards, the salesmen's record of cars actually on the premises. He didn't pull out the card for the newer tan metallic two-door, the one Merit had just seen the invoice for, but the card for the identical car in the back—the one Merit had driven. There were only a few differences in the cars really, so why should he worry? Merit had driven the car he would buy. Of course that car had the little bits of rust and the paint that didn't really match, but Merit didn't seem to care. The only substantial differences in the two cars were their age and price. Merit didn't know how to read the manufacturing date on a car—it's on a plate on every left front door—so it certainly wasn't Killer's fault he bought one that was ten months old. He hadn't checked the car's serial number either. And the price? The invoice Merit saw was for the newer car, the one with the three price increases. Killer would have no guilt pangs tonight. He would just pick up an extra $550 in profit. That was the difference in price in those "identical" cars.

As Killer finished his tale, appreciative laughter burst from Sam and Lanny. "Hey, Cherry, another round of the same for the man," Lanny volunteered.

"I hate to say it, Killer, but beautiful, just beautiful. Not interested in using your logic at Sam's finest or going into competition with Lanny, are you?" Sam jibed at Killer, peering at him over the rim of his glass. "No," Sam answered his own question, grinning. Then, digging a little harder, "Lanny probably wouldn't want you, afraid you'd skate him."

"Like hell." Killer slammed his glass on the table. A little teasing was okay, but Sam had touched on one of Killer's sermon subjects. "I've got no use, none, for those slimy bastards. People who skate and split their way to nice grosses ought to be shot. Just take DeLong and Buzz at our place. Well, not DeLong, he won't be troubling us anymore." Killer settled back and launched into his tale about the store's biggest skater. Forrest DeLong had probably known what the others were saying, but then he never paid much attention to what anyone said, including customers. And hell, why should he give a damn about other salesmen, even if what they said was true? But the other salesmen cared. Especially Killer.

"J. C.?" Killer was standing at J. C.'s office door. He had picked the time carefully, the time when J. C. was always in the worst of moods—early in the morning, before the cobwebs had cleared and the physical effects of the last drink were just beginning to wear off. Killer spoke again. "J. C., I need to talk to you a minute."

J. C. still didn't look up, but managed to say one word. "What?"

Killer took about two steps forward, just enough to clear the door, and began to recite his speech. "J. C., you've got to do something about Forrest DeLong. He has skated me on a deal—an old customer of mine. He's skated Ted. Hell, he even told Ted's customer Ted didn't work here any more; you know, when Ted was on vacation?"

J. C. looked up without saying a word, absolutely no expression on his face. J. C. didn't really like Forrest. Killer's complaint was the third one on him this month. Skaters like Forrest, the guys who deliberately take other salesmen's customers, were nothing but thieves to J. C. If somebody will steal a customer, he'll damn well probably steal other things, too, J. C. thought. But still J. C. didn't say a word. He pulled a cigarette from his pocket, opened a pack of matches with one hand, lit the cigarette with one hand, and turned his chair to the window. Why did he have to put up with all of this crap?

Killer didn't think he was getting anywhere with the conversation, but he kept on talking. "And the guy's not working the up system, either. He doesn't wait his turn like the others but sits on the lot in a used or new car and jumps out when an up pulls on the lot. Every time you ask him about it, he says, 'Oh, they were my customers. I waited on them yesterday.' Hell, he tried to pull that on my *daughter* yesterday."

J. C. liked that. Too funny. He turned his chair back toward Killer and picked up the phone. "Get out of here, Killer. I'll handle it," J. C. said as he pushed the paging button.

Forrest was standing on the used-car lot when he heard the page and took his time as he headed to the office. J. C. was standing at his door with the local newspaper's space saleswoman, but he turned to Forrest and spouted out with maximum enthusiasm, "Good morning, son! How are you doing? Here, I want you to meet this pretty young thing from the paper. Isn't she the prettiest thing you've ever seen?" J. C. did love to flirt with the pretty girls, and Forrest talked with them both for a while, finally following J. C. into the office, resting himself easily in a large armchair.

J. C. walked by the chair, smiling all the time, and put his hand on Forrest's shoulder, a reassuring touch. But as he began to talk, he slowly moved his hand over to Forrest's neck, squeezing just a little tighter as he talked. "Son, I've got something I want you to do for me, okay?" The words didn't really require an answer. "I want you to get your little ass out of this office. Outa the showroom. And off the lot. Don't let me see your fanny around here, again, okay?" J. C. was smiling as he lifted the guy up. He smiled until the office was empty again. And then he sat down. What a way to begin the day.

Most dealerships have their fair share of skaters, people who spend their time greeting ups on the lot, hoping to find one that has already been waited on by some other salesman and is now ready to buy. Skaters never get the other salesman for an up but rather sell the car themselves, never mentioning that little fact to the poor shmuck who waited on the customers before. Invariably the right salesman will see his customer's name up on the board but not *his* name as the seller. "What are you doing with my customer?" he'll yell. "I spent three hours with that guy the day before yesterday!"

The guilty party will usually feign shock. "Man, really, they didn't ask for you. How was I supposed to know?"

But skating is just one of the ways lazy car guys make money. Take Buzz. He's been at the dealership for over ten years and spent most of his spare time, which is considerable, buddying up to all those new kid salesmen that seem to come and go at the rate of three a week. He's a "split deal" expert. Buzz bends over backwards to let these guys know just how helpful he really is. "Whenever you have a problem, just find me, and I'll be glad to help," he tells them, like a good priest who cares for his flock. Invariably these greenhorns will talk a neighbor or some other friend into buying a car. But in the midst of the transaction, they'll forget something—the proper way to fill out the buyer's order or how to compute a difference figure—and run up to Buzz, breathless at the thought of selling their first car. Buzz will go right into the closing booth with them and do the paperwork himself, casually adding his name right by the name of the guy who needed his help. He will get half the commission for five minutes' work. "Kid, that's the *right* way to do it," Buzz explains when his little addition is noticed. "If you don't need my help, just take my name off and do it yourself from now on." The kid will leave Buzz's name there. And he'll keep coming to him, too. After all, Buzz is helping him, right?

By ten-thirty, Killer was alone in the booth in the Dead End, three empty glasses his only companions, or at least that's what he thought. "Hey, Mr. DeMarco, wanna buy me a drink?" Killer looked up, right into the face of J. C. It was the first time he'd ever seen the boss at the Dead End— J. C. liked the fancier places—and Killer didn't really know whether to smile or run. He smiled, half rising as he spoke. "J. C.! I'm sorry I didn't return your call, but I just got back from bird-dogging. Come on, sit down." J. C. didn't really look mad, Killer thought, he just looked real dry. J. C. sat down facing the men's john. "Boss, what are you doing here? I mean, you didn't come after me or anything, did you?"

J. C. grinned. He liked to see Killer nervous for a change. "I'll tell you what, I'm going to come across this table real quick if you don't get me a drink, okay?" Killer didn't wait on Cherry but went to the bar himself, returning with a double Scotch and soda.

J. C. drank it like cool water and started looking around the room and talking at once. "I want to tell you what, I hope Gower gets here pretty quickly," he said, pulling the glass to his mouth for one last taste. "That bastard said he'd be here at ten thirty on the nose."

"Jimmy Gower? I know him," Killer volunteered. "What's he doing in these parts of the woods?"

J. C.'s expression changed from mild to stormy quickly. He sat a moment before speaking. "You know that new guy on the used-car lot? Well, he frosted a car, and Gower put a figure on it, the Mercedes sitting in the shop. Gower won't buy it at that figure, now that he's seen the car."

Killer didn't say a thing; he'd heard about the Mercedes deal. Some couple had come in a few days earlier wanting to "trade down," to dump their big, new Mercedes 450 SEL 6.3 and replace it with "something really small—we want to be able to tow it behind our motor home," they'd told the salesman. And since the Mercedes was paid for, they expected to buy a small car "and get about $30,000 dollars in change."

The salesman had excused himself on the spot and run down the long hall that led directly to Davies' office. He didn't even knock on the door either but opened it just about as wide as his eyes. "Excuse me, but can I see J. C. just a minute? There's a guy in my office that wants *$30,000 DOLLARS!*"

For a moment the four men, interrupted in their card game, thought the place was being robbed. "What in God's name are you talking about!"

Oh, my God, the salesman thought, this is the first time Mr. Davies had even said boo to him. "I'm sorry, Mr. Davies, but there's a customer who's driving a new Mercedes, and he wants to trade it on one of the tin cans. He says his car is paid for, and he wants some money back, and I don't even know how to write up a deal like that. I mean, what do I do with him?"

J. C. pushed himself back from the table, carefully put his cards in his shirt pocket, and grabbed the guy by the shoulder. "Son, just calm yourself down; now, you go right back there and take the keys to their Mercedes up to the used-car department before you ride them—don't drive it up there yourself—and I'll be sitting in your office when you get back."

Davies watched this little conversation without saying a word until the salesman had left. "J. C., I'll be damned if we want that car on the lot. If the guy has a nice car, it could be worth forty. And nobody in this town, including the Mercedes place, is going to put a buying figure on it. Why don't you just tell that kid to send the people on their way?"

"Gary"—J. C. burped, he always burped after a few drinks—"Gary, you just leave this to me. I'm going to call Gower. He's got a phone in his car, and I'll bet the S.O.B. will buy it in a minute." J. C. picked up the phone and dialed 23, the paging number, cleared his throat, and said, "Used cars, dial one." He knew the call would come quickly—everyone stopped in their tracks when Mr. Davies' office was paging—but the used-car manager wasn't the one who answered the page. It was some new guy they'd just hired up there.

"J. C., I'm sorry, but Rax had to go out for a while—with Killer, he said. Can I do something to help?"

"Where in God's name did they go? No, I know *where*

they went. I'll tell you what you do, you call the Dead End and tell those sons a bitches to get their asses back here. And then you take those keys my guy brought up there and tell me how the Mercedes looks." He slammed the phone down and turned to Mr. Davies. "Gary, one of these days DeMarco is going to be out this door, I don't care *what* you say. There's no damn salesman in the world worth the crap he pulls off."

Gary Davies didn't say a word; he'd had this argument a hundred times with J. C. He also didn't give a damn what Killer did—as long as he kept selling cars. Dealers don't worry about the personalities or bad habits of their salesmen. Why should they? That's what the J. C.s of the world are for.

Davies headed to the door. "Come on. It's been a while since I've seen one of those things. Anybody that would want to trade a Mercedes for a tin can has just got to be crazy." He waited at the door for a few minutes as J. C. pulled out his wallet and fumbled through the cards and bits of paper shoved in there. J. C. found Gower's card and dialed the number that said "anytime, night or day," and told the guy's answering service to "have Mr. Gower call me as soon as he can, okay? Tell him we have a diamond Mercedes that he might want to put a figure on." Jimmy Gower was one of the best road hogs in the business. He specialized in only the nicest late-model used cars, and he was famous for putting a figure on those cars over the phone.

J. C. was feeling better as he walked out the door. After all, this was going to make a good story at the next automobile association meeting. Everybody at those meetings always had some "up" joke. But none of them could top this.

The new guy from used cars was standing by the car as they walked up. God, he'd never seen a dealer and a general manager on the lot together. He just stood there as J. C. and Davies opened the trunk, popped the hood, and finally opened the glove box. "I'll be damned, Gary, look at the sticker on this thing, will you?" J. C. said. The sticker had been carefully pulled off the window and folded neatly by the Mercedes service department. The list price was $55,000 dollars.

"J. C.?"

"Yeah?"

"Don't let Ted drive it home tonight!" Even the new guy laughed at that, an insider's joke. It was the policy of Mr. Davies' dealership for the salesmen to put customers out in their demos for the night and keep the people's trade at the store. This technique kept people from shopping any more. Salesmen would then drive the trade-in home. But that policy didn't seem quite right with a $55,000-dollar trade. The three of them headed to the showroom just as the salesman drove up and waved to the couple sitting in the back seat. J. C. was the first person through the door, heading straight to the phone. Gower was on hold.

"Jimmy, we've got a 6.3 here, current year, with about ten thousand miles on it. The car is a diamond; it looks like no one's ever done anything but look at it. And I'll be damned if we'll get it unless you put a good figure on it."

It takes a lot of guts to buy anything like a 6.3 sight unseen, but Jimmy spent fifteen minutes building a picture of that car in his mind. "J. C., did you check the molding around the sun roof? I need to know if there's any sign of leakage. And get someone to pull it in the shop. I want to know if there's any body damage at all, even a scratch."

J. C. sent the new guy to do both things. And though he

didn't know it at the time, it was a mistake to send a rookie. A very unfortunate mistake. He returned quickly. "J. C., there's not even a scratch *under* the thing, I'll stake my life on it! The whole underside looks just like it was undercoated just yesterday!"

Maybe the drinks had dulled his senses, but that fact never rang a bell with J. C. Even cars right off the truck have some mud or something on the undercarriage. But, based on the new guy's description, Jimmy Gower put $35,000 dollars on the car and told J. C. to lock it up in the garage. He'd pick it up in a couple of days. "Now, Jimmy, you understand, it's your car, not mine," J. C. said.

"Yeah, it's mine."

Gower had arrived at the dealership just six hours before J. C. entered the Dead End. He had a $35,000-dollar draft in his pocket and had been ready to hand that draft to J. C. personally—until he looked under the Mercedes. He hadn't said a word but opened the hood of the car and carefully moved his fingers along the firewall. He'd then opened the left front door and looked carefully at the seams of the doorwell.

"J. C.?"

"Yeah?"

"I get the feeling you gave me a glowing picture over the phone of a car that's been wrecked." Gower wasn't smiling.

J. C. looked shocked, and he was. "What do you mean, wrecked? This car is *new;* it's like I described it." J. C.'s words didn't portray the real fear in his mind: if the car had been wrecked, Gower wouldn't have to take the car, and the store would be stuck with a $35,000-dollar trade-in. Somebody would be in deep trouble. J. C. squatted and looked along the bottom of the doorwell as Gower talked.

"Look here—it's been repainted. It's a good job, but it has

been repainted. And look under here"—Gower was on his knees looking at the undercarriage—"that new undercoating is covering up overspray." J. C. said nothing. The guy was right. "This car has been hit *hard* on the side. Yes, it's been put back right," Gower said, "but I'll be damned if I can sell a 6.3 that's been damaged this much."

Gower had left without taking the car but had agreed to meet J. C. at the Dead End. He'd also agreed to put *some* figure on the car, and so he spent several hours calling his sources. That's why he was late—about two drinks late, according to J. C. But that was probably a good thing: J. C. was always a better salesman after a few doubles. J. C. and Killer both stood as Gower approached, both of them laughing as he made his way past the swinging fannies of two young things standing by the next booth.

"Jimmy, I've been drinking yours for you, I hope that's okay," J. C. said, shaking Gower's hand and pulling him into the booth in one motion.

"Hell, J. C., you may need some more, too—I'm having trouble getting a buying figure on that car. I've about run out of people to call."

J. C. figured on that statement. Gower was no fool; he knew he was in the driver's seat right then—there was no way J. C. would keep the Mercedes on his lot. No dealer in J. C.'s neck of the woods had customers for $35,000-dollar used cars, much less wrecked ones.

"Jimmy, now you know that's a damned nice car. And you also know I can't make the customer take it back. I might kill the S.O.B., but I'm stuck with the car. Just wait till he comes back in for service, though. Hell, he'll wait till hell freezes over. I want to tell you guys, the *real* crooks in this business are the customers. They all yell and scream if they think we've taken 'em for a nickel, and then they turn around and screw you to the wall with their trades! I'm telling you, they're all crooks."

No one at the Dead End would disagree with that sentiment, no one in the car business in fact, but J. C.'s sermon wasn't solving the problems of the 6.3. He realized that himself and quickly brought the conversation back to business. "Jimmy, no one tried to frost the car. I had someone else look at it, that was my fault, and the guy didn't know what he was doing. Rax, our best appraiser, wasn't around when we needed him—I think he was off with Killer, appraising a car or something—but it's really my fault." Killer's face bloomed red at that little aside, but he remained quiet.

"But, Jimmy, I'll tell you what I'll do. If you place that car for me at $35,000, I'll give you the pick of four other cars on the lot. And we've got some real nice ones, too, ones we'd never sell to a hog. Hell, Jimmy, you know you can sell the car out of state, and no one will know it's been hurt. And Killer and I will go with you right now to the lot—I've got booze there—and you can pick and choose as you want."

It was a good solution to a bad problem. J. C. would lose the profit that could have been made on the four used cars, but that was better than stocking the Mercedes or selling it to Gower at a loss. And Gower? He was covered both ways; he knew where to place that Mercedes for $35,000, wrecked or not. That's the secret of road hogs—they don't lay out money up front but rather act as brokers.

They walked the lot for twenty minutes, or rather, weaved through the cars, drinks in one hand and cigarettes in the other. The three looked like a group of concerned and slightly tipsy doctors, checking each patient in some hospital's charity ward. "Here, Jimmy." J. C. motioned him to a really nice but plain sedan, took a key from the large

keyboard lying on the roof of an MG, and opened the sedan's door. "Jimmy, you could do real well with a piece like
this down south." Four-door sedans are slow-selling items
in big cities, but they are popular in small communities.
"Jimmy, let me tell you," J. C. continued, "I don't really
want to sell this; Davies and I were going to ship it to
Lomax this weekend. But I said you could have any cars
you wanted"—J. C. grabbed Jimmy in a bear hug, the sure
sign booze was ruling his tongue and mind—"and you *can,*
son."

"Lomax? Why would you ship a car to Lomax?" Jimmy
asked.

J. C. looked off for a moment, glanced at Killer, and
smiled. "I'm going to tell you boys a secret. And I *don't*
want it to go any further. Killer, did you hear that?"
Killer's nod was a lie. J. C. probably knew that, but he
continued anyway. "Gary and I are buying George Norris's
Chevy store there."

Both Killer and Jimmy Gower looked at J. C. In the car
business, the buying and selling of stores is the hottest gossip item, even more juicy than stories about who's making
it with whom. "J. C., why in God's name would George
Norris sell that store? I do business with them, and they
sell every car they can get hold of. As a matter of fact, I
just sold them a couple of cars."

J. C. smiled. "Well now, Jimmy, how did they pay you
for them, by check or draft?"

"By draft. I've got them in the car now," Jimmy answered. There was a tone of uneasiness in his voice.

J. C. smiled again. "Well, Jimmy, I wouldn't deposit
those drafts for a week or so. Norris got caught with his
pants down. They pulled a surprise floor-plan visit on him
and caught him over $200,000 out of trust."

"How the hell could he be that much out of trust? I

mean, I know he was selling cars." Gower's voice betrayed nothing but anger. The two drafts sitting in his car totaled over $8000 dollars.

"Yeah . . . he was selling cars," J. C. continued, "but he's been bleeding money out of that store for over a year to keep his other operations going." Many automobile stores are continually out of trust. It's an easy way to increase working capital by using someone else's money—without their permission. Normally, as each floor-planned car is sold, the "mortgage" on that car is theoretically paid off. But people like Norris conveniently forget to pay off the sold unit. They take the customer's money, use it for operating capital, or take it out of the store entirely.

"J. C.?" Killer just had to get a few more of the details. "How did they catch him? I mean, did someone at the store slip up, or what?"

"Hell, no. One of the field reps had been in the store a few days earlier and noticed an awful lot of new cars with miles and state-inspection stickers on them." J. C. shook his head. "That usually works—I've even done it myself a few times when money is real tight. But I never had thirty-five cars out on I.O.U.s." Like most dealers, George Norris usually knew when the factory or finance boys would be snooping around, counting cars. As a matter of fact, he knew exactly when they were coming. Norris had a good friend at the finance company who would call him before each visit and say casually, "Oh, by the way, I'm in the office alone today. Everybody else is out counting cars." After each call, Norris would have his salesmen contact all customers who were driving floor-planned cars. The salesmen would tell each customer, "I'm sorry, but we've just received a recall letter on your car, some problem with the brakes. If you can bring it in tomorrow, we'll get it fixed, and you can drive my demo while we work on yours." By the time the car counters arrived, all of these "sold" units would be lined up nicely on the lot appearing "unsold." An automobile version of the shell game, of sorts: selling the cars and not paying off the mortgages to the manufacturer's lending institution. But this time the game had been interrupted.

"Well, J. C., I'll tell you one thing," Gower said. "I'm going down there tomorrow and get my two cars. To hell with their drafts."

J. C. shook his head again. "Jimmy, you can't do that. The bank has a man on the lot even during the night, and all sets of keys to every car, new and used, are in his possession. Hell, the salesmen can't even show a car without getting the keys from the guy. And if they sell a car, Norris has to physically hand over a check before the customer can drive away. I'm telling you it's real crazy down there."

It might be a crazy situation for the present owner, but it's really a nice situation for J. C. and Davies. Stores in this much trouble can be bought very cheaply. J. C. and Davies just have to pay Norris $35,000 dollars, and they'll be in business. The $35,000 isn't blue-sky, either—it's simply the real value of all the parts in the parts department and the book value of any service equipment. They will then form a new corporation, pump in $50,000 dollars in working capital, lease the same building, and open the doors as a completely new store. They will have an investment of no more than $100,000 dollars. Not bad. If the Chevy store is run properly, it will return that figure in six months.

The three men left the lot by midnight and drove again to the Dead End. The big drinker this time? Gower. The happiest guy? Killer. Though J. C. didn't know it yet, Killer had a plan. He wanted to move to Lomax as J. C.'s and Davies' sales manager. That small town really does need someone who's a pro in the business, Killer thought. And I'm tired of the rat race. I mean, it really must be easier to work people there. Hell, I can do battle with tobacco chewers as well as city slickers. It was the last thought Killer would remember from the night. But it was a pleasant one.

Do you live in the city? Or perhaps in a tranquil rural community? Big town or small, there's a Killer waiting for you. He may be quiet or loud, he may belong to your church or coach your kid, but he's there, hand on your wallet. If you intend to control the amount of dollars he'll so deftly lift from your pocket, you will need a plan. Something like the next part of this book—Battle Time!

PART II
Battle Time!

7

Some Preliminaries to Shopping

DOWN THE ROAD OF
GOOD INTENTIONS

During the last few years, a raft of well-intentioned publications have featured articles supposedly designed to clear up all the fog hanging over the car-buying process. Former used-car managers, salesmen, and even a couple of "serious" automobile traders have written books designed to accomplish the same thing. Unfortunately, most of these efforts have provided cheer and comfort to the wrong group of folks: the people who are selling cars.

For instance, one article entitled "How to Buy a Good Used Car" informs its readers that "a one-year-old car *can* cost twenty percent less than its initial purchase price." The article seems to imply that you'll be lucky to receive such a good deal. Well, anyone who swallows *that* little piece of advice will also be a candidate for your local Brooklyn Bridge sales contest. There is not a car made in America worth more than sixty percent of its original price at the end of the year. *Changing Times,* in January 1975, made even that advice relatively harmless. In authoritative style, the magazine suggested that you use one of the used-car books, such as the red book or the Kelly blue book, "before you make an offer" on a used car, adding proudly that "a few minutes of study will have you leafing through the book like a veteran." The article then concluded with a supposedly "good bargaining principle": "Offer $100 to $150 dollars less than the asking price and stick close to it." If I were in the used-car business, that article would be the first thing given to every customer on my lot along with some copy of a blue book or red book. I would be a very rich man in a short time, too. Used-car "books" don't tell anyone, including wholesalers, the value of a specific used car; a $150-dollar reduction in asking price is comical.

And then, there's *Money* magazine's justification for buying one of those rental-company used jobs: "Before it's put on sale, it gets a more thorough going over: *the engine is steam cleaned,* fluid levels are checked, and all systems are tested." [Emphasis added.] How nice. What does a clean engine have to do with the value of a used car? Absolutely nothing. Under the cleanest engine in the world can lurk an equally prime piece of junk.

This same article informs the reader that "The prices posted by Hertz, Avis, and National for their used cars usually aren't negotiable—the figure on the windshield is what you pay . . . [and] checks with rental-company used-car lots in three cities indicate that prices are indeed lower than those of local used-car dealers." I'm sure that statement alone sent droves of eager bargain hunters to their graves, for what the article *didn't* say was the most important thing: Sure, Avis's "fixed price" of $5500 was lower than the $5900 "asking" price at the used-car lots. But the used-car lots would have most likely cut their price to $5200—if someone bargained a little.

Like these articles, most of the "how to" books on the market seem to be filled with nice logical statements, too. One former car salesman's book begins a discussion concerning "fair profits" for the seller by stating that "most dealerships will be happy if you offer them a ten to fifteen percent profit on a car." Happy? How about happy as a pig in slop. Every dealership in America would die of ecstasy if its profit on each car reached that level. This same salesman goes on to say, "For heaven's sake, don't be a 'be-back'—one of those people who tell salesmen they'll come back the next day, but never do." What does this man want you to do? Does he want you to say, "John, even if I find a car at a lower price than the figure you've given me, I promise to buy a car from you"? Customers have enough insecurities as it is without having spurious morality trips heaped on them.

As a customer, your chances for survival in the car-buying and -selling maelstrom are next to none if you depend on general answers, pat formulas, and simplistic logic in planning your attack. Your chances are good, though, if you'll learn the right questions, the specific questions that *you* can answer. For instance, there is certainly no value in knowing that your salesman will be happy with a fifteen percent profit; a more appropriate piece of information would be "what is the *least* profit a specific dealership will accept on that new Olds Cutlass sitting there in the showroom." Or, why depend on the information in some book to tell you what your car is worth? Wouldn't it be wiser to know exactly how much your specific car is worth in wholesale dollars in your community *today*?

The first part of this book addressed the questions you should have about yourself as buyer, your present car, and your financing. The remaining portions of the book will help you use your answers, as you follow the correct procedures in shopping for and in negotiating the sale of your new or newer car.

These procedures are not hard to follow, but they will not exactly make you popular with salesmen—so what? As with any sale, the important thing to the seller is your money, not your friendship. Salesmen will be nice to you, laugh with you, support your ego to the fullest, as long as you are not threatening their opportunity to make the largest profit imaginable. But the moment you pull out a pad and attempt to discuss your purchase intelligently, most salesmen will be secretly cursing you under their breath. Why? Because they will have to work harder and longer with you than with most stiffs, and their profit will be less. Like most of us, car salesmen much prefer the path of least resistance when dealing with a customer. Accept that fact, and be prepared for at least small doses of contempt from that nice man. You will not only survive the transaction but you will also retain $300 or $500 or $800 dollars of your money in the process.

SOME PRELIMINARIES
ON ADVERTISING

J. C. flipped a cigarette in the puddle of water just by the front door to the showroom, opened the door, and headed to his office without once looking at any of the salesmen standing around in little clumps, each one of them quickly doing his best to look busy. Damn, things must be slow. It was a Saturday morning, usually one of the busiest days at the store, and J. C.'s lumbering body never made an appearance near the place on Saturdays. The showroom emptied as each one of the guys headed to his office and the phone. None of them really liked making cold calls, but it sure as hell beat a one-to-one session with the boss.

Killer had already been on the phone for an hour when J. C. settled behind his desk and opened his Thermos bottle of Bloody Marys, at the same time turning his chair around to the sample ad layouts on the chair just behind him. On that particular morning both men would be practicing their own particular version of the car-store lie. One thing was for sure: business had stopped dead in its tracks, and everyone was going to "bust ass" for the next six days. J. C. tipped up the Thermos and gulped. Gary Oliver Davies didn't care in the least that the first twenty-two days of the month had been record selling days. He didn't even care that Killer had nineteen cars out for the month.

"Damn it, J. C., we've written four deals a day for the past three days, and at least one per day couldn't be financed by the s.o.b.'s parents if their lives depended on it! Now, you find a way to get some people in this place, and you do it *today*."

Davies didn't yell much, J. C. thought, just every hour on the hour. He took another swig and picked up the ad that was running in Sunday's paper. It was a full-page ad. The headline ran: $300 IN CASH TO YOU AND A FREE TV WITH THE PURCHASE OF ANY OF THESE GAS SAVERS. The small asterisk by the headline was barely noticeable.

Just below the main head were three other nice promises. The truck department's ad said: $3000 DISCOUNTS ON ALL TRUCKS IN STOCK. The new-car department's subhead showed a picture of a big "zero" and proclaimed ANY CAR IN STOCK FINANCED WITH *NOTHING DOWN*. Another asterisk closed that heading too. The used-car department's head was just as enticing: ALL CARS FOR SALE AT PRICES BELOW NADA WHOLESALE. J. C. burped. "Maybe this will bring the queers from the closet," he said out loud, taking one final nip from the bottle.

Can You Believe Advertisements and Commercials?

Sure you can, just as much as you believe politicians. Again, it's usually the sin of omission that gets you. What automobile ads say is usually the truth; it's what they don't say that can hurt you.

Take the big headline in J. C.'s ad. Sure, the store will give customers $300 dollars. But they'll also do one of two things: lower the allowance on your trade the same amount or simply lower the discount on the new car $300 dollars. And the television? The little asterisk covers them there, too. The salesmen simply will say, "Folks, as the ad says, we only had a limited supply of TVs—and we just gave away the last one." Or they'll say, "We really *do* want to sell you the car—but at these figures, we just can't give you a TV."

The $3000-dollar discount on any new truck in stock is a true statement, too. But what the ad doesn't tell you is that *recreational vehicles, vans, and trucks are not required by federal law to have a manufacturer's "sticker price."* The dealerships can put any retail price they want to on trucks, thanks to a small loophole in the federal pricing regulations.

J. C.'s people will also finance any car in stock with nothing down. But the small asterisk at the bottom of the ad does qualify that somewhat. It says "with approved credit." The ad isn't talking about simply a good credit rating, either. Ads that say "nothing down" or "only $100 dollars down" neglect to tell you your house or furniture will be required as additional collateral to "qualify" you for the wonderful opportunity of buying something with nothing.

And finally there's the "below NADA wholesale" used-car gimmick. It is really a wonderful line that pulls them in every time. Of course, each of the particular cars in that ad is worth hundreds of dollars less than wholesale. The NADA wholesale book is the dealer's book, current wholesale prices as compiled by the National Automobile Dealers

Association. It divides the cars into categories, from "clean" to "below average," and the differences in prices in these categories are in the hundreds—sometimes over $1000 dollars. When the used-car department at J. C.'s store picked cars for this ad, they picked ones that were worth less than average but lifted the "clean" price from the NADA book.

All advertising in the car business is designed to convince you how much money can be saved by purchasing a car from a specific dealership. And have you ever in your life seen or heard any new- or used-car advertisement without the words "sale," "clearance," "year-end closeout," or "lowest price ever"? Of course not. Who would advertise "higher than usual prices this week," even though prices do go up and down?

And, of course, everyone is familiar with this classic: PUSH-PULL-DRAG YOUR TRADE TO OUR PLACE AND RECEIVE $800 DOLLARS IN TRADE. The smaller print then says, "on selected used cars and certain models of new cars." Doesn't the logic here bother you just a little bit? If you have some wrecked piece of junk worth $50 bucks, how can they afford to give you $800? Are the people simply trying to be generous? Maybe these folks are very religious and believe in charity to one and all? Maybe they believe in Saint Nick, too, but I doubt it.

"Push-pull-drag" works like this: the $800-dollar allowance applies to new cars with a large mark-up. If you drag in some wreck worth $50 bucks and want to trade it on a car with a $1600-dollar mark-up, the store will in reality give you $50 dollars for your car and discount the new car $750 dollars. The store is left with a profit of $850 dollars on the new car *plus* your $50-dollar trade. You are happy—after all you *knew* the old tub was worthless—and the store is happy, or rather ecstatic. What you didn't know is the funny part: the store would have been happy to sell you that same new car for a $300-dollar profit, whether you traded the junker or not.

On used cars the technique is modified. The used-car department will pick a group of used cars and simply add an additional $800 dollars in profit to their normal mark-up. For instance, one dealership featured a three-year-old Cougar in its ad. The Cougar cost the store $3000 dollars. The car would normally be priced at $3800 dollars, but for this ad, that price was raised to *$4600* dollars. If your trade-in is worth nothing, they still get $3800 dollars. Of course, the used-car department would be happy to sell the car for $3400 dollars in the first place.

Sad to say, people are drawn to ads like these as bees to honey. And many of them won't trade in junkers, either, but rather cars worth $400 or $500 or even $800 dollars. Since the ad promises to give you eight, some people still believe they are receiving a fantastic deal. But think just a moment: if you were trading in a $500-dollar car on the "$4600-dollar" Cougar, what would the dealership be making? $4600 minus $800 = $3800. And $3800 plus your $500-dollar trade is $4300 dollars—*a $1300-dollar profit.* Not bad at all.

But what about ads that advertise "$100" per month and $100 dollars down"? If the ad is simply featuring a specific car, rather than a group of cars, you'll probably find the car "sold" as soon as you drive to the store, since the car is used as a loss-leader. Some dealerships, however, are offering very low interest rates to help them move merchandise. But all of these "100/100" offers, regardless of their rates, have one thing in common: they don't provide you a free shovel—handy things when you've fallen in a bucket. The only people who fall for low down payment ads are the very poor or the very dumb. And no one reading this book is poor enough or dumb enough to need a car that badly.

Some dealers prefer even more dramatic forms of advertising silliness than those just discussed. One West Coast dealer has become a very rich man by wrestling bears on television and walking on the wings of aerobatic airplanes, just to convince you how badly he wants to sell cars. A Seattle dealer moves his merchandise by smashing windshields and destroying fenders on new cars. One Georgia dealer was famous for driving new sports cars through the plate-glass windows of his showroom. Unfortunately, whether dealerships use J. C.'s version of the truth or the maniacal marketing of the dealers we've just mentioned, the result is always the same: like gnats to a flame, people just come in droves, hypnotized by that mythical pot of gold at the end of the rainbow.

Whether for new or used cars, don't trust ads and don't believe the advertised price is a good one. It may be, but that's for the seller to know and for you to find out. One thing is certain: even if the price is a good one, someone is going to try to make more money from you.

What About Ads from Individuals Selling Their Cars?

If you are planning to buy a used car, classified newspaper ads can be a very productive source for locating a car, but not a price. Many classified ads are also placed by salesmen, not individuals. Smart salesmen will drive a nice used car from their lot home on the weekend to try to sell it.

Incidentally, Killer had a copy of Sunday's ad in front of

him, too. He had asked for it the night before, and his request had brought a smile to J. C.'s face. Mr. DeMarco might not have the boss's personal esteem, but he knew how to work him. The ad was on Killer's desk, by an open phone book turned to the name "Smith," and Killer cleared his throat as the phone rang. "Hello, Mrs. Smith, this is Robert DeMarco. I just wanted to tell you that your new car arrived yesterday and will be ready for delivery on Monday morning. Would ten o'clock be a good time for the two of you to come down?"

Killer had never talked to these people before, and certainly there was no car waiting on them, either. The voice on the other end of the phone confirmed this. "I'm sorry, but you must have the wrong Smith. Were you calling Allen C. Smith?" The voice was a little surprised but friendly, so Killer continued.

"Oh, ma'am, I'm sorry. I was trying to reach Allen *D.* Smith. I sure hope I didn't bother you."

"Oh, no," she volunteered, "I wish we *were* getting a new car; our old one is honestly on its last legs."

Killer liked the sound of that. "I'm sorry to hear that. What type of car do you have?" His tone was that used more frequently by morticians.

"Oh, it's a three-year-old LTD, a blue one."

"Mrs. Smith! I think someone up there is really watching after us today! I have a customer looking for a used LTD right now. Even though you may not be interested in trading right now, I might be able to *sell* your car for you at a retail price. And then you *could* afford to buy a new one, especially on Monday. You know, we're having this special sale then; after you buy a car, we give you back $300 dollars in cash and a color TV!"

Not all of the "wrong numbers" proved so productive as

this one. But the Smiths did come in on Monday, and Killer immediately gave them a demo to drive for the morning while he "showed" their car to his imaginary prospect. They spent three hours driving the demo and didn't even seem upset by the fact that Killer's "prospect" had already purchased some other car. That, too, was an old trick in the business. After spending several hours in a shiny new car, most prospects' sense of good judgment seems to pale. The Smiths would just trade their old tub, anyway. Killer made a really nice deal. And just think how many Smiths are left in the phone book.

WHEN DO CAR PEOPLE REALLY HAVE SALES?

They never do and they always do. If "sale" means a low price, you can have that any time. If "being taken" means someone made a lot of money on you, that can happen at the best sale in town. All car salesmen are going to attempt to make a *maximum* profit on you, even if the car you are interested in is marked down to dead cost. They may give you less on your trade; they may sell you "add-ons"—high-profit things such as "glazing" or rustproofing; they may finance you at a higher rate—by some method, they will try to make more money.

Sales *may* be a fun time to shop for a car, as we discuss in the next section. But you will normally be wise to forget about sales. Forget about easy-payment and low-downpayment plans. Your objective should be to get the lowest price on the car you are buying, the highest dollar for your car if you trade, and the most advantageous financing. If you do these things, you will always be purchasing a car at a *true* sale price.

WHEN'S THE BEST TIME TO BUY?

It was two days before "show time," the intro date for the store's new cars, and J. C. was chairing the sales meeting again. Or at least, he was chairing this special meeting at closing time on Saturday, and every damned salesman had been told to be there *or else.* J. C. had also passed the word that all the service mechanics and writers—even the parts men—had to be there and every single one of these people was nervous, especially after catching one quick glance at the boss. He was nearly frothing at the mouth, standing up in the front of the room by one of the store's videotape machines.

No one needed to call the meeting to order that day. Everyone was dead still and silent as J. C. began to speak, or rather, to thunder. "Sloppy! This place is the damnedest bunch of pigs I've ever seen in my life, and I'll be damned if we're going to Intro Day without being a tight place. Every single one of you is going to know what's new and saleable about every single car. Now, I'm going to show you a tape. And if there is anyone in this room who doesn't watch every second of it, memorize every technique, I'll be damned if that person will be here long. Killer, pass out these pads."

Killer took the yellow legal-sized pads and started passing them down each row as J. C. continued. "And one other thing: Starting tomorrow morning, *no one* is to put a date on any of their deals. And *everyone* is to tell their customers all new cars will take three days to get ready for delivery. I'm talking about all the deals on current cars, not the show cars." No one said a word, though few knew the significance of J. C.'s request. The front row of lights was turned off, and as J. C. pushed the start button on the machine, he repeated himself. "Now damn it, *learn these techniques!*" He said that just as the first picture came on the screen. It took about three seconds for most of the guys to figure out what was going on. They were watching *The Devil in Miss Jones.* J. C. liked a good joke every now and then.

In the midst of J. C.'s joke, though, one important piece of information was passed out in that meeting—the matter of the dating of buyer's orders at show time. When the next year's cars are introduced, the vast majority of manufacturers give their dealers an extra four or five percent profit on all leftover new cars in stock from the previous year. Called a carryover allowance, it is important to the dealers, to put it mildly. But many dealerships like to cheat just a little bit. Why should they sell a car a few days before showdate, before it earns that extra five percent profit? So, what do these dealers do? They fudge the paperwork. If a deal is written on a car four or five days before showdate, the paperwork on that deal, including the buyer's order, isn't processed until showdate. The IBM cards that are supposedly sent to the manufacturers the day a car is sold are held to showdate, too. Yum. Dealers just love this little sleight-of-hand.

Though this carryover allowance is meant to be an incentive for dealers to stock more cars at the end of the model year and then sell them for less money, don't expect to see any of this money in your pocket. Dealers are very jealous of both this end-of-the-year "holdback" and their normal two or three percent holdback, and they seldom share this profit with their salesmen, much less customers. If you are aware of the largess, however, you will be in a stronger position to negotiate your deal.

But is it a good idea to wait until year-end to buy a car in the first place? As with most things in the business, the answer is yes and no. During the course of a year, all manufacturers raise their prices on every car line by hundreds of dollars, price increases usually much larger than any savings you may earn by waiting. But if the year-end is the time you plan to buy anyway, you can certainly buy a leftover for less money than the models just appearing. And *if* you trade cars again two or three years down the road, and are trading for another leftover, you won't be hurting yourself. Many people will make the mistake of trading cars during the last month of a model year, then trading cars again in thirteen months. On the used-car market, that thirteen-month-old car is *two* years old. If the same car had been traded during the twelfth month, it would have remained a one-year-old car and been appraised as that.

So, are there any "best times" to buy a car? If you remember that car people will always make more if you let them, and if you guard against that, timing can be important.

Car Store Sales. The prices may not really be lower at sales, but the pressure to sell is greater. For instance, advertising and promotional expenses need to be recouped, and sales managers are continually under the gun of gaining "extra deals"—more sales than usual for the time period to pay for the added expense. At sale times a good bargainer may not get a better deal but may have an easier time negotiating that deal.

Before Christmas. Most people's minds are on other things at Christmas time, and many dealerships' sales drop dramatically. Managers are more inclined to take smaller profits during this time.

When Car Sales in General Are Low. When the economy and other factors depress the car business as a whole, competition is at its fiercest for those few customers who do buy *new* cars. As we've discussed, used-car sales are usually highest at times like this.

At Monthly Pressure Times. Car salesmen are under two great pressures. One is the pressure of the dealer, who expects his salesmen and managers to sell every day. When business is slow—when it's pouring down rain, for instance—the sales manager's neck is under the guillotine, and you would be surprised how much money some people save. Salesmen refer to rainy-day buyers as "fairies"—weird folk who only come out in the rain, invariably with a pad in hand. That's okay, though. You can afford to put up with this contemptuous attitude for enough bucks, right?

Another good time to buy a car can be the last of the month. Dealerships keep profit-and-loss statements on a monthly basis, and sales people can get a little desperate toward the last of the month if forecasts aren't being met. Even if the month has been a successful one, you will probably come out better—any deals made then are pure gravy.

If you really want to be mean, go down to a dealership thirty minutes before closing time on a rainy night on the last day of the month. You'll either get a really great deal or a really black eye.

REMEMBER: A really smart car buyer can usually get the same deal any day or month. It's just easier to negotiate during pressure times.

8

Jumping Into the Fray: Shopping the Right Way

"Damn it!" The bright blotch of blue ink had spread over six inches of Killer's shirt before he noticed it. "Why in God's name is it always a new shirt?" He said it out loud. Not that anyone was listening—saying it out loud just seemed to let out more anger. Killer pulled his car off the first exit and headed back home. Maybe he should have stayed there, too, but he didn't. After all he was supposed to meet some lady and her husband, a lady who was definitely going to buy a car—or at least that's what she said. Gloria Wright had called him the night before and set an appointment for ten this morning.

"Hell, I'll sell them a car and buy *two* new shirts," he thought, as he headed once again to the store, speeding just a little bit more than usual. About a mile from the store, Killer flipped open the glove box and grabbed one of those small liquor bottles airlines dispense regularly. The tasty juice was down his throat in a swallow. Killer didn't know it, but even three of those liquid tranquilizers would not make this day any better.

He didn't really like the couple from the beginning, from the moment Jim Wright pulled out his pad. Hell, the guy was probably a pipe smoker, too. Everyone in the business knows that pipe smokers, those thoughtful, nonemotional

S.O.B.s, are some of the hardest people to make money on. And every single one of them seems to have a pad glued to his palm. Killer also didn't like their attitude. These people didn't want to be led the least little bit but knew exactly which cars interested them. As a matter of fact, they knew the *one* car that interested them, and the damn thing didn't even have a bonus on it.

"Folks, I know you like that car, but you know, we've been having a little trouble with the transmission on that model. Let me show you something that could be a lot better value for the money," Killer said. Like a car with a "spiff," a cash bonus: *that* was Killer's idea of value.

But Wright answered just as quickly. "Thanks, Mr. De-Marco, but we've done enough reading and riding to be satisfied with our choice. Now, why don't we go to your office and get to business. We have an appointment with another salesman at noon."

Oh, God, this guy was going to be a pain. He probably *did* have an appointment with someone else.

Killer grabbed a buyer's order as soon as the Wrights were seated and began to fill out each line. This normally was a good tactic. Before talking price, he liked to have the entire order completed except for the trade allowance. Then, after discussing price for a few moments, Killer would fill in the allowance "offer" acceptable to his customers, turn the pad around, and simply say, "Why don't you okay these figures for me?" Most people would sign without thinking, very easy. But hell, the Wrights didn't let him write one line.

Gloria made the point. "Mr. De Marco, it isn't necessary to fill that out just yet. Why don't you take our car and have it appraised? We may be just wasting your time until we know that figure, don't you agree?" She smiled, a friendly smile. Killer smiled back as he took the keys, a very plastic smile, and headed out the door.

"Jim?"

"Yeah, honey?"

"Should we have told the man our highest wholesale of-fer on the car is $4700?" Forty-seven was the figure put on the car by a used-car lot not too far from the dealership.

"No. Maybe they will put even more on the car—you never really know. And anyway, I want to see if the guy lowballs us!" Jim Wright was beginning to enjoy this; he was the driver, rather than an unwilling passenger, for a change. They both were luckier than they knew, too. Killer's office wasn't bugged, like many offices in other car stores.

Killer returned within ten minutes, sat down, and began to write figures on a blank sheet of paper on the desk, seem-ingly preoccupied with the magical figures. Then he looked up, smiling again, and spoke. "Mr. and Mrs. Wright, I've got an excellent appraisal on your car! We have normally been taking in cars like yours for $4200 dollars, but let me ask you this: If I could allow you $5000 on the new car, really $1000 more than usual, would you buy that car? Of course the boss will have to approve something like this, it's so much higher, but would you buy the car today?"

Killer had spoken the words in one continuous stream, and the Wrights nearly fell for it. But as the word "allow" exited his mouth, alarm bells began to ring in the Wrights' ears. Gloria turned to Jim, and both of them began to speak at once, the echoes of a miniature Tower of Babel filling the room. All three laughed, but Killer's laughter didn't really match the slightly quizzical look on his face. Why had they reacted so quickly?

"Mr. DeMarco," Jim said firmly, "thank you for the generous offer. But we are not really interested in allowance—we asked you to have our car appraised. Now, what was the appraisal on the car, if you don't mind telling us? We'll talk about the discount on your car after we discuss our car, if that's okay."

Killer froze for a second, all the little cubbyholes up there in his mind opening wide, ready to throw out answers that worked every time. The real big cubbyhole, the one containing sarcasm, was trying to open, too, but Killer mentally pushed the door shut and locked it. So what if these people were know-it-alls? So what if they didn't want to do it the right way, or rather the dealership's way? Killer's mouth opened, and he hesitated perhaps another second. "Jim and Gloria—I hope it's okay if I call you that—let me tell you something. I can see that you are very intelligent car buyers, and *that's* refreshing. So many people don't know the first thing about buying cars." The line always worked. Get their attention with a compliment, and then do a number on them. Killer continued, "And of course we can discuss the value of your car first, the real value. As you probably know, our buyer's orders aren't designed to show discount on a new car and then actual wholesale value on your car—Mr. Davies, our owner, doesn't want to make it too easy on customers, you know—but I'll handle that." Another good line. The owner was the enemy, and Killer was the good guy, a lamb in wolf's clothing, of sorts. Right.

"Now, about the wholesale value of your trade," he continued, "our used-car manager personally drove the car and placed a wholesale value of $4400 dollars on it." Killer continued talking before anyone could speak, confident he was heading in for the kill. In truth, he was heading fast to the ground, tail high in the sky. The car had really been appraised for $4600; he was just lowballing them a little. Everyone could be taken just a bit, he was sure of that. Killer didn't know about the Wright's $4700-dollar offer. "And, Jim and Gloria, let me tell you: that's really more than the car is worth. The used-car man put such a high figure because he has a customer for the car." Killer smiled.

But the Wrights weren't smiling at all. "You know, Mr. DeMarco, maybe we are just wasting your time. You see, we already have a much higher offer than $4400 on the car. If you don't think your people can do $300 or $400 dollars better, we'll just sell the car ourselves; I've done that many times before."

Gloria agreed with that sentiment, adding, "Jim, why don't we do that? And anyway, I want to look at the other new car; we could do that on the way. And, Mr. DeMarco, we can always buy a car from you without trading."

Gloria Wright's words pulled Killer back from the fog, and he spoke. To the experienced ear, his voice now betrayed just a little impatience, too. Customers weren't supposed to be talking like this. "Ma'am, before you do that, let me go back up to the used-car lot. Maybe they can do a little better. Now you folks just make yourselves at home."

At home? Hell, they were more comfortable than Killer at the moment. He headed back to the used-car lot and grabbed Timothy Raxalt. "Rax, I need another $100 at least, on this car. The people say they have got it sold to someone for $4700 or $4800. What do you think?"

Rax didn't look at the car but at Killer. He had heard that line so, so many times. "Killer, I'm going to rename you Chicken Little. It's a damn nice car but I am not going to put another dime in it just to make *you* a higher gross. Now, go trade for the thing at $4600."

"Damn it, I'm telling you the straight. Now, do you want

me to send them on their way, or do you want the car at $4700?"

"What's got into you, man? Can't you allow them a little more?"

"Hell, no—the damn people won't talk allowance. I'll tell you what, though. Let me try one more thing. But then if they don't agree, can I go ahead and figure the deal from $4700?"

I don't really think the Wrights had noticed the tone in Killer's voice or knew how much their approach to buying a car was messing up the mind of our number-one salesman. But they might have had some hint when Killer returned. His shirt pocket was again stained in that same blue ink, and not once did Killer notice it. He was talking as he entered the door.

"Folks, the used-car department is going to call me in a minute—they are trying to do a little better—but do you really want to sell your car to someone else? After all, the paperwork can be pretty tricky, and—"

"Mr. DeMarco," Wright interrupted in mid-sentence, "we've handled the paperwork before, as I said. You don't need to worry about that. Plus we will be selling the car to a dealer just down the road. They'll be doing the paperwork this time."

Killer was hanging from the cliff of calm with one hand, and even those five fingers were beginning to slip. He agreed to give them $4700 for their car. And then he started to discuss the new car. *That's* where he would stick them.

"Now folks, on the hardtop . . ." Killer laid the stock card for the particular car on the desk, pushing it around with his finger until it faced the Wrights. It was a loaded car: power windows, cruise control, the works. As they looked at the card, Killer caught one last glance at the coded cost figure in the corner. Or rather, the packed figure. Killer knew it contained a $300-dollar profit. "Now as you can see, this car lists for $10,600. But let me show you something. See this figure in the corner? It's the coded cost of the car. We are *never* supposed to show that figure to customers but, since you are knowledgeable people, why don't we simply add a profit to that figure?"

It always worked before; Killer was sure the Wrights would say yes, add a small profit to that figure, and—zap—pay that profit plus the $300-dollar pack.

Wright shook his head yes, and, for the first time, Killer smiled a real smile. "Mr. DeMarco, that certainly sounds fair to us. Would a $200-dollar profit be acceptable?"

God, he had them! "Well, I can't say for sure what my boss will accept, but why don't we write it up, and I'll go argue with them a little. After all, I won't make any money if you don't buy at some figure, isn't that right?" Another standard, logical question. Wright shook his head again, and Killer started to write.

"Oh, Mr. DeMarco . . ." Killer looked up just in time to see Wright reopen his pad. "If you don't mind, we've calculated the true cost of the car ourselves. I'd like to check our figure against the card's figure." Wright's words were as calm and self-assured as Killer's usually sounded. Killer ran his right hand through his hair and pulled his tie loose. His other hand? It was in the cookie jar, so to speak. Wright compared the two figures, looked off into space, and then began to talk. "You know, Mr. DeMarco, I'm afraid your bosses are pulling the wool over your eyes. If my figures are correct, and I'm sure they are, your card 'cost' is about $300 dollars or so higher than the actual invoice." Wright looked at Killer without blinking and just sat there. "But, I'm sure your bosses just made a mistake, don't you think?" Killer lifted his eyebrows and shrugged, doing his best to look surprised, nod agreement, and disavow any guilt with his movements. He instead looked like the smoking gun itself.

Wright continued, "But since we seem to have agreed on a $200-dollar profit, why don't we just take *my* figure and add $200 dollars to that? As you can see, we have the cost of every single item on the car, and our list figures for those items match your list figures." Wright laid his pad in front of Killer and turned the stock card back around.

Killer didn't touch them but looked down for a moment and began to speak. He really didn't sound too enthusiastic, however. "Mr. and Mrs. Wright"—he dropped the first-name bit—"my company will look at any offer. If you are saying you *will* buy a car at that figure, I believe the total would be $8900 dollars, let's do write it up and I'll take it to the manager. But Mr. and Mrs. Wright"—he looked at Gloria, hoping to find a little moral support there, instead finding a nice frozen smile—"the manager will not even consider an offer this low without a deposit. It's a policy, and I can't do a thing about it. If you will give me a deposit, I'll go in there and fight for us."

Mrs. Wright's expression didn't change, but Jim's face dropped any pretense of a smile. "No, Mr. DeMarco, I'm sorry, that won't do. We didn't come to this dealership to waste your time or ours. And, quite honestly, I am not interested in an hour of offers and counteroffers. I'll be happy to sign the buyer's order, but there will be no check until your man has approved the price."

As soon as Killer left the office, Gloria turned to Jim, a look of concern on her face, and said, "Jim, what if they won't approve it without money? You know, I really do like the car, and even if we did have to pay a little more, we could afford it." These two never argue, but her words nearly started one. "Look, we have gone this far. Now let's be patient. Let's keep emotion out of it!" His words made sense. After all, Killer had enough emotions right then for all three of them.

He sat down in the manager's office, looking like some forlorn puppy. Don had seldom seen him like this. "Killer, what is wrong with you? I mean, did they bite you or something?"

"Screw you! I'm telling you, I haven't seen anyone like these people in six months. Here, here's what the guy will do. And he says he'll walk if I try to bump him. He won't give me a deposit, either, until you sign the damn thing." Killer threw the buyer's order across the desk and sat there, immobilized.

"Killer, I know why you're giving this car away," Don said. "You're worried about your shirt."

Killer looked down and saw the patch of blue ink, and started laughing. "Oh, man, I just *knew* this wasn't going to be my day. Hell, I'm going home as soon as these jerks leave. Well, come on, tell me what you want to do."

"What's their trade like, can we make any money on it?"

"Hell, yes, it's a cherry from the word go."

"Well, will Rax put any more money in it?"

"No, I already got him up a hundred, and he is strong in the car."

"Well, are you going to get any financing? Have you tried to sell them glazing or a warranty? Killer, you know you can knock them dead on something."

"Don, I'm telling you, the people won't discuss financing or anything until you sign the order. Now, what do you want me to do, put their asses on the road, or sell them the car? Hell, *you* come on in with me if you want."

During his four years at the dealership, Don Burns had never been asked to go in on one of Killer's deals. There had really been no need to go in, either; Killer didn't leave money on the table. Burns would have normally taken the deal just to get the trade. But this was a good chance to show the master a few tricks. Burns picked up the buyer's order, looked at the $200-dollar profit figure, and headed out the door with Killer in lukewarm pursuit. Gloria was flipping through one of those car brochures as they entered, and Jim Wright stood up, shaking Burns' hand, returning his smile, too. "Folks, Don just wanted to have a chance to meet you—why don't we all sit down?" Killer said, with about as much enthusiasm as someone meeting his in-laws for the first time.

Don began to speak, the words a replay of countless other T.O. situations. This time he was using the "logical and fair" approach, which seemed to work best on people like this. "You know, Mr. and Mrs. Wright, I believe you are fair people, am I correct?" Both nodded their heads slightly, and Burns continued. "Let me tell you a little about what it costs to run a dealership this size. We have a hundred and twenty employees here. All of them receive benefits above and beyond their earnings. We also have nearly $2,000,000 dollars' worth of cars sitting here, and as I'm sure you know, we pay interest on every one of them. For instance, the car you folks like so much cost, as you said, $8937 dollars. Our interest on that car runs just about one percent over prime, or about one point five percent of its cost per month. That particular car started costing the dealership interest payments about two and a half months ago—as you can see on the stock car, the car has been here about three months, but we receive a two-week grace period on each car before the interest starts. But during the past two and a half months, we have paid on this specific car approximately $336 dollars in interest.

"Now, you have offered to pay us a profit of $200 dollars. If we sell you the car for that profit, we're really losing money on this transaction from the beginning. But there's more. I have to be paid something. Bob here has to be paid something. The title clerks in the office have to be paid for doing your paperwork. My point is simple. Your offer isn't really a fair one, is it?"

The expression on Don's face would have reminded you of Saint Peter's face as he sat there at the pearly gates, gently asking each petitioner, "Now, are you *really* a nice man?" Killer looked equally sincere. During this entire sermon the Wrights simply sat there, good members of the flock listening patiently to the shepherd.

Jim Wright cleared his throat and responded, "Mr. Burns, you are a convincing man." Don had him, Killer thought. "But even at that figure, you know you are making money." Don's mouth couldn't move fast enough to keep Wright from continuing. "Now, before you interrupt, let me tell you what I mean. I know the 'cost' figure, the real invoice figure, has a couple of percent extra profit built into it. I also know you are going to sell my trade and make at least $500 dollars on it. And I also know that we will buy rustproofing and undercoating, and you will make money on that. I am willing to pay you that profit, since it would cost me the same thing to have the car done at one of the independent places. I am willing to let you have my trade, even though it would be easy for me to retail it. Mr. Burns, I'm also willing to pay you the $25-dollar 'title and documentary fee,' even though that little bit of work certainly doesn't cost $25 dollars. Now, if you don't think I am paying a fair profit, that is certainly your right. We have an appointment down the road, as I mentioned to Mr. De-Marco, so perhaps those people will think my offer is fair."

Burns had only one more shot in his gun, but that bullet was wasted before the trigger was pulled. "Mr. Wright, what you say may be true, I don't really know. The dealer doesn't tell us those things. And I'm not saying we won't sell you the car at your figure, either. Oh, by the way, were you folks planning to finance the car here?"

"No, thank you." Gloria answered, even though Burns was looking at Jim. "We've already checked the various sources, and our credit union will be handling the transaction. As a matter of fact, the money is already in our checkbook, right here." Gloria laid the checkbook on the table. It was the stripper's last garment. Killer's tongue slipped by reflex over his lips as Don continued.

"Well, what I will do is talk to J. C. Hollins, our general manager." Don paused. "But there is probably one thing you can do to assure Mr. Hollins will accept your offer. You see, he really does want to know that offers like this are serious. I believe what we should do is this: let me figure up the total cost of the car, including tax. If you will give me a check for the entire amount, I'm sure the sight of that check will convince my boss to approve your offer. I know it sounds silly, but money does talk in this business." Don was determined to do at least one thing right. If he could get the couple's money to keep them from running out, maybe J. C. would actually come in and argue with these flakes himself. People seldom go running out of stores if their checks are still in the manager's office.

Wright shook his head firmly. "Mr. Burns, I not only won't give you a check for the full amount now, I won't give you more than a $100-dollar deposit, at most. *If* our offer is approved. I prefer to give you all the money only *after* I check out the car before we pick it up. I like to know the car is completely ready before taking delivery. And, quite honestly, I'm not interested in talking to anyone else, though your boss may be a nice man. That would be a waste of his time and ours."

Killer and Don Burns were probably thinking the same thing, slowly savoring how nice it would be to choke these people, to pull their fingernails out one by one. The two of them left the office with the buyer's order showing the same $200-dollar profit—supposedly to visit J. C. They didn't have any deposit, either, much less a check for the full amount. "Well, Don, what do you think?" Actually Killer wasn't feeling all that bad at the moment. At least Burns hadn't sweetened the deal either.

But Burns was feeling lousy. He really did need the deal even though the gross was nothing. Business was slow. And the used-car boys needed the trade, too. He signed the order quickly and said, "Here, take the damn thing back in there and get me their deposit," pushing the paper into Killer's hand.

Killer returned to the office, another one of those plastic smiles glued to his face, and concluded his little visit with the Wrights, shaking both their hands and finally saying, "Now folks, we'll have the car ready for you by six tomorrow afternoon. And I look forward to seeing you then."

God, was that a lie.

Wouldn't you like to do it like that? You will. These people succeeded in beating the system because they did their homework: they took the time to shop their own car and learned its true value—using the steps outlined in Chapter 4; they shopped their financing sources, too—just as we outlined in Chapter 5.

The Wrights also spent a good deal of time finding a

couple of specific cars that fitted their needs, and then computed the cost of those cars carefully. That's why Killer
couldn't fool them with artificial cost figures. And that's
what we are going to look at now: where to shop and how
to compute cost.

SHOPPING:
IF YOU PLAN TO BUY A NEW CAR

If you plan to buy a new car, you will have an easier time
of it because the variables are fewer than when shopping
the used-car market. First, consider dealerships close to
your home or work. Some people purchase a new car sixty
miles from home and then spend much more in gas having
the car serviced under warranty than they saved in the
actual purchase—if they saved anything. And don't think
you can automatically buy a car far from home and then
have it serviced at the dealership next door. Most cars are
sold with two separate warranties. The "adjustment" warranty is usually for ninety days or so and includes problems
such as squeaks and rattles, air leaks, and alignment. Since
all adjustment warranties are the responsibility of the *selling* dealer, the expense is paid by the selling dealer. Obviously other dealers will not incur expenses for your
selling dealer.

Your car's regular warranty has some restrictions, too.
Normally, other dealerships are not required to honor regular warranty work if your selling dealer is located closer
than fifty miles to the dealership at which you wish to have
the work done. Some service departments will honor anyone's warranty work, but don't count on it. Warranty
work, even regular warranty work, is relatively unprofit-
able for the dealer.

Once you have determined the make or makes of cars

that interest you, locate at least two dealerships for each make. Car stores have personalities, just like the rest of us. Usually a new-car store's personality is determined by the dealer, and since many dealers are S.O.B.s, you need the option of comparing similar stores' attitudes and tactics. One store may have a friendly, laid-back way of taking you, and a similar store six miles away may emulate the tactics of Vlad the Terrible, the true-life model for Dracula. Good old Vlad was famous for having troublesome villagers boiled alive at his dinner table.

Different stores will usually have different inventories of cars, too. Some stores are "color queer": the person who does their ordering may be partial to blues and light colors, and fill their lot with nothing else. Others stock mainly dark colors.

If you are buying new, it is not important to worry about a specific store's profit policies or their trade-in policies at this stage. For shopping purposes assume that you will get the best deal from any store.

What About Service Departments? Obviously, you would do well to buy from a store with an honest and efficient service department. Equally obviously, service departments are hard things to evaluate. They are like restaurants: great food one night and slop the next. But if you are concerned with a particular store's service, take the time to meet their service manager. If the guy hides behind an oil drum as you approach, go someplace else—he probably has a complex from all his service problems. If he'll talk to you straight, explain their service policies, and treat you for what you are—his meal ticket—you may have found a good service operation.

Ask specifically about loan cars or the availability of a courtesy bus. Find out if his service department works on an appointment basis. Don't be shy. Don't think you are wasting the man's time. Remember, he will make more money if you buy the car from his store.

What Do Those Pretty New Cars Cost the Dealer?

This is how it used to be: You were standing on a lot looking at a great big Chrysler New Yorker and a very small Dodge Omni. A salesman walked out and offered you a twenty percent discount on the New Yorker as you were standing there. No dummy you, you told the guy you would buy the Omni if he would give you a twenty percent discount. The guy had had a bad day. He decked you. What did you do wrong?

Until 1980, though many people thought to the contrary, each car line manufactured by each company had a vastly different margin of profit, or discount structure, as car people refer to it. Large cars, such as Chryslers, had twenty-three percent margins or larger, and many small cars had margins of twelve percent or less. For several decades both the manufacturers and dealers were happy with this setup. After all, big cars were everyone's goal in life, and big cars were the hot sellers at every store in town. Those small little jobs were grudgingly kept on dealers' lots as an accommodation for the weirdos who actually thought it was fashionable to be seen in a tin can.

But, beginning in 1974, something very strange began to happen in the minds of customers who for years had been "normal": even the most blue-blooded, dyed-in-the-wool Americans, the folks who drove Electra 225s and Mercury Gran Marquis, began to trade down to Buick Skylarks or Mercury Cougars. The dealers became nervous. After all, those smaller cars only carried mark-ups of seventeen or eighteen percent, not twenty-three. By 1976 the folks who normally drove Skylarks and Cougars were trading down, too. Customers who had normally bought cars with seventeen percent margins were buying cars with fifteen percent mark-ups. And, good Lord, by 1979 even *those* people were trading down to cars with ten and eleven percent mark-ups. What was happening? A Communist plot to undermine the economy? Some sick love affair with tiny things engendered by those rotten Japanese? Seemingly overnight, car lots were filled with enormous tanks covered in cobwebs, and all of those nice, fat profit margins just weren't doing the dealers any good at all. Is that fair?

Of course not. And though the dealers and manufacturers may be a little slow to catch on to reality, by Intro Day 1980, every manufacturer had begun to correct this injustice. Luxury and family-sized cars (industry euphemisms for "big," a nasty, nasty word these days) appeared on the showroom with smaller margins of profit. Small cars appeared with sticker prices high enough to choke a giraffe—and much of that increase, naturally, was simply a larger profit margin. Small cars that once carried mark-ups of ten percent proudly showed off their new fifteen percent profit stickers to one and all.

This change was big news in the auto world. *Automotive News,* the bible of the industry, proudly proclaimed, "The American auto makers, taking a cue from the imports, seem to be moving in the direction of common dealer discounts, the same discount on all sizes of cars." *Automotive News* breathlessly described the courage of General Motors, for instance, in cutting the discount rate on Cadillacs from twenty-five percent to nineteen, the discount on Corvettes from twenty-four to twenty percent, and proudly stated that GM had "settled on an eighteen percent discount on all its intermediate and regular-size cars, down from nineteen, twenty-two, or twenty-four percent." GM president E. M. Estes spoke of this radical change in pricing structure as if he were talking about landing men on Mars: "We didn't get to a common discount [for all cars] but we got close enough this time." Estes also said, "We didn't see any way to do just one [discount], although I think we came close." It's hard to lower the profits on the big ones, even though they aren't selling too well, isn't it? Thank goodness the prices were raised on those little tin cans. I mean, the boys in Detroit need all the help they can get.

All of this changing of price structure may not seem very important to you, but you are wrong. Because Detroit has finally decided in one area to emulate the foreign makers who have always had one discount for their car lines, dealerships have also decided to change a few of their selling tactics—to emulate the imports again, naturally. First, dealers would like you to think that small cars can't be discounted. After all, the import stores don't have price wars. Beginning in 1980 salesmen were drilled relentlessly in this nice little lie. Salesmen were also reminded that many customers really believe small cars have very small discounts. No one was encouraged to tell the customers those discounts were now close or equal to full-size car discounts.

So, what do they cost? There are two answers to the question. Use the first answer, What Cars Cost by Car Line, to help you determine the range of cars you might be interested in buying. If you are thorough, use the second answer, What a Specific Car Costs, to determine *exactly* what a specific car cost a dealer. Chapter 9, Negotiating the Sale, was designed for either method of calculating cost.

What Cars Cost by Car Line. Pages 343 and 347 in the Appendix provide formulas for quickly determining, within one or two percent, the invoice price, or "cost," of most foreign and American cars. These formulas will require your help; you will need to copy the *base* list price and the total dollar amount of all options from the window of the cars you like. Then look up the make (like Chevrolet) and model (like Monte Carlo) in the Appendix. Multiply the sticker price by the number listed by that car. This figure will be the amount of profit in that particular car. Some cars have *two* numbers by them. These cars have different margins of profit for the base car and options. Simply use the two numbers to develop the profit in the base car and options, and then add your answers for the total.

EXAMPLE

1. A Chevrolet Monte Carlo has a sticker
   price of $10,000. $10,000
2. The number by Monte Carlos in the table is .15.
   Multiply the list price by .15 and you
   have the "margin," or profit—$1500.
3. Subtract that figure ($1500) from the sticker price.   −1,500
4. What remains is the "invoice" price. $8,500

Remember: the formulas will provide you with a good guide, but they will not give you the exact cost of a particular car.

What a Specific Car Costs. "Very specific" describes the method the Wrights used for arriving at the cost of the new car they wished to buy. Gloria was mainly responsible for this step. The family had all decided that a two-door sedan was their most practical choice, and two particular cars seemed to fit their needs. After the family conference Gloria visited two dealerships for each car, telling each of the salesmen the same thing, which happened to be the truth: "Hello, I hate to tell you, but I'm not buying a car today at any price! We *are* going to buy a car within the next few days, though. Now, could you let me drive one of those sedans sitting over there?"

At the end of each test drive, she copied down *all* the information from the sticker of each car, the stock number of the car, the salesman's name, and the name of the dealership. Then she headed home.

"Gloria, are you sure you copied off the total figure from the *manufacturer's* sticker, not the dealer's sticker?" The dealer's stickers were always higher, of course; they usually contained a charge for "dealer preparation," even though the cost of dealer prep is built into the actual invoice of the car; rustproofing and undercoating charges were there, too, and many times there was a charge for "glazing." You would think that new cars would disintegrate on the spot if they weren't "protected" with all this crap.

"Yes, I copied down the right price. Now, it's your turn to get to work." Jim was sitting at the kitchen table studying a small paperback book that listed the cost of every single car and option sold in America. He also had a piece of paper for the two cars now under consideration. Listed on each sheet were the options on each car and their list prices, the figures from the window sticker. Jim first checked these list figures with the figures listed in his book. They matched. "Hey, honey, you *did* buy the right book, after all. You bought the one with all the latest price increases. But I like the old prices better! Why don't we use that book?"

Gloria looked at him. "Jim, that's crazy. How are we going to know the real cost if we use an old book?"

"But the older prices are *so* much lower. Think of all the money we'll save!" Jim loved the look on her face—Gloria really looked ready to kill now. But he was just playing with her; it was one of the stupid things that drove her crazy and made her laugh at the same time, like the time he looked her straight in the eye and said "I'm going to buy a boat! One of the guys down at work tells me that boats are going up in value, and, since that must be true, we can buy a $100,000-dollar boat, keep it until we can sell it for $200,000, and then we'll be rich!"

Jim turned back to the book. Within an hour, he had figured the exact factory cost of each car to the penny. He checked the book's list prices against the list prices from the window of the cars once more, pushed his chair back, and sighed. "Hey! Gloria! I've done it again. I've figured the cost right!" The Wrights now possessed the three most important pieces of information in any car transaction: what their used car was really worth, where the best financing was available, and what each new car cost. No question was hard to answer, either. Especially the cost of the new cars.

Like Jim and Gloria, if you really want the nitty-gritty, you're going to have to make a visit to your local drug or bookstore and spend three bucks, to boot. Hidden away there on the shelves is a book called *Edmund's Car Prices Buyer's Guide*. This little book is a gold mine for the curious car buyer—it shows you nice fuzzy pictures of every car sold in America and tells you what each car and its options list for and cost. There is an "American Automobile" edition and a "Foreign Car" edition. It is an automobile fancier's delight, a straightforward, meaty compendium of raw facts. It is, unfortunately, also the home to several ads for computer-buying services and "price quotation" companies. Buy the book, follow the steps outlined in the following, and you will determine the exact cost of just about any car. But don't pay any attention to the ads unless you've read the section on car-buying services beginning on page 257 of this book.

How to Use Edmund's. (1) First, find a few cars in the book that appeal to you by flipping through the picture section. Use these cars for practice only—once you actually begin to shop, you will be figuring the cost of a specific car and options, but for now, find something that appeals to you and turn to the pricing section for that particular car. All cars are listed alphabetically by make—Buick before Cadillac, Lincoln before Mercury.

(2) Take a sheet of paper and "create" your ideal car. List the make and model of the car at the top of the paper. We'll assume for practice purposes you are going to create a Chevrolet Citation.

(3) Now make two columns on your paper. In the first column, put the "list" or retail price of the base car and write under that the name and list price of all options you would like on your ideal car. It's important to write down these list prices, even though you will be dealing with cost figures. The list prices will enable you to compare the list price of the same options with those from an actual car. If they don't match, you have a book with old prices.

EXAMPLE

CHEVROLET CITATION FOUR-DOOR HATCHBACK

Item	List Price	Base Cost
Car without options	$5153	$4484
2.8 engine	225	187
Air-conditioning	564	468
Automatic transmission	337	280
TOTAL	$6279	$5419

Now, you have the list price and base cost for the Citation. But at least two things need to be added to the base cost to determine the true "cost" of the Citation. The first is a charge for dealer advertising. Yes, you are charged for all those nice commercials. This figure varies, but averages about $50 dollars per car. The second charge is for "oil and gas"—the manufacturers, those chintzy folks, aren't satisfied merely charging you thousands for a car; they want you to pay for the gas and oil necessary to drive it from the plant onto a truck. Most manufacturers charge under $25 dollars for this privilege, but let's assume $25 dollars. By adding these two items to your total basic cost, you have the real cost of the vehicle:

Total basic cost	$5419
Advertising	50
Gas and oil	25
Cost of car	$5494

There's one more thing to add, though: transportation. Transportation will vary by model of car and distance of the dealership from the factory. Once you have actually begun to shop, that figure will be on the window sticker of each car. Add it to the "total cost of the car."

The Wrights' experience has shown you how to compute the cost of specific cars that interest you. After you have visited the dealerships and taken down the specific information for the cars that interest you, you can, by using *Edmund's* actually determine exact figures for those cars, with these exceptions.

(1) Manufacturers include in the base cost of their cars a charge for dealer preparation and handling. Many dealers will try to charge you for preparation again and will insist on adding an additional $100 or $200 dollars to the list price of their vehicles. Don't fall for this. If you would like, read them *Edmund's* notation on dealer preparation and handling.

(2) Because manufacturers change prices several times during the year, it will be important for you to have the newest copy of *Edmund's*. You can verify the validity of your book by comparing the "base list price" for a specific car, the top figure on the window, with the base list price of the same car in *Edmund's*. If your book is outdated, simply note the difference in the base prices and add that to your total cost figure.

(3) If you are considering a "leftover" new car, a new car left over from the previous model year, the dealer's profit margin will usually be *five percent more* than the margin listed in *Edmund's*. This five percent is simply an incentive for the dealer to stock more new cars at the end of the model year. To adjust your cost figure down, simply multiply the *list* price by five percent and deduct that figure from your "total cost of the car." Most salesmen don't know about this little bonus to the dealers; you might want to enlighten them.

(4) Automobile manufacturers periodically give their dealers other "incentives" on slower-moving cars. These are usually unadvertised bonuses to encourage dealers to lower their prices. Of course, they don't, preferring to retain these bonuses as additional honey for the pot. You and I don't know which cars may have these incentives either, but we can assume most slow-moving, unpopular cars may have them. If, for instance, you are considering a large gas guzzler, take these incentives as a given when you begin to bargain.

(5) Don't forget the normal dealer "holdback." All new cars have an extra two percent profit built into their invoices. Neither you nor the salesman ever sees this money—another spiff for the boss—but remember it's there when you begin to bargain.

Does all this sound too complicated? It isn't. If you will

take your time, remain patient, and *think,* you will easily determine the true cost of a new car. But even if you miss the mark slightly, you'll still be ahead of the game. Our approach to buying, Negotiating the Sale (Chapter 9), provides you with the best way to deal close to any car's cost. By giving you specific tactics for specific situations—for example, if you are trading in your old car and financing a new car—we will show you how to use and modify the information in this chapter for your needs.

"Add-Ons"—Are They Worth It?

New-car dealers have found new toys to improve their profits. They are called "add-ons" and encompass just about every conceivable low-cost, high-margin item the wildest mind could conceive. Add-ons have two things in common: they are put on the car by the dealer, and they always make the dealers lots of money. For example, there is "glazing," the new "miracle" coating supposedly designed to protect your car from the Devil's breath itself. Or "custom stripping," usually $3 dollars' worth of material and $20 dollars' worth of labor disguised with a $200-dollar price tag. And, of course, there's rustproofing and undercoating, another item that may cost the dealer $35 dollars including application, but that sells for the handy price of $150 to $200 dollars. Do you really need those extra stripes? Is the paint job so lousy it needs "glazing" to survive? And do you really need extra rustproofing and undercoating in your neck of the woods? Again, why are you spending thousands of dollars for a car only to have some dealer tell you your money isn't really buying a car that won't rust?

But as if the add-ons weren't bad enough themselves, most dealers leave you little choice in the decision-making process. They glaze new cars the moment the car hits the lot, rustproof and undercoat it, and stripe it without once asking the potential buyer *if* he wants these goodies. You'll see all their high prices written or typed on the sticker right by the manufacturer's sticker, a *fait accompli*. And you will hear your salesman say with a straight face, "You, of course, will have to pay for them." Nope. In Chapter 9, Negotiating the Sale, we don't mention the add-ons when your offer is computed. If you really feel that rustproofing and undercoating is something you would have purchased anyway, feel free to add the price for that "service" to your offer. If you like to be silly, even add the price for "glazing" to your offer. But don't feel obligated to add *anything*. Remember that all add-ons simply add a large amount of profit for the seller and a very small amount of cost.

Other Nice Ways to Be Taken: Car-Buying Services and Leasing

They make it sound so easy. Car-buying services say they will "help" you by taking all the mystery from the car-buying process. For a mere $7 or $10 dollars, these services will send you a computer printout of the "exact" car you want to buy. Their printout will give you the list price and cost of every single car in America—right! And some of the services will actually sell you a car for around $100 dollars above "cost." The appeal, or rather the spiel, is alluring; and during recent years, the President's consumer-affairs advisers and well-meaning publications such as *Changing Times* have lauded these noble companies for their service to mankind. *Changing Times* proudly proclaimed that if "you are armed with the knowledge of how much potential profit the sale involves, you can saunter into the show-rooms and bargain with confidence." "Saunter" is such a classy word. If you believe *Changing Times,* that computer printout will immediately transform you into Gary Cooper in *High Noon*. Even *Edmund's Car Prices*, the most straightforward guide in the business, allows these services to advertise in their books. *Edmund's* does place a small disclaimer in each edition, stating, "The computerized pricing services herein are not operated by nor are they the responsibility of the publisher." A nice way to wash your hands.

If you are planning to order a car—not buy one already on someone's lot—and if you don't have a trade, buying services can take some of the work from your transaction. Any of the services will send you a checklist for a specific car, and within the week will send you back the cost of that car, including transportation. We tell you how to figure the cost yourself, but have at the services, if you're the lazy type.

Should you have a trade-in, forget it; most of the dealerships signed up by these services *will*, as an accommodation, as they so politely put it, take your trade off your hands. Of course, they'll lowball you on your car and turn their $100-dollar profit into a $400- or $500-dollar profit. As we've discussed, simply knowing one part of the car-buying puzzle, the cost of the car, won't help you much.

But won't the nice "personalized" printout help you shop for a car? After all, it will tell you the cost of a specific car and model. No it won't. It's virtually impossible to find identical cars to match one printout. Actual cars on the lot will be hundreds less or hundreds more than your one example, and simply adding or deducting the difference won't give you true cost. You will fare much better by using the costing methods outlined herein.

Car-buying services also can't normally sell you the "hot" cars for a real discount. The best-selling gas misers and fanciest sports cars are seldom included in their selection. When they do agree to sell you for a hundred over, they tack on a few little things, too. Like a delivery charge of $75 bucks or so. And many quote you "$100 over" prices for the city of Detroit, not your own hometown. What would it cost you to make a quick flying trip to Detroit to pick up your new beauty?

A few of these services are even more imaginative in their plots to help you. "We'll sell you a car for *less* than a $100-dollar profit," they say. But these same services require you to finance the car with them at very profitable rates, require you to purchase equally profitable life and accident and health insurance, *and* require you to buy an even more profitable extended warranty. The "bargain" is, in reality, a very poor deal.

Don't waste your time. If you are ordering a car, buying straight out and paying cash, consider ordering a printout from one of the services. You will probably buy a car for the same price the rest of us will who work the system. But, other than this specific instance, don't let these people do a number on you.

What About Leasing a Car? Many people believe that leasing is one sure way to surmount the problem of dealing with salesmen, their trade, and the car-buying process. As sure as the sun shines, most of these people are taken, too. If you plan to lease, *shop your leasing quotes* from the various sources. If you are trading your car for a leased car, insist that each potential leasing company tell you the exact amount each is allowing for your trade. If possible, don't trade—sell your car.

Ordering a Car

If you are buying straight out, not trading your car, it makes sense to order. First, you'll have the exact car you like. But, more importantly, you will probably pay less; dealers don't pay floor-plan interest on ordered cars. Because of that, most sellers will accept smaller profits.

If you are planning to trade your car, ordering can be a little more complicated. The seller will appraise your trade at the time your new car is ordered but will insist it be reappraised when your new car arrives. Because several months can pass before ordered cars arrive at the dealership, the value of your trade could drop substantially—at least that's what the dealer will probably tell you. If possible, insist that the wholesale figure on your trade be a firm one. Better yet, why not sell your car yourself?

"Demos" or Demonstrators

Demos are new cars driven by salesmen, managers, and other employees of a dealership. All of these cars are "new" in the legal sense only—they have not been registered to an individual but are still the property of the dealership or floor-planning institution.

Many customers actively seek out demos, believing these cars are less expensive than new ones. Nine times out of ten that belief is false, too. The average dealership's profit on demos is just as high as its profit on new cars. Other folks seem to prefer demos because they believe the "kinks" have been removed. These people assume dealership employees spend large amounts of time caressing and caring for their wheels—another dangerous assumption. Most dealership employees are careless with these cars because they don't own them and will be driving them for only a few months.

So, what's the advantage of buying a demo? There is none. Even though most manufacturers provide at no extra cost a new-car warranty on demos, the manufacturers can't erase the mileage on these cars. At trading time, you will probably pay a penalty for those miles, too.

If you negotiate properly, you'll buy a *really* new car for the cost of these slightly used ones.

SHOPPING:
IF YOU PLAN TO BUY A USED CAR

Buying a used car can be one of the smartest moves you can make. It is also, unfortunately, one of the dumbest moves many people make. Because those people don't accept the fact that shopping for a used car is *not* like shopping for a new car. Yes, used-car buyers will need to bargain for a good price, and yes, they will have to choose the seller with care—just like new-car buyers. But price and seller are not the most important factors in the used-car process. What have you gained if the price on a specific car is low and the seller is President of the Better Business Bureau, but the internal organs of your bargain—the things you cannot see and cannot judge easily—are junk?

The paramount factor in choosing a used car is the condition of that particular car. If it is sound mechanically, it's worth more money than a bargain vehicle; if it really checks out thoroughly, *who* sells it to you isn't important—a good used car from your neighbor or even the local fly-by-night lot is better than an average car from your Cadillac dealer.

It sounds easy enough: just buy a good one. The process of finding that car will probably be long and frustrating, much more so than finding a new car. Unless you are a gambler at heart, stop reading about used cars *unless* you are willing to follow a few suggestions that will probably be unpleasant to implement. Go buy a new car, spend that extra money, and be happy. The used-car field isn't a ball-game for flighty folks at all; it's for thorough ones.

We are going to be discussing the used-car hunt and purchase in detail, but first, think carefully about these few "givens"—suggestions that all smart used-car buyers have accepted since the first used car sat on anyone's lot.

(1) You must put away your shyness. If you are the type of person who feels that asking things of sellers, making notes, and generally taking time to know a particular purchase is an imposition, change that feeling right now. You are probably getting ready to spend thousands of dollars, and it is not only silly, it's poor, poor business to spend money without really knowing what your money is buying. The only safe approach to buying a used car assumes that you have a *right* to know everything about that car before signing anything. If the seller doesn't agree with this approach, go somewhere else. Say good-bye, leave, and don't be embarrassed, either. Many sellers will imply that only *amateurs* check out a car; they will tell you, "Of course, the car isn't perfect, that's why it costs less," giving you a look normally reserved for the town moron. Bull hockey. Shopping for a used car never should include too much concern for the seller's feelings. Invariably he will have absolutely none for yours. Remember that used-car people are concerned only with your money, not your friendship.

(2) You will need a pencil and a checklist. Two checklists are provided in the Appendix. The first list, the one you will be using, will help you take the emotion out of the buying process. It provides you with sixteen easy things to check on any used car which will help you determine if that car is as beautiful under the skin as it may be on the surface. Because all used-car operations make the exterior of their cars as beautiful as possible in order to take your mind off

interior sicknesses, this checklist will be your first protection from the thousands of junkers sitting proudly on lots across the country.

(3) You will need to wear old clothes. Don't laugh—if you are really going to check out a used car, you will definitely get dirty and probably greasy. But so what? So what if the guys on the lot laugh a little when you crawl under the car a foot or two? Would you get a little dirty to save $300 or $500 or $800 dollars in repairs the moment you buy a used car? Let them laugh. *You* can laugh all the way to the bank.

(4) You will need a mechanic. Your checklist will tell you many things about a car, but unless you have a shop in your backyard, you really can't check most of the important and less obvious problem centers in a car. The second checklist in the Appendix provides your mechanic with a short list of must things you will need to have checked before you buy any car.

Choose your mechanic before you begin to shop. You may already have one you trust. If not, your favorite gas station may have one. Car-care centers and tire shops usually have them. Your neighbor may know a good one. Before you begin to shop, find one and give him a call. If you like, read him the list of items from the checklist and ask for a price to check your prospective car. Normally, a mechanic will check these items for under $35 dollars and also provide you with an estimate of the cost to repair any problems. *Having a mechanic is the most important thing you can do as a used-car buyer.* Though the seller may not admit it, the mere fact you plan to take a car to a mechanic will lessen his natural desire to stick you with a piece of junk. You will also be in a much better position to negotiate price once a specific car has been checked. And you, you smart thing, will know what repairs will be needed on any car, and how much those repairs will cost, before you buy. Which brings us to the final given.

(5) Expect things to be wrong with every car. As they say, wear and tear *is* the reason used cars cost less. But, if you know that a really nice car needs a complete brake job for $300 dollars, the car might still be the best buy *if* you plan that expenditure as part of your purchase price. If a specific car you like needs a dozen things fixed at a cost of $700 dollars, that car might be a good purchase, too, *if* you plan that expenditure as part of the purchase price.

If you will accept these five points as a given, you will be a smart used-car buyer and will in all likelihood outsmart the foxiest seller in the world. Most sellers will accept this approach to buying a car, too. Just remember: those who won't do it your way, who refuse to have their car checked by a mechanic "for insurance reasons" or other easy cop-outs, are not people you will do business with. Regardless of their smile, okay?

Why All This Work Is Worth It

You've been warned about the hard work. If you're still game, let's consider more specifically why this drudgery may be worth it. The only logical reasons to buy a used car are price and depreciation—or the lack of it. Unless you plan, and I mean are sure, to keep a car for a long time, a *new* car is probably one of the worst investments in the world. As a matter of fact, 99 out of 100 new cars will drop *forty percent* in value the day they're driven home.

If you purchase a used car wisely, you won't face such drastic losses. The only "depreciation" you'll face the moment you drive off the lot will be the amount of profit you've paid on the car. For instance, if you pay $6500 dollars for a used car with a wholesale value of $6000 dollars, your car will be worth $6000 the moment you own it, a depreciation of less than ten percent. If you maintain the car well and drive it for a year, it will probably depreciate another ten percent. But, even at the end of those twelve months, you'll still be far ahead of the new-car game.

Why It's Harder

In the first place, used-car buyers must function in a less than pleasant environment. From road hogs to small independent lots to new-car operations, the used-car business would make Boss Tweed's activities pale in comparison. Most people who have shopped used cars know this. They have experienced firsthand the seedy characters and odiferous atmosphere of corner lots that could pass for deserted junkyards.

Used-car dealers these days just love to brag about the changes in their business, about the vast degree of professionalism newly present. They point to the "new car" warranties now being offered on their merchandise or speak with great pride about new state and federal regulations that protect the customer. What they don't say is the more telling truth: virtually every "protection" now offered used-car buyers was shoved down the throat of used-car dealers after a struggle by consumerists for nearly two decades. What they don't tell you about are the loopholes strategically placed in protection regulations by their own lobbyists. Though you may have to triple your caution and make "Caveat Emptor" (let the buyer beware) a cardinal rule, you can surmount these difficulties to make a good deal. Unfortunately, the difficulties go further than these:

as a used-car buyer, you will face five other discomfiting variables.

(1) Each used car is an original. Don't think you'll find an identical car down the road. Yes, you may find the same year and make and model, maybe even the same color, but the car can be as different as the Gabor sisters. Used-car operators use similarity to their advantage continually. They may, for instance, advertise a nice low-mileage car for $5000 dollars, and then sell you a virtually identical car with high mileage and hidden body damage.

(2) Used cars don't have fixed wholesale values or asking prices. You will have a very difficult time "shopping" the price on any used car. Asking prices change with the wind. They invariably go up if you plan to trade your car. They invariably go down if you look like you are going to walk.

(3) A great car may be at a rotten lot. And vice versa. You can't automatically assume that the fly-by-nighters sell only junkers, and you certainly can't assume new-car operations will always have the most dependable cars.

(4) It takes time to check out a used car. Most of us evaluate a used car on the basis of its looks. We make decisions involving thousands of dollars based on cursory evaluation rather than careful examination. Or worse, we let our emotions rule the decision-making process. Choosing a used car will involve lots of time and a small amount of money, but it's worth it.

(5) Financing rates vary tremendously on used cars. In automobile lingo, the "spread" is much greater. On new cars, for instance, the percentage spread between the cost of money and the highest legal rate that can be charged for money is usually two percent. But the spread on a two-year-old car can be *ten* percent. If you plan to finance a used car, you must shop for the lowest rate for that particular *year* car. Do not agree to finance a car from the

seller, even if the seller plans to use your own bank as the source; you *will* pay more for the money.

The Importance of Loan Value

Used cars obviously don't have set "invoice" prices. Cars of the same year and roughly equal condition can vary in value hundreds of dollars, depending on mileage and color—even on the time they were traded in. For instance, used station wagons are normally at a premium before the summer begins. Many folks trade for wagons then, planning on a nice family vacation in their newer tub. But in the fall buyers seem to look for smaller cars, hardtops and four-cylinder jobs to use for work and short trips. Station-wagon wholesale values drop dramatically at that time.

This variation in wholesale value poses a problem for lending institutions: what would be a generally safe amount of money to loan on a used car? Lending institutions have historically wanted to loan less than the true wholesale value—a nice way to protect their loans—but haven't had the manpower to actually determine the wholesale value of particular cars.

Over the years, lending institutions developed a "loan value" formula as a safe compromise for setting loan limits. They began to loan eighty percent of the "average clean wholesale" price for all cars of a particular make sold at auctions. For instance, if the average clean wholesale figure for all three-year-old Chevrolet Monte Carlos last month at sales around the country was $5000 dollars, lending institutions would loan $4000 dollars on those cars. Loan value is affected by a car's general condition, mileage, and options such as air-conditioning, power steering, and power windows.

Since it may be impossible for you to know the true

wholesale value of a particular used car sitting on someone's lot, the loan value figure can at least give you a good
indication of the worth of the car. We will be using loan
value as our benchmark in the examples in the next chapter. However, because some cars are actually worth *less*
than their loan value, we'll always be offering *less* than
loan value, raising our offer slowly from that figure. Your
financing source will determine the particular loan value of
specific cars for you.

Used-Car Sources

If you are lucky, you will find a car that suits your need
without once visiting a lot. Dealers will, of course, tell you
just the opposite: Never buy a car from a friend or neighbor—it won't have warranty, you will lose a friendship, and
in all likelihood will be "cheated" by your erstwhile buddy.
Chicken feathers. No warranty from an acquaintance is
better than most warranties provided by your neighborhood lot. Review these sources and consider giving the first
few a try before walking on that lot.

(1) People you know. Do you have neighbors who trade
cars regularly? All of us have friends who trade every two
or three years. Wouldn't it be better to consider offering
that person more money for his car than any dealership
will give him? If you can find a friend or neighbor who is
planning to trade, shop his car with him as we have indicated and then offer him a profit. Both of you will be better
off—your friend will be receiving more than wholesale for
his car and will be able to buy a new car with less hassle.
And you will have a nice used car with absolutely no hassle. Some smart used-car buyers regularly buy the same
person's trade year after year. Could that make sense for

you? The paperwork involved in person-to-person dealing is less involved than at your friendly used-car lots, even if the seller owes money and you prefer to finance.

(2) Bulletin boards at work. Your chances of finding a nice car by reading those little notices are just as good or better than your chances of finding a nice car on some lot. Unfortunately many people who attempt to sell their cars like this are in the bucket—they owe more on their cars than their actual value. But that's the seller's problem, not yours. Once you have agreed on the wholesale figure plus a fair profit, the seller is obligated to pay off his car.

(3) Classified ads and "shoppers." Sure, it will take a little time to call those ads and personally inspect each car. But hidden away in those funny little messages are many good cars that can be bought at very reasonable prices.

Incidentally, don't for a minute think that all classified ads are placed by *individuals* selling their own cars. Some used-car operations pay housewives a fee to act as "fronts" for a particular car, instructing them to tell potential buyers, "Of course, I put every mile on this beauty." Don't be shy if you plan to search the classifieds. Ask the party specifically, "Is the car titled in your name?" Ask to see the title if you are uncomfortable with the person's answer. If the car is the property of a used-car dealer, you probably won't be buying a bargain—and *may* be buying a wrecked vehicle. If you are still interested, *go to the selling dealer*—don't accept the easy words of his representative.

FAIR WARNING: Ignore any friend, bulletin board notice, or ad that says "assume payments" or "$500 down and assume payments." These people are obviously *deep* in the bucket. They can't sell their car to some used-car operation because they would have to *pay* an operator to take their car. They can't sell their car to an individual for a lump sum for the same reason. Don't fall for this line, or you will automatically leap into the bucket yourself.

(4) New-car dealers. Most of the used cars on their lots were trade-ins, an important fact in itself. One of your most important questions in any used-car transaction is, "Who was the previous owner, and how do I call him?" Dealerships should know that information. If you plan to buy a car from any new-car operation, insist on this name and number.

New-car dealers can also be held more accountable than used-car dealers. Their operations are more visible in the community, and the caliber of their salesmen may be just a shade above the strictly used boys. As with all used-car operations, it will be important for you to select the cars that interest you. Don't be led by the nose. Salesmen are not interested in selling you one particular car that might fit your needs; they are interested in selling the car with the highest likely profit or bonus for *them*.

New-car dealers also offer you the advantage of their own service departments. You certainly won't receive any price breaks on service, but you might have a better chance of buying a car with less problems if you are dealing with a lot that has an in-house service operation.

(5) Used-car dealers. Look for large lots that have been in business for years. Once you've found a few with nice selections, call your local Better Business Bureau. The Bureau will tell you if complaints have been lodged against those particular lots. If the complaints have been numerous, either forget that lot or plan to have your mechanic check their cars twice. *Always insist on knowing the previous owner of cars at any strictly used lot.* Many independent lots purchase virtually all of their cars from new-car dealers and "road hogs," wholesalers who travel from city to city peddling individual cars. A "bought" car may be a fine

piece of merchandise, but shy away from them unless you can locate the previous owner. Road hogs make their living by taking questionable cars to new market areas.

(6) Rental agencies. These people must have good public relations organizations working for them. Countless articles have praised them as the used-car-buyer's salvation. These articles enthusiastically tell you how helpful their selling procedures are. For instance, rental agency used-car operations just love to brag about their "one price" method of selling. They tell you how much nicer it is to forego dickering. And they are right—it is nice for them.

But not for you. You are paying a nice hefty profit, probably more than a reasonably comparable car on some other lot. They tell you "our cars are cheaper because there are no middlemen." Incorrect. Rental agencies determine the true wholesale value of their cars and then add their profit to that figure, as all used-car boys do. So, who's getting the good deal? The seller, of course. Rental agencies also tout their "twelve-month warranties." It's the same warranty offered at most used-car lots these days.

Rental agencies are no better or no worse than many other sources. Shop them carefully. Decide if you really want a car that's been driven by several dozen people, too.

(7) Red lights. Do you remember the last car you saw with a "for sale" sign and a price sticking in the back window? Don't try too hard, but do notice these rolling advertisements. If you see a pretty nice-looking car, it might be worth a call, or at least a yell across lanes.

Checking Out a Used Car

Most people's idea of checking out a used car is simply to walk around it slowly, kicking each tire vigorously in the process—an evaluation that usually results in nothing more than a sore foot. Some people are a little more thorough in their inspection—they will blow the horn, turn on the radio, or lift the hood. The hood lifters are some of my favorite shoppers, too. Invariably, these people will raise the hood and simply stand there staring, as if waiting for a "hello" or some other appropriate engine-to-person salutation. Several years ago our used-car department wired many of our cars to do just that, installing small tape recorders engineered to speak when the hoods were opened. One day a nice old lady drove up to the lot and asked her salesman to open the hood of that cute little car over there, the "one with the flower on her antenna." She laid her purse on the fender and leaned in toward the air filter just as a plaintive voice rose inches from her face. "I'm thirsty! Could I please have some oil?" The lady didn't jump but rather slowly straightened her body, raised her right hand to cheek, and dead-panned, "I think she's an oilaholic." We liked that lady.

Professional appraisers at most dealerships are never quite this flippant when putting a figure on a car; their job is the real essence of the automobile business. And Rax, Killer's favorite man on the used-car lot, knows that, too. His ritual is always the same. "First, I determine if anything needs to be spent on the car's drive train—the engine, transmission, and so forth. I crank it up, and let the engine idle for a few minutes, listening for clatter or other unusual noises in the engine. Then I slip the transmission into neutral, then reverse, then neutral, then reverse. If there's any motion there, clanking, you've got transmission problems, at least in that gear. Then I do the same thing, from neutral to drive.

"I've also got a road that serves as my 'drag strip.' After the car is warm, I bring it to dead still, kick the accelerator to the floor, and look out the window, behind the car. If there's smoke back there, she's burning oil. And valve jobs are expensive. An easier way to check for that, especially if it's dark, or on a busy road, is to simply rub your fingers inside the exhaust pipe. If there's oil there, you know the same thing. If I find anything mechanically wrong with the car, I make a little note on how much it'll cost to fix it. I make the same type of notes about the *outside* of the car, too. If the paint's dull, will it buff out or will it need a new coat? If there's body damage, can it be hammered out or will the piece need to be replaced? I also look very carefully for rust. Usually the best places to look are leading edges under the hood and around the doors, really any place where water or salt can accumulate. Then I add up all the money it'll take to put the car in shape and deduct that from a fair wholesale value of the car when it's ready to go on the front line."

Anyone who plans to trade an old car should be familiar with at least some of the factors Rax has been talking about. If you plan to trade for a new car, you'll need the information to prepare for the battle surrounding the value of your trade.

If you are a used-car buyer, you are a fool if you don't know the inside of a used car. In all likelihood, most will appear very healthy on the outside. But you must know about all the hidden things that are more important than looks. So use the two checklists—one for you and one for your mechanic—provided in the Appendix.

9

Negotiating the Sale: Specific Tactics for Specific Buyers

WHAT IS A "FAIR" DEAL?

One of the best general managers I know says and believes this: "If the customer is happy and we are happy, *that's* a fair deal." Unfortunately, there is a problem with his logic: the house will always *know* what it did to you—how much money it made. The vast majority of customers *think* they are satisfied. And the vast majority of those people would commit murder if they knew the truth. Be wary of your deal if you see the manager pouring your salesman champagne and hear shouts of glee through the walls.

It's a cruel world out there, you've worked hard for your money, and all those dealers are living in fancy houses, so let's define "fair" in the buyer's terms, for a change: the least dollar any particular seller will take for a specific car. That figure may include a $100-dollar profit or a $400-dollar profit; you won't know until you bargain a little, but always assume a seller will say "yes" only if the deal benefits him. This chapter on negotiating the sale assumes that fact. It will show you how to negotiate price *until* the seller says "yes." It's important to approach "fair" from this point of view rather than a fixed percentage of profit, because most dealers' definitions can also change because of factory incentives and contests. At times, a dealer will happily sell a specific car for less than $100 dollars' "profit," and within days, refuse to sell the same car for less than a $500-dollar profit. But, regardless of the final figure any seller will take for a specific car, remember he will be making more money than you think.

If you are the type of person who absolutely refuses to dicker over price, if you are determined to offer one firm price only, offer the seller a maximum profit of three percent of the list price. And I said maximum. If the dealer absolutely refuses to take your offer, raise it a percent if you like, but don't go above that figure. Go to another dealership. Car dealerships survive on churning their money, turning cars over quickly. Don't fall prey to sob stories, even in "bad" car years. Smart dealers make money in the worst years—they don't need your sympathy. Car people will attempt to convince you no business can live on very small profits, two or three percent or less, and they are right. But follow this logic for a moment: if you are looking at a $10,000-dollar car, don't think the dealer paid $10,000 for it, or even the invoice cost of $7700 dollars. The vast majority of new-car automobile dealerships floor-plan their cars; they do not own them outright. Most dealerships' new cars are owned by their financing institutions, such as Ford Motor Credit or GMAC. When the new car you want to buy was ordered, the car was shipped to the dealer on consignment. The dealer pays only interest, high interest, on the invoice price of the car. For instance, that $10,000-dollar car will probably cost the dealer $1800 dollars a year in interest, or $150 per month for each month the car sits on his lot.

If the car has been on his lot for three months, the dealer

has an investment of $450 in the car. If you pay the dealer three percent profit, and the dealer adds to that three percent the profits built in and hidden in the invoice, his gross will be over $800 dollars. Now subtract the $450-dollar interest and $70-dollar commission to the salesman. The dealer has a net cash increase of $280 dollars on an investment of $450 dollars. A fifty percent return on his investment—in three months. Can you do that with your money?

So, what's a fair deal? When you know the seller is taking the least amount of money, *that's* a fair deal.

HANDLING HIGH-PRESSURE TECHNIQUES

Dealerships, especially large ones, are masters at using high-pressure sales techniques. Salesmen wear you down, confuse you, curse you out behind your back, and generally don't give a damn about you once you've bought a car from them. Since most of us have felt many of these pressures before, it's hard to imagine a car transaction that is simple, clean, and to the point. But that's exactly what your next transaction will be, if you've read this book carefully. And if you decide to stick with these basic ground rules, right now before you enter the negotiation.

(1) Have all your facts on paper when you go to the dealership. If you know the true wholesale value of your car, the amount of your Available Cash, and your financing terms *before* you shop, salesmen won't be able to lead you on some mini-safari around their lot. If you plan to shop for a new or used car, you'll know the dollar range of cars that fits your budget.

(2) Don't fall for "if" questions. It may not sound like a high-pressure technique, but it's really the *highest* pressure

technique. "If" questions are simply designed to suspend logic. For instance, anyone would be inclined to say yes to "If I can sell you a $10,000-dollar car for $5000 dollars, will you buy it?" Of course you would. But logic dictates the reality. No dealership can do that. When salesmen use the "if" approach, *take control of the conversation* and don't commit. Simply smile and say, "I don't know."

(3) Insist on straight answers. Obfuscation is the name of the car game. If you ask the wholesale value of your trade, don't accept some mumbled answer about "allowance." Many salesmen will tell you cars "just don't have one value. The value of your trade will be determined by the car you want to purchase." Say good-bye to people like this and leave.

(4) Don't be "worked." If your salesman needs reinforcements, if he insists upon having his "team captain" or sales manager talk to you, tell the man in no uncertain terms you would prefer to deal with him alone or not at all.

(5) Do things in your sequence, not theirs. In order to understand a car transaction, you will have to control the order in which information is gathered. Many salesmen will tell you, "Oh, no, before we have your car appraised, we always fill out the buyer's order." Say no. Follow the steps outlined in Stalking and the Kill, page 278. If someone insists on changing your order, thank them and say good-bye.

If you follow these steps, *you* will be in control, not the salesman. You will probably find that most salesmen and dealerships won't like your approach, but they will be nice to you. Remember: any dealership would rather sell you a car on your terms than miss a sale. It's the most important pressure you can bring to bear.

YOUR HOUR UPON THE STAGE:
THE IMPORTANCE OF PLAY-ACTING

Have you ever met someone you really didn't like at a party, but managed passably to be nice to that person? Or, in your own particular job, have you ever said the "right" thing, rather than expressed the thought really on your mind? If you have, you'll have no problem dealing in the car world, for dealerships are the world's greatest arena for amateur actors. Salesmen do it every day—like Joe Girard, "the world's number-one car salesman," as he's fond of claiming in his book. Girard sells more cars than most dealerships and proudly proclaimed in a *Newsweek* article that he would "do anything to make a sale. I'll kiss the baby, hug the wife. It's nothing but an act." Customers do it every day, too. Even the most intimidated Caspar Milquetoast in the world usually forgets to tell his salesman little things that might adversely affect the value of his trade-in.

Rather than condemn the process, however, why not accept it for what it is? Car negotiations are simply polite tugs-of-war. One side is fighting mightily to make lots of money. The other side is trying to conserve money. And neither side has much sympathy with the other's plight.

STALKING AND THE KILL:
THE NEGOTIATION

When you were in school, did you ever fudge a little on exams? Perhaps read the "Cliff Notes" version of some novel rather than the real thing? Or were you the type who memorized answers rather than understood concepts?

Well, you may have graduated with honors using those tactics in school, but you can't cheat on the final exam in this game. Unless you've done your homework thoroughly you'll stumble, fumble, generally make an idiot of yourself, and lose money in the process—no fun at all. But:

(1) If you've shopped your car,

(2) If you've shopped your financing rates,

(3) If you're comfortable developing Loan Cash and Available Cash figures, and

(4) If you are prepared to develop cost figures—read on.

We're going to walk through, step-by-step, each buying situation. Pick the one that fits your particular need and go directly to that section. The Appendix also contains these same steps in much abbreviated form. You may want to refer to them once you are comfortable with the entire buying process. *After you've read your section, turn next to the section on Warranties: New and Used, page 312.*

If you are planning to finance your next car, review these terms before going to your section:

1. *Loan Cash*

   The lump sum of cash your payment will buy. For instance, 36 payments at $172 at 8 percent add-on will buy you $5000 in Loan Cash.

2. *Equity*

   The wholesale value of your car minus your payoff. For example, if the wholesale value is $5000 and your payoff is $3500, your equity is $1500.

3. *Available Cash*

   Your Loan Cash and equity (or cash down payment) added together. This figure tells you how much car you can buy.

4. *Difference*

   The final selling price of their car minus the wholesale value of your car.

If You Are Financing, Buying a New Car, and Trading the Old

Let's walk through a typical transaction. We'll say that you've shopped your present car, arriving at a value of $5000. Its payoff is $3500. We'll assume eight percent add-on was your best financing rate and that you have decided to finance for three years. You want to pay $172 per month.

(1) Compute your Available Cash (Loan Cash plus equity). For shopping purposes, your Available Cash is the important figure. It tells you the maximum amount of car you can buy, including tax, tag, title, and all other charges. By using this figure while shopping, you won't have to be concerned with the effect of your trade, since its real value is *already included in your Available Cash figure*. Our figure is $6500.

(2) Go to two different car stores and look for specific cars that interest you. Find at least two cars at each store and ask your salesman for a demonstration ride. Don't discuss price. Don't be "if-ed" to death; simply find two cars you like and drive them. When you've finished your demonstration ride, copy down all the information from the price

sticker on the window. Remember, don't pay any attention to the dealer's sticker. Copy information only from the manufacturer's sticker. Take down the name and price of everything, including freight. Ask your salesman to give you the stock number of the car. Write that down by the name of the dealership and your salesman. Ask him to give you the amount of any miscellaneous charges, such as title fees. Ask him how tax is computed. For instance, is tax paid on the total price of the new car or on the difference figure? Don't be talked into *anything* during this visit; simply thank your man and leave. Once you have visited two stores, go home and relax for a while.

(3) At home, write down the price information and stock number of each car on a clean sheet of paper and compute the cost of the car and all its options. We'll assume you've found a car that lists for $7300, and have figured a true cost for the car and options of $5800. When you've done this, total the following:

Cost of the car and options	$5800
Transportation charge	175
Title fees and miscellaneous charges	45
TOTAL COST	$6020
The maximum profit you will pay (for our example, we'll assume $350)	350
YOUR MAXIMUM OFFER WILL BE	$6370

(4) Now, check to see if you are over or under budget. Don't forget that tax will need to be added to your offer. But for now, simply check your Available Cash against your offer:

Your Available Cash	$6500
Your offer on the new car	6370
AMOUNT OVER OR UNDER BUDGET	$130 *under*

(5) Now compute your *difference* figure. Remember, the difference will be your method of checking their figures.

Your offer on the new car	$6370
Wholesale value of your car	5000
DIFFERENCE	$1370

Use these five steps for each one of the cars you have driven. And then put the following information in your pad. You will need it at the store.

A. Write down the location, stock number, and color of each car. By that, write down your offer on the car and your trading difference on the car.

B. Write down the wholesale value of your car. You'll only need to write this once, since the wholesale value won't change.

C. Write down your Available Cash figure once, too.

Dealing With the Store. You don't have any reason to be nervous now, for you have more information at your fingertips than your salesman. Go back to the store and see him. Make an appointment if you like. Let him show you the two cars again, and if both cars were in your price range, make an emotional decision on which car you really like the best. Enjoy! This is the only time your heart rate should affect your negotiations. Once you have decided on *the* particular car, head to the salesman's office. Be nice. Smile and laugh. But remember that *you* must control the order of the next few minutes. Do it like this:

(1) Tell the salesman to have your car appraised. Don't tell him your wholesale figure either, but review that figure in your mind. When the guy returns, speak before spoken to. Look him in the eye, and think positive thoughts.

(2) Ask your salesman for the appraisal on your car. Let him know you want their wholesale offer, *not* an allowance

figure. If the figure is lower than your wholesale value, tell him. But don't tell him the amount; give him room to come up as much as he will. If the figure is higher than your figure, smile. You are ahead of the game. If his offer never equals yours, tell him your figure. Tell him who gave you the figure. If necessary, remind your salesman that his used-car boys can sell your car to the same people you would sell it to. If he still won't accept your figure, go to your other dealership. If he finally agrees to your figure or offers you more, write his offer in your pad.

(3) Make your offer on the new car. The figure is on your pad. Don't be afraid for him to see your pad, either. Salesmen are invariably thrown off-guard by customers who actually know what they are doing. If you are smart, offer him *less* than your figure; give him room to dicker a little. But don't go over your maximum figure. Once the two of you have agreed on a figure, write it down in your pad. Put it by your original offer for that particular car.

(4) Stop and check your difference figure. Deduct *his* offer on your trade from the agreed price of the new car. If this difference figure is more than your difference figure, you are losing money. If the figure is lower than your figure, you are making money. If the figure is an acceptable one to you, go to the next step. If it is not acceptable, continue to negotiate or go to your other dealership.

(5) Tell him to write it up. Once the salesman has completely filled in the buyer's order, look at the difference figure on the order. If you don't see it, ask the salesman to point it out to you. That figure must agree with the one you have just computed.

Most buyer's orders are not designed to show cash offers on a new car and wholesale figures on used cars. Your salesman will probably indicate, for instance, that you are buying the new car at sticker price but receiving more than wholesale on your trade. That's okay *if* the difference figure is the same.

(6) If the difference figure is the same, sign the buyer's order, but do not give him a deposit. Tell him you will give him a check *when* the deal is approved by a manager. The salesman will probably insist on a deposit. Tell him it's your way or not at all. Remember: a deposit before you have an approved deal is their way of keeping you there while they work you.

(7) If the salesman returns with a signed order, give him a deposit. If he returns with his boss or insists himself your offer is too low, tell him again you will not be raised. If he keeps insisting, raise your offer $50 dollars, if you wish. But don't be raised more than once. If you are determined not to be raised at all, say good-bye. Head to your other dealership.

(8) If you are not financing the car at the dealership, arrange the best time for you to pick it up. If you are financing the car at the dealership, be prepared to talk with their finance manager. Remember, you already know the number of months and the interest rate. You have already made a decision on insurance. Don't let the finance manager change your terms. Before you leave his office, confirm the amount to be financed, and take that figure home with you. If the amount to be financed is not exactly the same as your projected Loan Cash, compute the payment when you get home and take that figure with you when you pick up the car. It should be within pennies of his payment.

If You Are Financing, and Buying a New Car Without Trading

You're going to have an easy time of it.

(1) Determine your Loan Cash. Let's assume you have

shopped financing sources and found eight percent add-on interest money. You plan to pay $172 dollars a month for 36 months. Your loan cash would be $5000.

(2) Determine how much money you intend to pay down. If you're smart, you'll pay at least twenty-five percent down—in this instance, $1250. If you don't plan to pay twenty-five percent down, you will have to pay a sum equal to or larger than the total of the profit on the new car, your taxes, and other expenses.

(3) Now, total your Loan Cash and down payment. That figure is your Available Cash, how much car you can buy, including tax, tag, and any other charges. In our example, Available Cash is $6250.

(4) Go to two different car stores and look for specific cars that interest you. Find at least two cars at each store, and ask your salesman for a demonstration ride. Don't discuss price. Don't be "if-ed" to death; simply find two cars you like and drive them. When you've finished your demonstration ride, copy down the item and price of everything on the window sticker. Remember, don't pay attention to the dealer's sticker. Ask your salesman to give you the stock number of the car. Write that down by the name of the dealership and your salesman. Ask the salesman to give you any miscellaneous charges, such as title fees. Also ask him how tax is computed. Is it figured on the *list* price of the new car, or the discounted price? Don't be talked into anything during this visit; simply thank your man and leave. Go home and relax for a while.

(5) Once you are home, write down the price information and stock number from each car on a clean sheet of paper. Compute the cost of the cars and all their options. We'll assume you've found a car that lists for $7300 dollars, and have figured a true cost for the car and options of $5800 dollars. When you've done this, add the following:

Cost of the car and options	$5800
Transportation charge	175
Title fees and other miscellaneous charges	45
TOTAL COST	$6020
The maximum profit you will pay (for our example, we'll assume $350)	350
YOUR MAXIMUM OFFER WILL BE	$6370

(6) Now, check to see if you are over or under budget.

Your Available Cash is	$6250
Your offer on the new car is	6370
AMOUNT OVER OR UNDER BUDGET	120 *over*

You are over budget. *Plus,* you've still got to pay tax and other fees. If your state charges four percent sales tax on the total selling price, you will owe tax of $254. You are over budget a total of $454. Can you afford that? Can you pay your overbudget figure with your own cash? If not, your payments will go up dramatically. If you refigured your payments, they would be $186 rather than $172.

Let's assume that you don't want to spend that much. Remember that this car *listed* for $7300. You'll need to find a car that lists for about $400 less, if you plan to stay in budget. Let's say that you have found a car listing for $5850 instead. You have computed the cost to be $5400. If you use step five to refigure your offer and step six to check your budget, you'll find you are now $280 under budget. Nice! You are under budget enough to pay your taxes and perhaps take a trip in your new wheels, to boot. Put $5970, the new offer, in your pad.

Dealing With the Store. You really don't have any reason to be nervous, now. You know more than your salesman. So, call up the store that's home to your favorite cars, and make an appointment to see your salesman. Go see him.

(1) Look at your favorite car again. If you would like, don't feel shy about asking to drive it. Decide if it's the car you really want to own.

(2) Tell your salesman you would like to go to his office and talk price. Don't wait for him to drag you to his office, take the initiative. Remember, you must be in control.

(3) Pull out your pad once you are in his office. He won't like your pad, but that's okay. The more uncomfortable he is, the more in control you are. Tell your salesman that you are prepared to make an offer on the car. Tell him it is a *firm* offer. Tell him your offer doesn't leave any money on the table. Use that phrase, too.

(4) Make your offer and insist that he take it to his manager. Let him write it up, but *don't* give him a deposit. Even if he insists, don't do it. Tell him there are other dealerships down the road who don't require a deposit until both parties have agreed on a figure.

(5) Before signing, compare the total sale price to your Available Cash. For instance, using our last example:

Your Available Cash	$6250
Your offer	5970
Sales tax (assuming 4 percent)	238
Other miscellaneous charges	50
AMOUNT OVER OR UNDER BUDGET	$8 over

You are overbudget $8 dollars. Not bad at all.

(6) If the salesman returns with a signed buyer's order, give him a deposit. If he returns with his boss or insists himself your offer is too low, insist on your offer. If your salesman will actually let you leave on your figure, consider budging a little. But don't budge much. If you make a counteroffer, make only *one*. Tell the salesman it is your

final offer. Do not let them "work" you. If your final offer is not accepted, thank the man and say good-bye. Head to your other dealership. If your final offer is accepted, and you're within budget, pat yourself on the back. You have survived.

(7) If you are not financing the car at the dealership, arrange the best time for you to pick it up. If you are financing the car at the dealership, be prepared to talk with their finance manager. Remember, you already know the number of months and the interest rate. You have already made a decision on insurance. Don't let the finance manager change your terms. Before you leave his office, confirm the amount to be financed and take that figure home with you. If the amount to be financed is not exactly the same as your projected Loan Cash, compute the payment when you get home and take that figure with you when you pick up the car. It should be within pennies of his payment.

If You Are Financing, Buying a Used Car, and Trading the Old

Before reading any further, tell me the truth: did you really work through the chapter on used cars, or did you just read the headings? If you cheated, go back and read the chapter carefully—you're a candidate for the slaughterhouse. If you did it right the first time, read on.

Remember that there is no set value on any used car, no accurate book to tell you what a particular car is worth. Remember, also, that you must be prepared to dicker quite a lot. Remember, finally, that "asking price" always includes a very healthy profit: for dickering purposes, always assume a nice used car has a mark-up of $600 to $1000 dollars *regardless* of its wholesale value or asking price.

Now, let's walk through a typical transaction. We will assume you've shopped your car and found that it's worth $1500 wholesale. You owe $500 on the car. We'll also assume your best financing rate is eight percent add-on and you plan to pay no more than $150 per month for 24 months.

(1) Compute your Available Cash (Loan Cash plus equity). For shopping purposes, your Available Cash is the important figure. It tells you the maximum amount of car you can buy, including tax, tag, title, and all other charges. By using this figure while shopping, you won't have to be concerned with the effect of your trade, since its real value is *already included in your Available Cash figure*. In our example, your Available Cash is $4100.

(2) Decide on three or four sources, using the guides in the chapter on buying a used car. Include at least one new-car dealership.

(3) Visit the lots and look for cars with *asking* prices a few hundred dollars higher than your Available Cash figure. Do *not* tell the salesman you are trading. Used-car operations raise the prices of their cars if they feel you are going to trade. Do not tell them your Available Cash figure. As you find cars with asking prices close to your figure, take time to drive them. Take with you the checklist from the Appendix, and look for obvious problems with the car. If you still like the car after a test drive, write down the stock number and a description of the car. Write down the asking price, the name of the person you are dealing with, the miles of the car, and any options that may add to loan value, such as a vinyl roof, air-conditioning, power windows, or cruise control. Then thank your salesman and go home.

(4) Call a local bank or credit union and ask for a loan

officer. Tell the officer the year and model of the car. Then ask him the minimum interest rate and the maximum number of months the car can be financed. Write that information down and keep it in your pad. You'll want to compare it to the rate you need in determining your Loan Cash. Now, accurately describe the car to him. Give him the options and mileage, and then ask for the loan value of that particular car. Put that figure in your pad, too.

(5) Compare the seller's asking price to the loan value of the car. We'll assume you've found a car with an asking price of $4600 and a loan value of $3800. The spread is their *probable profit*—in this instance, $800.

(6) Compute your "best probable" difference figure. Subtract the wholesale value of your car from the loan value of the seller's car.

The loan value of the seller's car	$3800
The wholesale value of your car	−1500
EQUALS YOUR BEST PROBABLE DIFFERENCE	$2300

When we begin to negotiate, we will be trying to be close to this difference figure or below it. Put the figure in your pad; it's your most important figure.

(7) Go back to the lot and tell your salesman you have decided to trade your car. Though it may not do any good, tell him you want the actual wholesale value of your car, *not* an allowance figure. He'll probably be surprised you know the difference. And then tell him you would like to take his car to your mechanic. Leave your car with him for ransom. If your salesman won't agree to this, don't buy the car. If he agrees, take a clean copy of the Mechanic's Checklist in the Appendix and drive to your mechanic's shop. Don't forget to add to the checklist any specific problems you have noted in your pad. Before leaving the shop, ask for an estimate to repair the car to your satisfaction.

Put that figure in your pad, and take a coffee break.

(8) Your Available Cash is $4100. But you may now have a repair bill, if you buy the car. Let's assume the repairs were estimated to cost $300. To stay in budget, you will need to *subtract* the estimate from your Available Cash ($4100 minus $300). Your new Available Cash figure is $3800. Make that adjustment and head back to the lot.

(9) Don't let your salesman do the figuring when you return, but ask him directly how much he is giving you for your car. Subtract that from his "asking price" and determine his difference figure. We'll assume he actually appraised your car for $1500.

Asking price	$4600
His figure on your car	−1500
HIS DIFFERENCE FIGURE	$3100

(10) Now, compare his difference figure to your "best probable" difference figure. The balance will be how much more money he wants for the car than you are planning to spend. That figure is also his profit, most likely.

His difference figure	$3100
Your "best probable" difference figure	−2300
HIS PROBABLE PROFIT	$800

(11) If by some act of God, his difference figure is the same as yours, don't automatically agree to buy the car. Every salesman's first offer, regardless how low it is, has a cushion in it. Offer the man $200 or $300 dollars less. You should be smiling on the inside, too.

If his figure is close to your figure, only $200 or $300 dollars above, tell him that the figure is $400 or $600 dollars away. Always compromise and split the difference on any offer.

(12) At some point in the discussion, your salesman is not going to budge. When he reaches that point, check these things:

A. His probable profit. Subtract your difference figure from his. We'll assume he agreed to $2650.

His final difference figure	$2650
Your "best probable" difference	2300
HIS PROBABLE PROFIT	$350

For a nice used car, that's a very reasonable profit.

B. Can you afford it? Add these items together and determine how much you will owe the seller.

His final difference figure	$2650
The payoff on your old car	500
Tax (we'll assume 4 percent, use your own state's rate)	106
YOU WILL OWE THE SELLER	$3456

C. What will be your total expenditure? Subtract what you will owe the seller and the repair estimate from your Available Cash:

Your Available Cash	$3800
What you owe the seller	—3456
The repair estimate	— 300
AMOUNT OVER OR UNDER BUDGET	$44 *under*

You're in good shape.

(13) If you've determined this is the actual car you want to buy, discuss warranties. Be sure you are familiar with the section on warranties before opening your mouth, or you'll probably find your foot resting on your molars.

(14) If the salesman's final offer fits your budget and the warranty is satisfactory, have him write it up. Tell him

you'll take the car at that figure. Once the salesman has completely filled out the buyer's order, look at the difference figure. If you don't see it, ask the salesman to point it out to you. That figure must agree with your final difference figure. Make sure the warranty is written. If the figure is the same, sign the buyer's order, but do not give him a deposit. Tell him you will give him a check when the deal is approved by a manager. The salesman will probably insist on a deposit. Tell him it's your way or no way at all. Remember, a deposit before you have an approved deal is their way of keeping you there while they work you. If the salesman returns with his boss or insists himself your offer is too low, tell him you will not be raised. If he insists, and if you really like the car, raise your offer $50 dollars, if you wish. But don't be raised more than once. If you are determined not to be raised, say good-bye.

(15) If you are not financing with the seller, arrange the best time to pick it up. If you are financing with the seller, be prepared to be worked again. Remember, you already know the number of months and the interest rate. You have already made a decision on insurance. Don't be talked into changing your mind. Before leaving, confirm the amount to be financed, and take that figure home with you. If the amount to be financed is not exactly the same as your projected Loan Cash, recompute the payment when you get home and take that figure with you when you pick up the car. It should be within pennies of his payment.

If You Are Financing, and Buying a Used Car Without Trading

Before reading any further, tell me the truth: did you really work through the chapter on used cars, or did you just read the headings? If you cheated, go back and read the chapter carefully. You're a candidate for the slaughterhouse. If you did it right the first time, read on.

(1) Determine your Loan Cash. Let's assume you have shopped financing sources and found eight percent add-on interest money. You plan to pay $150 per month for 24 months. Your Loan Cash would be $3100.

(2) Determine your down payment. If possible, plan to pay down thirty percent of your Loan Cash figure. If you can't afford that much cash from your pocket, you will need to pay down a sum equal to the total of the profit on the car, tax, and other charges. In our example, we'll assume you will pay a $300 profit. We'll also assume that your Loan Cash figure is also the loan value of the car. For shopping purposes, you can assume the same thing: compute your tax on your Loan Cash figure. Then allow $100 for other miscellaneous charges. In this instance, your down payment will need to be $524, figuring four percent tax on your Loan Cash.

(3) Now, determine your Available Cash, the total of your down payment and Loan Cash. This figure will be the total amount of money you can spend, including tax, tag, and all other expenses. In our example, your Available Cash is $3624.

(4) Decide on three or four car sources, using the guides in the chapter on buying a used car. Include at least one new-car dealership.

(5) Visit those lots. Look for cars with asking prices $400 or $500 above your Available Cash figure. Don't tell the salesman your price range. Virtually all used-car salesmen have a very bad habit of raising asking prices up to your figure. When the salesman asks you, "Well, what were you thinking about spending?" just tell him, "Well, it depends on the car," and smile. Let's assume you have found a car

with an asking price of $4200. Take it for a drive. Use the checklist in the Appendix, and look for obvious problems with the car. If you still like it after your test drive, write down the stock number and description of the car, the mileage, and the name of the person you are dealing with. Write down any options that may add to loan value, such as automatic transmission, air-conditioning, vinyl roof, or power windows. And then thank your salesman, saying good-bye in the process.

(6) Call a local bank or credit union and ask for a loan officer. Tell the officer the year and model of the car. Then ask him the minimum interest rate and maximum number of months the car can be financed. Write that information down and keep it in your pad. You'll want to compare it to the rate you used in determining your Loan Cash. Now, accurately describe the car to him. Give him the options and mileage, and then ask for the loan value of that particular car. Put the figure in your pad, too.

(7) Now, compare the seller's asking price to the loan value of the car. We'll assume loan value was $3200. The spread is their probable profit.

Asking price	$4200
Loan value	3200
PROBABLE PROFIT	$1000

You want to pay as little of that profit as possible. You want to buy the car for a figure as close to loan value as possible.

(8) Determine your offer. Since you would ideally like to buy the car for loan value or less, decide the *maximum* amount you are willing to pay over loan value and add the two figures. In our example, your maximum profit will be $300, loan value is $3200, and your maximum offer will be $3500. Remember that tax and other charges must be added to that figure.

(9) Now, head back to the lot and tell your salesman you would like to take his car to your mechanic. Leave whatever car you are driving as ransom. If your salesman won't agree to this, don't buy the car. If he agrees, take a clean copy of the Mechanic's Checklist and drive to your mechanic's shop. Don't forget to add to his list any specific problems you have noted in your pad. Before leaving, ask your mechanic for an estimate to repair the car to your satisfaction. Put that figure in your pad and take a coffee break.

(10) Your Available Cash is $3624. But you may now have a repair bill, if you buy the car. To stay in budget, you will need to *subtract* the estimate from your Available Cash. Let's assume your repair bill was $300. Your new Available Cash figure is $3324. Make that adjustment and head back to the lot.

(11) Lead the salesman to his office. Don't be led, take the initiative. Offer the man *less* than loan value. When the man counteroffers, don't accept his figure. Compromise; offer to split the difference with him.

(12) At some point in the discussion, your salesman is not going to budge. When he reaches that point, compare his final offer to your Available Cash. Let's assume his final offer is $3300.

Your Available Cash	$3324
His final offer	3300
AMOUNT OVER OR UNDER BUDGET	$24 *under*

You're in pretty good shape. Don't forget that tax will need to be added to that figure. Can you afford the car?

Now, compare his final offer to the loan value of the car. The answer, in this instance $100, is his probable profit. Is that figure satisfactory? It should be, Jesse James.

(13) If you've determined this is the actual car you want to buy, discuss warranties. Be sure you are familiar with

the section on warranties before opening your mouth, or you'll probably find your foot resting on your molars.

(14) If the salesman's final offer fits your budget and the warranty is satisfactory, have him write it up. Tell him you'll take the car at that figure. Once the salesman has completely filled out the buyer's order, check the figures. Make sure the warranty is written. Sign the buyer's order, but do not give him a deposit. Tell him it's your way or not at all. Remember, a deposit before you have an approved deal is their way of keeping you there while they work you. If the salesman returns with his boss or insists himself your offer is too low, tell him you will not be raised. If he still insists, and if you really like the car, raise your offer $50 dollars, if you wish. But don't be raised more than once. If you are determined not to be raised, say good-bye.

(15) If you are not financing with the seller, arrange the best time to pick it up. If you are financing with the seller, be prepared to be worked again. Remember, you already know the number of months and the interest rate. You have already made a decision on insurance. Don't be talked into changing your mind. Before leaving, confirm the amount to be financed and take that figure home with you. If the amount to be financed is not exactly the same as your projected Loan Cash, recompute the payment when you get home and take that figure with you when you pick up the car. It should be within pennies of his payment.

If You Are Paying Cash, Buying a New Car, and Trading the Old

Let's walk through a typical transaction. We'll say that you've shopped your present car, arriving at a value of $7000.

(1) Compute your Available Cash (your cash plus the

value of your trade). We'll assume you're flush this year and have allocated $8000 dollars in cash. Your Available Cash is $15,000. For shopping purposes, that figure is the important one. It tells you the maximum amount of car you can buy, including tax, tag, title, and all other charges. By using this figure while shopping, you won't have to be concerned with the effect of your trade, since its value is included in your Available Cash.

(2) Go to two different car stores and look for specific cars that interest you. Find at least two cars at each store, and ask your salesman for a demonstration ride. Don't discuss price. Don't be "if-ed" to death; simply find two cars you like and drive them. When you've finished your demonstration ride, copy down all the information from the price sticker on the window. Remember, don't pay any attention to the dealer's sticker. Take down the name and price of everything, including freight, and ask your salesman to give you the stock number of the car. Write that down by the name of the dealership and your salesman. Ask him to give you the amount of any miscellaneous charges, such as title fees. Ask him how tax is computed. For instance, is tax paid on the total price of the new car or on the difference figure? Don't be talked into anything during this visit; simply thank your man and leave. Once you have visited two stores, go home and relax for a while.

(3) At home, write down the price information and stock number of each car on separate sheets of paper and compute the cost of each car and their options. We'll assume one car lists for $17,500, and costs $14,100. When you have figured the cost, total the following:

Cost of the car and options	$14,100
Transportation charge	375
Title fees and miscellaneous charges	50
TOTAL COST	$14,525

The maximum profit you will pay (in our example, we'll assume $500— you make the real decision)	$500
YOUR MAXIMUM OFFER WILL BE	$15,025

(4) Now, check to see if you are over or under budget. Don't forget that tax will need to be added later. But for now, simply check your Available Cash against your offer:

Your Available Cash	$15,000
Your offer	15,025
AMOUNT OVER OR UNDER BUDGET	$25 *over*

After taxes, you're going to be hundreds over budget. Can you afford that? Since you are the flush type, we'll assume you don't worry about things like taxes and will happily pay it.

(5) Now compute your *difference* figure. Remember, the difference will be your method of checking their figures.

Your offer on the new car	$15,025
Wholesale value of your car	− 7,000
DIFFERENCE	$8,025

Use these five steps for each one of the cars you have driven. And then put the following information in your pad. You will need it at the store.

A. Write down the location, stock number, and color of each car. By that, write down your offer on the car and your trading difference figure.
B. Write down the wholesale value of your car. You'll only need to write this once, since the wholesale value won't change.
C. Write down your Available Cash figure once, too.

Dealing With the Store. You don't have any reason to be nervous now, for you have more information at your fingertips than your salesman. Go back to the store and see him. Make an appointment if you like. Let him show you the two cars again, and if both cars were in your price range, make an emotional decision on which car you really like the best. Enjoy! This is the only time your heart rate should affect your negotiations. Once you have decided on *the* particular car, head to the salesman's office. Be nice. Smile and laugh. But remember that *you* must control the order of the next few minutes. Do it like this:

(1) Tell the salesman to have your car appraised. Don't tell him your wholesale figure, either, but review that figure in your mind. When the guy returns, speak before spoken to. Look him in the eye, and think positive thoughts.

(2) Ask your salesman for the appraisal on your car. Let him know you want their wholesale offer, *not* an allowance figure. If the figure is lower than your wholesale value, tell him. But don't tell him the amount; give him room to come up as much as he will. If the figure is higher than yours, smile. You are ahead of the game. If his offer never equals yours, tell him your figure. If necessary, remind your salesman that his used-car boys can sell your car to the same people you would sell it to. If he still won't accept your figure, go to your other dealership. If he finally agrees to your figure or offers you more, write his offer in your pad.

(3) Make your offer on the new car. The figure is on your pad. Don't be afraid for him to see your pad, either. Salesmen are invariably thrown off guard by customers who actually know what they are doing. If you are smart, offer him *less* than your actual figure; give him room to dicker a little. But don't go over your maximum figure. Once the two of you have agreed on a figure, write it down in your pad. Put it by your original offer for that particular car.

(4) Stop and check your difference figure. Deduct *his* of-

fer on your trade from the agreed price of the new car. If this difference figure is more than your difference figure, you are losing money. If the figure is lower than your figure, you are making money. If the figure is an acceptable one to you, go to the next step. If it is not acceptable, continue to negotiate or go to your other dealership.

(5) Tell him to write it up. Once the salesman has completely filled in the buyer's order, look at the difference figure on the order. If you don't see it, ask the salesman to point it out to you. That figure must agree with the one you have just computed.

Most buyer's orders are not designed to show cash offers on a new car and wholesale figures on trades. Your salesman will probably indicate, for instance, that you are buying the new car at sticker price but receiving more than wholesale on your trade. That's okay *if* the difference figure is the same.

(6) If the difference figure is the same, sign the buyer's order, but do not give him a deposit. Tell him you will give him a check *when* the deal is approved by a manager. The salesman will probably insist on a deposit. Tell him it's your way or not at all. Remember: a deposit before you have an approved deal is their way of keeping you there while they work you.

(7) If the salesman returns with a signed order, give him a deposit. If he returns with his boss or insists himself your offer is too low, tell him again you will not be raised. If he keeps insisting, raise your offer $50 dollars, if you wish. But don't be raised more than once. If you are determined not to be raised at all, say good-bye. Head to your other dealership.

If You Are Paying Cash,
and Buying a New Car Without Trading

You're going to have a very easy time of it.

(1) Decide just how much money you plan to spend on a car. Let's say you would like to spend $6250. That figure, obviously, is your Available Cash.

(2) Go to two different car stores and look for specific cars that interest you. Find at least two cars at each store, and ask your salesman for a demonstration ride. Don't discuss price. Don't be "if-ed" to death; simply find two cars you like and drive them. When you've finished your demonstration ride, copy down the items and prices of everything on the window sticker. Remember, don't pay attention to the dealer's sticker. Ask your salesman to give you the stock number of the car. Write that down by the name of the dealership and your salesman. Ask the salesman to give you any miscellaneous charges, such as title fees. Also ask him how tax is computed. Is it figured on the *list* price of the new car or the discounted price? Don't be talked into anything during this visit; simply thank your man and leave. Go home and relax for a while.

(3) Once you are home, write down the price information and stock number from each car on a clean sheet of paper. Compute the cost of the cars and all their options. We'll assume you've found a car that lists for $7300 dollars and have figured a true cost for the car and options of $5800 dollars. When you've done this, add the following:

Cost of the car and options	$5800
Transportation charge	175
Title fees and other miscellaneous charges	45
TOTAL COST	$6020

The maximum profit you will pay (in our example, we assume $350— you decide the real profit)	$350
YOUR MAXIMUM OFFER WILL BE	$6370

4. Now, check to see if you are over or under budget.

Your Available Cash is	$6250
Your offer on the new car is	6370
AMOUNT OVER OR UNDER BUDGET	$150 *over*

You are overbudget. *Plus*, you've still got to pay tax and other fees. If your state charges four percent sales tax on the total selling price, you will owe tax of $254 dollars. You are over budget a total of $454 dollars. Can you afford that?

Let's assume that you don't want to spend that much. Remember that this car listed for $7300 dollars. You'll need to find a car which lists for about $400 dollars less, if you plan to stay in budget. Let's say that you have found a car listing for $6850 dollars instead. You have computed the cost to be $5400 dollars. If you use step three to refigure your offer and step four to check your budget, you'll find you are now $280 dollars under budget. Nice! You are under budget enough to pay your taxes and perhaps take a trip in your new wheels, to boot. Put $5970 dollars, the new offer, in your pad.

Dealing With the Store. You really don't have any reason to be nervous, now. You know more than your salesman. So, call up the store that's home to your favorite cars and make an appointment to see your salesman. Go see him.

(1) Look at your favorite car again. If you would like,

don't feel shy about asking to drive it. Decide if it's the car you really want to own.

(2) Tell your salesman you would like to go to his office and talk price. Don't wait for him to drag you to his office, take the initiative. Remember, you must be in control.

(3) Pull out your pad once you are in his office. He won't like your pad, but that's okay. The more uncomfortable he is, the more in control you are. Tell your salesman that you are prepared to make him an offer on the car. Tell him it is a *firm* offer. Tell him your offer leaves no money on the table. Use that phrase, too.

(4) Make your offer and insist that he take it to his manager. Let him write it up, but *don't* give him a deposit. Even if he insists, don't do it. Tell him there are other dealerships down the road who don't require a deposit until both parties have agreed on a figure.

(5) Before signing, compare the total sales price to your Available Cash. For instance, if your Available Cash were $6500 and your final offer on this car were $6050, the comparison would look like this:

Your Available Cash	$6500
Your final offer	−6050
Sales tax (assuming 4 percent)	− 242
Other miscellaneous charges	− 50
AMOUNT OVER OR UNDER BUDGET	$242 *under*

You are in good shape. Let the man take the buyer's order to his boss.

(6) If the salesman returns with a signed buyer's order, give him a deposit. If he returns with his boss or insists himself your offer is too low, insist on your offer. If your salesman will actually let you leave on your figure, consider budging a little. But don't budge much. If you make a counteroffer, make only *one*. Tell the salesman it is your final offer. Do not let them "work" you. If your final offer is

accepted, and you're within budget, pat yourself on the back. You have survived.

If You Are Paying Cash, Buying a Used Car, and Trading the Old

Before reading any further, tell me the truth: did you really work through the chapter on used cars, or did you just read the headings? If you cheated, go back and read the chapter carefully—you're a candidate for the slaughter-house. If you did it right the first time, read on.

Remember that there is no set value on any used car, no accurate book to tell you what a particular car is worth. Remember, also, that you must be prepared to dicker quite a lot. Remember, finally, that "asking price" always includes a very healthy profit: for dickering purposes, always assume a nice used car has a mark-up of $600 to $1000 dollars *regardless* of its wholesale value or asking price.

Not let's walk through a typical transaction. We will assume you've shopped your car and found that it's worth $1500 wholesale. You have decided to spend $3100 in cash.

(1) Compute your Available Cash (your cash plus the value of your trade). For shopping purposes, your Available Cash is the important figure. It tells you the maximum amount of car you can buy, including, tax, tag, title, and all other charges. By using this figure while shopping, you won't have to be concerned with the effect of your trade, since its real value is included in the figure. In our example, your Available Cash is $4600.

(2) Decide on three or four sources, using the guides in the chapter on buying a used car. Include at least one new-car dealership.

(3) Visit the lots and look for cars with *asking* prices a

few hundred dollars higher than your Available Cash figure. Do *not* tell the salesman you are trading. Used-car operations raise the prices of their cars if they feel you are going to trade. Do not tell them your Available Cash figure. As you find cars with asking prices close to your figure, take time to drive them. Take with you the checklist from the Appendix, and look for obvious problems with the car. If you still like the car after a test drive, write down the stock number and a description of the car. Write down the asking price, the name of the person you are dealing with, the miles of the car, and any options that may add to loan value, such as a vinyl roof, air-conditioning, power windows, or cruise control. Then thank your salesman and go home.

(4) Call a local bank or credit union, and ask for a loan officer. Tell the officer the year and model of the car. Accurately describe the car to him. Give him the options and mileage, and then ask for the loan value of that particular car. Put the figure in your pad.

(5) Compare the seller's asking price to the loan price of the car. We'll assume you've found a car with an asking price of $4800 and a loan value of $3800. The spread is their *probable profit*—in this instance, $1000.

(6) Compute your "best probable" difference figure. Subtract the wholesale value of your car from the loan value of the seller's car.

The loan value of the seller's car	$3800
The wholesale value of your car	−1500
EQUALS YOUR BEST PROBABLE DIFFERENCE	$2300

When we begin to negotiate, we will be trying to be close to this difference figure or below it. Put the figure in your pad; it's your most important figure.

(7) Go back to the lot, and tell your salesman you have

decided to trade your car. Though it may not do any good, tell him you want the actual wholesale value of your car, *not* an allowance figure. He'll probably be surprised you know the difference. And then tell him you would like to take his car to your mechanic. Leave your car with him for ransom. If your salesman won't agree to this, don't buy the car. If he agrees, take a clean copy of the Mechanic's Checklist in the Appendix and drive to your mechanic's shop. Don't forget to add to the checklist any specific problems you have noted in your pad. Before leaving the shop, ask for an estimate to repair the car to your satisfaction. Put that figure in your pad, and take a coffee break.

(8) Your Available Cash is $4600. But you may now have a repair bill, if you buy the car. Let's assume the repairs were estimated to cost $300. To stay in budget, you will need to *subtract* the estimate from your Available Cash ($4600 minus $300). Your new Available Cash figure is $4300. Make that adjustment and head back to the lot.

(9) Don't let the salesman do the figuring when you return, but ask him directly how much he is giving you for your car. Subtract that from his "asking price," and determine his difference figure. We'll assume he actually appraised your car for $1500.

Asking price	$4800
His figure on your car	−1500
HIS DIFFERENCE FIGURE	$3300

(10) Now, compare his figure to your "best probable" difference figure. The balance will be how much more money he wants for the car than you are planning to spend. That figure is also his profit, most likely.

His difference figure	$3300
Your "best probable" difference figure	−2300
HIS PROBABLE PROFIT	$1000

(11) If by some act of God his difference figure is the same as yours, don't automatically agree to buy the car. Every salesman's first offer, regardless how low it is, has a cushion in it. Offer the man $200 or $300 dollars less. You should be smiling on the inside, too.

If his figure is close to your figure, only $200 or $300 dollars above, tell him that the figure is $400 or $600 dollars away. Always compromise, split the difference on any offer.

(12) At some point in the discussion, your salesman is not going to budge. When he reaches that point, check these things:

A. His probable profit. Subtract your difference figure from his. We'll assume he agreed to $2850.

His final difference figure	$2850
Your "best probable" difference	−2300
HIS PROBABLE PROFIT	$550

For a nice used car, that's a very reasonable profit.

B. Can you afford it? Add these items together and determine how much you will owe the seller.

His final difference figure	$2850
Tax (we'll assume four percent, use your own state's rate)	114
Miscellaneous charges	50
YOU WILL OWE THE SELLER	$3014

C. What will your total expenditure be? Subtract what you owe the seller and the repair estimate from your Available Cash:

Your Available Cash	$4300
What you owe the seller	−3014
The repair estimate	− 300
AMOUNT OVER OR UNDER BUDGET	$986 *under*

If you can bargain that well, you should go into the car business.

(13) If you've determined this is the actual car you want to buy, discuss warranties. Be sure you are familiar with the section on warranties before opening your mouth, or you'll probably find your foot resting on your molars.

(14) If the salesman's final offer fits your budget and the warranty is satisfactory, have him write it up. Tell him you'll take the car at that figure. Once the salesman has completely filled out the buyer's order, look at the difference figure. If you don't see it, ask the salesman to point it out to you. That figure must agree with your final difference figure. Make sure the warranty is written. If the figure is the same, sign the buyer's order, but do not give him a deposit. Tell him you will give him a check when the deal is approved by a manager. The salesman will probably insist on a deposit. Tell him it's your way or no way at all. Remember, a deposit before you have an approved deal is their way of keeping you there while they work you. If the salesman returns with his boss or insists himself your offer is too low, tell him you will not be raised. If he insists, and if you really like the car, raise your offer $50 dollars, if you wish. Don't be raised more than once.

If You Are Paying Cash, and Buying a Used Car Without Trading

Before reading any further, tell me the truth: did you really work through the chapter on used cars, or did you just read the headings? If you cheated, go back and read the chapter carefully. You're a candidate for the slaughterhouse. If you did it right the first time, read on.

(1) Determine how much you plan to spend. Let's say, for example, $3700.

(2) Decide on three or four car sources, using the guides

in the chapter on buying a used car. Include at least one new-car dealership.

(3) Visit those lots. Look for cars with asking prices $400 or $500 above your cash figure. Don't tell the salesman your price range. Virtually all used-car salesmen have a very bad habit of raising asking prices up to your figure. When the salesman asks you, "Well, what were you thinking of spending?" just tell him, "Well, it depends on the car," and smile.

Let's assume you have found a car with an asking price of $4200. Take the car for a drive. Use the checklist in the Appendix and look for obvious problems with the car. If you still like it after your test drive, write down the stock number and description of the car, the mileage, and the name of the person you are dealing with. Write down any options which may add to loan value, such as automatic transmission, air-conditioning, vinyl roof, or power windows. And then thank your salesman, saying good-bye in the process.

(4) Call a local bank or credit union and ask for a loan officer. Tell the officer the year and model of the car. Accurately describe the car to him. Give him the options and mileage, and then ask for the loan value of that particular car. Put that figure in your pad.

(5) Compare the seller's asking price to the loan value of the car. We'll assume loan value was $3200. The spread is their probable profit.

Asking price	$4200
Loan value	3200
PROBABLE PROFIT	$1000

You want to pay as little of that profit as possible. You want to buy the car for a figure as close to loan value as possible.

(6) Determine your offer. Since you would ideally like to

buy the car for loan value or less, decide the *maximum* amount you are willing to pay over loan value, and add the two figures. In our example, your maximum profit will be $300, loan value is $3200, and your maximum offer will be $3500. Remember that tax and other charges must be added to that figure.

(7) Now, head back to the lot and tell your salesman you would like to take his car to your mechanic. Leave whatever car you are driving as ransom. If your salesman won't agree to this, don't buy the car. If he agrees, take a clean copy of the Mechanic's Checklist, and drive to your mechanic's shop. Don't forget to add to this list any specific problems you have noted in your pad. Before leaving, ask your mechanic for an estimate to repair the car to your satisfaction. Put that figure in your pad and take a coffee break.

(8) You have $3700 to spend. But you may now have a repair bill, if you buy the car. To stay in budget, you will need to *subtract* the estimate from your cash. Let's assume your repair bill was $300. You now have only $3400 to spend, if you plan to stay in budget. Make that adjustment and head back to the lot.

(9) Lead the salesman to his office. Don't be led, take the initiative. Offer the man *less* than loan value. When the man counteroffers, don't accept his offer. Compromise; offer to split the difference with him.

(10) At some point in the discussion, your salesman is not going to budge. When he reaches that point, compare his final offer to your cash. Let's assume his final offer is $3300.

Your cash	$3400
His final offer	3300
AMOUNT OVER OR UNDER BUDGET	$100 *under*

You're in pretty good shape. Don't forget that tax will be added to that figure. Now, compare his final offer to the loan value of the car. The answer, in this instance, $100, is his probable profit. Is that figure satisfactory? It should be, Jesse James.

(11) If you've determined this is the actual car you want to buy, discuss warranties. Be sure you are familiar with the section on warranties before opening your mouth, or you'll probably find your foot resting on your molars.

(12) If the salesman's final offer fits your budget and the warranty is satisfactory, have him write it up. Tell him you'll take the car at that figure. Once the salesman has completely filled out the buyer's order, check the figures. Make sure the warranty is in writing. Sign the buyer's order, but do not give him a deposit. Tell him you will give him a check when the deal is approved by a manager. The salesman will probably insist on a deposit. Tell him it's your way or not at all. Remember, a deposit before you have an approved deal is their way of keeping you there while they work you.

If the salesman returns with his boss or insists himself your offer is too low, tell him you will not be raised. If he still insists, and if you really like the car, raise your offer $50 dollars, if you wish. But don't be raised more than once. If you are determined not to be raised, say good-bye.

WARRANTIES, NEW AND USED

Why isn't anything simple in this business? Like warranties: why can't manufacturers or new-car and used-car dealer associations develop some standards or guidelines to protect the consumer? They could, but they won't. As with many things in the business, warranties are not designed to protect the buyer but rather to protect the seller. With a very few exceptions, car warranties not only protect the seller, but they also provide the most convoluted definitions and exceptions in the English language. We are going to look at most of the pitiful offerings separately; keep in mind, though, this very sad fact: along with all the other negotiations in the car-buying process, you will probably need to negotiate a better warranty, too.

New-Car Warranties. Two specific "free" warranties apply to every new car sold in America. One is the "adjustment warranty." Adjustment warranties are provided by the selling dealer, not the manufacturer, and supposedly cover items such as squeaks and rattles, air leaks, alignment, and other minor annoyances. Because the selling dealer provides this warranty and pays for the work himself, many dealers are loath to spend much time correcting those little problems that affect most new cars. Dealers also limit the time period for minor adjustments—usually no more than ninety days. If you are concerned with rattles, you will do well to talk with a dealership's service department before purchasing a car. Ask the service manager specifically if *all* problems with your new car will be fixed for free. Note the time limit on these repairs. Smart car buyers keep a small note pad in their new cars and list each problem the moment it develops. You would be wise to do the same and provide your service department with a written list of all minor adjustments.

All new cars in America also provide a basic manufacturer's warranty. Most of these warranties protect the major components of each car for a minimum of twelve months or twelve thousand miles. Should your car need repairs under the manufacturer's warranty plan, these repairs will be paid for by the manufacturer—and that's the rub. Most manufacturers pay a lower hourly service rate for warranty repairs than the service department charges individuals; consequently, the service department makes less money on this work. So, which cars normally are serviced first? The paying customers, of course. Warranty work is shuttled to the end of the line, and you are left sitting in "the customer's lounge"—a nice name for the best imitation of the Black Hole of Calcutta—reading a six-year-old copy of *Modern Bride*. You can do something to lessen this problem, but you will need to act *before* you sign anyone's buyer's order. Make it clear to your salesman and his manager, if necessary, that you plan to sit in *their* offices—unshaven and undeodorized—wasting the time of everyone in sight should you be detained in the service line.

There is one other "free" warranty no dealer will volunteer to discuss, the "secret warranties" provided by virtually all manufacturers. Both dealers and manufacturers even deny that such warranties exist, but they do. Called "policy adjustments" or "goodwill service," they apply to widespread problems with old Chevrolet Vegas, or the universally bad head gaskets on certain model Hondas. Dealers and manufacturers like to keep these little free services from the general public to save money, as usual. But, should you have a major problem with your car after the normal factory warranty expires, be loud and visible in your complaints. If your selling dealer refuses to help you with a problem, write the manufacturer's customer service office. The addresses of these offices are located in the owner's manuals for cars produced after 1979.

What About Car Service Contracts? Every new-car dealership in America offers its version of a breakdown insurance policy. These policies are designed to extend the protection on carefully selected portions of your car for a number of years. And invariably, they are advertised heavily by the manufacturers as the best thing since the promise of the second coming. None of these advertisements addresses the really important question: why does a brand-new car need protection from self-destruction after twelve months or twelve thousand miles? Why should you pay for an insurance policy on an $8000- or $10,000-dollar purchase? Do the manufacturers really think their offerings are going to fall apart? No. The manufacturers have simply found *another* way to make money on you, bimbo. If your new car is properly maintained, any major problem at twenty thousand or thirty thousand miles should be the responsibility of the seller, don't you think?

Let's assume you don't agree and really do want to purchase a service contract. If you were to look at most of these policies carefully, you would notice the biggest lie in the first paragraph. "Coverage provided for three years," or "coverage provided for five years" is prominently underlined or captioned. But read on a little further to find the truth: coverage *always* begins *after* the normal factory warranty on your car has expired. Your three-year warranty is really a two-year warranty; your five-year warranty is really a four-year warranty.

And then look at the items not covered by your policy: normal service isn't covered; radiators, fans, fan clutches, and fan motors are not usually covered; most electrical problems are not covered, including power windows and seats; your transmission clutch and its related parts are not normally covered; the carburetor is usually not covered. Of the thirteen major service contracts generally available, *none* really protects you from further expense.

For all this magnificent noncoverage, companies charge you from $185 dollars to $995 dollars. All of them but one also charge you a "deductible" for each visit to the service department.

For most people planning to buy a new car, a service contract will be a waste of money. But if you are the type comforted by insurance, even bad insurance, have at it. Just remember, you'll be betting your expensive new toy won't really sing past the first year. But take heart: most of these policies do provide money for a rental car *if* yours stays in the service department overnight, which normally means it's very sick. You can take that rental car to the nearest bar and toast the night away; include a toast to the state of American engineering while you're at it.

The Biggest Joke: Used-Car Warranties. If you are buying a used car, the negotiation of a proper warranty is something you'll need to do before you sign anything. But negotiate for the warranty *after* you have agreed on a price. Many people insist on something approaching real protection before agreeing on price and are unknowingly stuck with a "service pack." For instance, if you should insist on a full ninety-day warranty, your seller will be happy to provide that. But you will pay a higher price for the car. The seller will give you a $4000-dollar car for $4400 dollars and bank the extra $400 as "insurance" against future repairs. Since the seller has neglected to tell you he's raised the price, he is covered on both ends: if the car needs repairs, you have paid for them in advance; and if the car doesn't need repairs, he has an extra $400 dollars in profit. You want to buy that car for $4000 dollars *and* receive the best warranty. After agreeing on price, begin your battle by asking for the best of the following warranties first; negotiate downward only after long and intense discussions.

(1) One hundred percent warranty on all mechanical parts. This warranty won't cover your radio, squeaks and rattles, or leaks, but it will cover just about everything else. Try for a ninety-day, one hundred percent warranty. Be

happy if you get a thirty-day or sixty-day warranty. If your used car has major problems, they'll usually show up within thirty days. This is a hard warranty to get any seller to agree to, but try for it. By just asking for the best warranty, the seller will be less likely to offer you some of the really rotten "warranties."

(2) One hundred percent drive-train warranty. The drive-train encompasses your engine, transmission, and rear axle. It does not include your braking system or air conditioner. Drive-train warranties are fairly common in the business, but most sellers will try to give you a fifty-fifty drive-train warranty. Say no; it's a lesser option. Aim for a one hundred percent drive-train warranty as your minimum coverage. Again, try for ninety days, but accept thirty or sixty.

(3) Fifty-fifty warranties. If sellers were honest, fifty-fifty warranties would be acceptable under most circumstances. But many dealers will agree to provide this coverage, then simply raise the price of the repair one hundred percent. You, friend, are left paying the full bill. Another version of the fifty-fifty warranty is the "parts and labor" split: you agree to pay for the labor, and the seller agrees to pay for the parts. Unfortunately, the price for labor is conveniently raised far above its normal cost, in most instances. And since labor is the largest portion of most repair bills, you are doubly stuck—nice. Sellers can do this because they require you to have service work done in their shops or in places of their choosing.

If a fifty-fifty warranty is your only choice, consider doing this before actually taking your car to the seller's shop for repair: Take the car to some other shop and ask them for a written estimate for the same work that needs to be done. Then take your car to the seller's shop and ask for an estimate before the work is done. If there is a substantial difference in the two estimates, you are being taken again. If you don't really cotton to confrontations with the service manager, show him your other estimate up front. You might make the guy a little more honest. On any fifty-fifty warranties, insist on coverage for at least ninety days.

(4) Repairs "at cost." This type of warranty is worthless, because who defines cost? How can you check the definition of "cost"? Don't accept this favor.

(5) "As is." Unless you are deliberately buying a piece of junk, don't buy any car "as is." Most dealers will actually attempt to make you sign a statement acknowledging your stupidity when you agree to "as is" purchases. Your signature waives virtually every single right of recourse, even if the car blows up *before* you drive it off the lot.

Regardless of the type of warranty you finally negotiate, insist that the full conditions of the warranty be placed in writing, either on the buyer's order or on a separate sheet of paper signed by the manager, not by the salesman. Salesmen can promise you anything, even sign their personal guarantee in blood, but they cannot obligate the seller to honor their promises.

Implied Warranties. For both new and used cars, many courts are beginning to enforce the principle of "implied" warranties. New cars are more strongly protected by the principle, but you should consider *any* car to be covered by implied warranty. This principle states that any car you buy can be safely purchased on the assumption that it is roadworthy and will perform for a reasonable amount of time without undue expense or trouble on your part. Some states have developed specific implied warranty definitions, but most are developing guidelines slowly. Should you purchase a car that honestly fails to give reasonable service, first have a talk with your seller. Mention the implied warranty concept. If the seller is uncooperative, tell him you are filing a written complaint with one or all of the organizations or officials listed in the Appendix. Normally, a seller will help you with your problem rather than enter into sticky ethical battles with the various agencies responsible for consumer protection.

Used-Car Service Agreements. These will normally cost you more than service agreements on new cars, and they invariably cover less. But if your mechanic has indicated that major problems could develop down the road with your purchase, consider buying a service agreement. If you purchase one of these insurance policies, still insist that the seller provide his own warranty for the longest period of time possible. In all likelihood, the seller will tell you this is a duplication of warranty, and will not be inclined to provide his own protection. Don't accept that answer. If the seller's warranty does duplicate your service agreement, he will be protected. But if the problems should develop that are not covered by the service agreement, you may still be protected.

Whether given by the seller or paid for by you, warranties are no better than determination to receive a fair shake during each visit to the service department. Be a nice person, be an honest person, but especially be an insistent person when it comes to your rights.

A NOTE ON DEPOSITS

Regardless of the car you plan to purchase, don't give the dealer a big deposit. Car people are like the rest of us, they need incentive. Let's assume you signed up last night for the perfect car and gave the man a check for the total purchase price. You return to the dealership the next day to pick up your car and notice a funny noise in the air conditioner and a small scratch on the hood. The salesman says they will, of course, take care of both, but the body shop is busy for two weeks, and the mechanics are busy right now. Can you bring the car back at six in the morning sometime next month?

What can you do? You've paid for the car. Don't think you can stop payment on the check, either. They've probably "hammered" it, taken it to the bank for certification. If you had paid a $100-dollar deposit instead, your car would be in the plant before the eye can blink, and mechanics would be swarming over the air conditioner. To car people, a car isn't sold until all the money is paid. Keep your deposit low, and turn over the rest of your hard-earned dough or sign that contract when you are satisfied the car is right.

SIGNING THINGS

Most dealerships are very smart when it comes to the moment of signing. They seem to invariably pick the very second your heart is beating wildly, your lips are smacking in anticipation, and your common sense is visiting in a neighboring state; *then,* and only then, will your salesman or finance manager stealthily slide the large mound of papers under your quivering hand and say, "Sign here, and here, and here." Most of us could be signing away our inheritance or rights to conjugal visits and never know the difference.

If you have survived to the signing stage, if you've really followed the steps carefully, don't blow it now. Sober up quickly and consider each of these points carefully. Most dealerships won't alter things you sign—but many will put things in front of you that shouldn't be signed.

(1) The buyer's order. Your buyer's order shouldn't be a scratched up piece of paper; it should be a clean, neat sheet of paper with every important piece of information filled in. It's important: many customers have been taken because the major record of their sale was too scratched over and through to stand up in court. Remember, this is a *contract*. If you are not financing at the dealership, it is the only contract. If you are financing at the dealership it is a conditional sales contract that will be replaced by the financing contract—but it is still the only record containing important information about warranties and a few other tidbits.

Make sure your buyer's order contains the following information. Take this list with you to the dealership, if necessary.

a. The date
b. Year of cars (yours, too, if you're trading)
c. Make and model of cars
d. Serial number of cars
e. Asking price
f. Trade allowance (if you're trading)
g. "Difference" figure (if you're trading)
h. Amount of your payoff
i. Taxes
j. Amount to be financed
k. Other fees
l. Complete warranty statement (if a used car, if no other warranty statement is provided)
m. Number and amount of payments (if you are financing at the dealer)
n. APR (if you are financing)

If the buyer's order is completely filled out, *check it.* Do the figures match those on your pad? Are the financing figures as you have agreed? Are the years and makes of cars right? Are the serial numbers right? The serial number on the car you are purchasing is important: remember Killer's little trick. Then and only then, sign the buyer's order. Be sure you have an *exact copy,* and *keep that copy* with your other car papers. You'll need it soon to check the financing contract, if you finance, and you may need it later if you have problems.

(2) Mileage statements. You will be asked to sign a mileage statement for your trade-in. The statement should be completely filled out *including* the mileage. Many salesman will leave the mileage blank and happily inform you the figure will be filled out later. Baloney. You go to the car and write down the figure. Your mileage statement makes *you* liable for the actual mileage on your trade. If you let the salesman leave this figure blank, a sneaky salesman or store could run the miles on your car back, enter the false figure, and sell the car. If the new buyer should discover this, *you* can be sued, not the dealer—because you signed it blank, dummy.

The seller will also provide you a mileage statement on his car. If you are buying a new car, the mileage should obviously be low. It should also match the figure on the odometer. Again, insist that the statement be filled out completely. If you are buying a used car, the seller is obligated to give you a copy of a statement signed by the previous owner. If there is no mileage statement from the previous owner, *don't* buy the car. Insist that copies of both mileage statements be given to you.

(3) Powers of attorney. You will be required to sign "limited powers of attorney." Normally, you will be asked to sign two of these, one for the car you are purchasing and one for the car you are trading. These powers of attorney simply give the seller the legal authority to change titles. If

you have already signed the buyer's order, it's okay to sign the powers of attorney blank—many dealerships must type these up to satisfy state law—but at least ask that they be filled out before you sign, especially if the people you are dealing with make you feel a little "greasy."

(4) Finance contracts. All finance contracts, especially those used by dealers, will remind you of *War and Peace*. The back of every single page is just loaded with all types of unusual protection for the financing institution. For instance, most contracts say your car can be repossessed even if you pay your payments on time—the institution simply needs to feel that their loan is in jeopardy. Most of these contracts also state that your car cannot be driven or "domiciled" out of your state without the permission of the financing institution. Friendly people you are dealing with, right? They really trust you. Unfortunately, you can't do much about all this fine print, but you do need to check several things on the front of the contract. *Take your buyer's order with you* when you go for the actual signing, and check the following things:

a. Is the serial number the same as the car on the buyer's order?
b. Is the "amount financed" the same?
c. Look at the "finance charge" section. This section contains the total amount of interest, the charges for insurance, if you wanted it, and other charges such as state documentary fees. If there are any charges here you don't understand, ask what they are.
d. Look at the APR. Is it the same rate you agreed to?
e. Look at the amount and number of payments. Do they agree with your buyer's order? Be sure this section does not contain a "pickup payment." Some dealers will attempt to make a little extra money by adding an extra payment due

within a week or two. For instance, if you have agreed to pay thirty-six payments of $100 dollars, their contract will read "thirty-six payments of $100 dollars and one payment of $80 dollars." Unless you have agreed to a pickup payment, stop doing business with these people—they are trying to cheat you. Get your money, tear up all the paperwork, and run to your Better Business Bureau.

(5) Warranty Agreements. If you are purchasing a service agreement on a new or used car, you will probably be required to sign the agreement. Most of these agreements are *not* transferable to the next owner of your car. Before signing, review again the coverage that is supposedly being provided.

If you are buying a used car, many dealers will provide you a separate piece of paper detailing their particular warranty for that car. Many times, this paper will not detail any specific agreements you may have made with the seller. For instance, your salesman may have told you air-conditioning is covered under the warranty. But your sheet of paper may simply state "One hundred percent drive-train warranty for ninety days." Air conditioners are not covered on drive-train warranties. Make sure the seller writes down specifically such exceptions. Make sure the warranty is signed, too, by a manager, *not* by the salesman.

10
Lomax

It began as the sweetest of dreams. Killer had fallen in the bed, rolled on his back, and sighed, his fall rocking the bed like some giant jelly bean making hard contact with a bowl of Jell-O.

"Honey, are you okay?" Killer's better two-thirds asked.

"Lilly, I feel fine, just fine. Guess what's happened?"

"What?"

"J. C. and Davies have bought the Chevy store in Lomax. And honey . . . ?"

"Yes?"

"I'm going to be the new sales manager there, or at least I'm going to ask to be. What do you think of that!"

"Bob, why do we want to move to a small town? And can't we talk about this tomorrow?"

"Lilly, I'm tired of the rat race. And I hear the people in small towns are really nice." Killer's definition of nice is "easily taken," but Lilly didn't know that. She is much like some Mafia don's wife who thinks her husband sells olive oil for a living. At the moment, however, she was a sleepy don's wife.

"That's fine, honey, whatever you say. Oh, does the Dead End have a branch there?"

"Lilly, that isn't fair! You know I work there. Now good night, princess."

Lomax. Robert DeMarco, Sales Manager. His dream took him quickly to the big office overlooking the showroom. Killer was holding his first sales meeting with the six young men hired to become the mirror of the master. "Now, men, we're going to work *my* system here, like I said. It's all so simple. We use niceness and logic, and we win every time. I'm even going to show you how to do it with the first customer who comes in this morning. When I finally get that customer in my office, all of you head in the next room. I'll leave my intercom on, so you can hear." Killer dismissed the men and walked on the lot, a satisfied smile marking his career as a manager.

Within minutes an older Chevy pulled up. The driver was a woman in her mid-thirties—blond, slender, breathtaking, and friendly. Oh, God, what a way to start a career, Killer thought.

"Hello, ma'am, I'm Robert DeMarco, the sales manager. How can I help you today?" Killer said "sales manager" as if the title meant "I'm the greatest thing since canned heat." The lady was obviously impressed.

"Well, isn't this nice," she said. "I was so nervous coming here—it's the first time I've bought a car by myself—and who should help me but the manager himself. I hope it won't bother you that I'm a rookie buyer."

"Oh no, ma'am, that won't bother me at all," Killer replied quickly, an understatement, to say the least. "I'm sorry, ma'am, but I missed your name."

"Oh Mr. DeMarco, *do* forgive me. My name is Jo Wright."

At that point in the dream, Killer should have awakened. But he didn't, and some creature hidden away in his brain quickly pushed the "bad dream" button. But not before Killer's last remark. "Well, Jo, I hope it's okay if I call you Jo—well, I'll tell you what. You are our first customer at the *new* Lomax Chevrolet. And I *personally* want you to know that you have been treated fairly. If we don't, I'll *give* you the car!"

She quickly found the perfect car and just as quickly drove it. Killer appraised her old Chevy and walked casually to his office with the beautiful lady at his side. He noticed that the door to the adjoining room was closed and thought, Good, the guys are in there.

Jo sat quietly across from him, right leg resting comfortably on left, watching as he began to fill out a buyer's order.

"Well, Mr. DeMarco, what do we do now?" Jo volunteered cheerily.

Killer wrote "$1500" on the "trade" line of the order and pushed it around to face her. He was smiling. The car had been appraised at $2200. "Jo, as you can see, I'm going to give you a really enormous allowance on your car." He smiled again. But Jo wasn't returning the gesture.

"Allowance! Mr. DeMarco, I'm not interested in allowance! I want to know what my trade is worth in wholesale dollars, and it's certainly worth more than $1500. As a matter of fact, it's worth $2200, isn't it? What are you going to do next? Try to fool me with the cost figure of your car?"

Killer was stunned. He looked back at the buyer's order, Jo's last name jumping from the page like a dagger to the heart. He stuttered, "You . . . you . . . are you by any chance . . . ?" He looked up and saw a couple standing by her. They looked too familiar. Jim and Gloria Wright.

Lilly DeMarco opened her eyes and listened. Killer, still sleeping, was emitting the moan of some wounded animal. Beads of sweat were popping on his forehead. "Bob? Bob!" Lilly reached over and shook him gently. But the dream was not to end that quickly.

"Mr. DeMarco," Jo said, "do you remember these people, my aunt and uncle?" She was smiling now. But the eyes that had appeared so beautiful moments ago were red and glaring, the teeth sharply pointed. "Do you remember these people, MR. MONSOON!"

Killer's office quickly filled with perhaps twenty customers, the only buyers during Killer's entire career who had really defeated him in car transactions. Each carried a placard emblazoned, "K.O. Killer" or "Kill Him! Kill Him!" All were chanting, "Killer! Killer! Killer!"

Jim Wright leaned across the desk, pounding his fist just under Killer's running nose and drippy eyes, and yelling, "We know your name, Killer Monsoon! We know your game! And we've all moved to Lomax!"

Killer's moans sounded like the dying rumbles of the army of evil, and Lilly began to shake him violently, a shake that coincided with the joggling Jo was administering at that moment.

"A free car! A free car!" Jo yelled, grabbing the keys for the new Chevrolet and running from the office. Killer tried to run too, but he was blocked by the twenty maddened buyers, and then his own salesmen, who were yelling, "Rotten! Rotten! Rotten!"

"Stop!" Killer bounced awake in the bed, sweat pouring from his body as from a broken pipe. He rubbed his neck.

"Honey, are you okay?" Lilly asked.

Killer looked around the room, slipped his feet to the floor, and headed to the kitchen. "Yeah, yeah, I'm okay," he said over his shoulder. "Lilly, forget what I said about Lomax, okay? I don't think small towns are for me."

Scraps of the nightmare roiling in his head, Killer paused with his hand on the refrigerator door, staring at its blank white front. Surely *that* hadn't been scrawled on the back window of the fleeing Chevy. Surely not. Not TAKEN AT LAST.

APPENDIX

Checking Out a
Used Car

Do you remember when Richard Milhous Nixon appointed some of his own to conduct an "objective" investigation of Watergate? He learned the definition of objective from friends in the used-car business, obviously. Used-car dealers will tell you their cars have "been checked out from top to bottom," place fancy stickers on many cars windows proclaiming their top-notch condition, and then head for the hills the moment you drive back in with your first problem. Invariably, your problem just isn't one of the things their "service specialists" checked out. Tsk tsk.

If you will adhere to the first checklist carefully yourself, and have your mechanic adhere to the second, you won't need these folks' help, and will discover just about every skeleton in any car's closet. The first checklist will require some judgment calls and a good amount of objectivity on your part. Copy the items and take them with you as you shop. Take a flashlight, too.

Things to Check Out Yourself

(1) The name of the previous owner. Insist on a name and number. If the seller resists, ask to see the title. If he still resists, don't buy the car. The previous owner's name

and address should be on the title. Call the owner and ask specifically, "What were the major problems with the car when you owned it." Don't ask the owner *if* he or she had problems, assume there were problems. You'll get a more direct answer. Note the problems, if any, and add them to your Mechanic's Checklist.

(2) Check the exterior of the car. Kneel down by each front fender and look down each side of the car. Look for ripples in the metal or dull paint. Either could indicate the car has had body damage. If the ripples or bad paint cover an area larger than twelve inches, make a note for your mechanic to check the frame of the car. Also look directly at the damaged area and check for the match of the paint. Are you satisfied with the paint job? When you call the owner, ask him, "How badly was the car wrecked? Again, don't ask him *if* the car was wrecked. If the car had damage to the frame or engine compartment, you would do well to look for another car. If you are still interested in the car, plan to drive it at least half a day.

(3) Check the moldings around the bumpers, grill, wheel wells, and windows. Are any missing or damaged? Cosmetically, is the car a well-kept car? Are there signs of small paint bubbles accumulating around the moldings? If you see these small rust bubbles, ask the seller to punch through them firmly with a screwdriver. If the screwdriver continues through the entire piece of metal, the car is rusting from the inside out, and will probably require major body work. If the bubbles are only surface bubbles, repairs will be less costly. *Any* rust indicates the presence of salt. Be conscious of other rust as you check the car.

(4) Open and close all doors. Do they open and close properly? If a door needs to be forced to close, the door may have been hit in an accident. Look carefully at all metal on the bottom and inside of the doors. Are paint

bubbles present, or are other signs of rust evident? Many doors begin to rust through along the bottom first. If rust is present there, ask the seller to use his screwdriver again. Normally doors with rusted through bottom edges will continue to rust even after repairs. If you buy such a car, you may eventually need to replace the doors. Look at all rubber moldings on the doors and adjacent surfaces. Are they brittle or cracked? Rubber moldings are expensive to replace. Make a note.

(5) Open the trunk. Look carefully at all inside edges. Is there rust present? If so, check it with the screwdriver. Look at the interior walls of the trunk. Are there stains present? Stains are an indication of leaks. If possible, lift up the trunk mat and check for rust. Check the spare tire. Does it match the other tires, i.e., is it a radial if the others are radials? Will the tire make a satisfactory spare? If the tire doesn't match or is barely serviceable, make a note and insist on a different spare. Make sure a jack is in the trunk.

(6) Check the wheels wells and undercarriage. Turn the steering wheel completely to the right and look in the left well. Do the opposite for the right well. Are there signs of rust? Are there signs of fresh undercoating? Many sellers will simply spray over rust. Take a screwdriver or knife and scrape away a small portion of the undercoating. If rust is mixed in with the undercoating, don't buy the car—you are probably dealing with a shyster. Check the real wheel wells, too. Then look under the car with your flashlight. Check the muffler system with the car running. Are fumes escaping at any point along the system? Are the holes larger than a pinpoint? If so, the system will probably need to be replaced rather than repaired. Has the underside of the car been freshly undercoated? If so, forget the car or plan to spend an hour or so scratching undercoating from the various surfaces. Used-car sellers have absolutely no incentive

to undercoat their cars other than to hide things. Most rustproofing and undercoating companies won't guarantee or perform their work on used cars because the product actually seals in rust; it does not stop it.

If the car is a front-wheel drive vehicle, look for welding seams along the frame or underbody. Welds can indicate a wrecked car, or worse, *two* wrecked cars. Some less-than-reputable dealers are actually taking two wrecked cars and welding them together—and not telling the potential customer. Don't buy a car with extensive welding seams *unless* it's checked out first by a body shop. If the seller has failed to inform you of welding work, do the rest of us a favor and report the incident to your local Better Business Bureau.

(7) Check all glass and plastic. Is any broken or cracked? In many states, a cracked front windshield must be replaced. The seller should be responsible for the expense. Check the headlights, parking lights, and taillights. Are they cracked or broken? All broken light covers will need to be replaced.

(8) Check the wiper blades. Are they cracked or pitted? They are cheap to replace, but make a note and determine who will replace them.

(9) Check the vinyl roof. Look for lumps. Under every lump is a mountain of rust. If the lumps are really numerous, don't buy the car unless the seller will pull the roof and repair the rust. Rust under vinyl roofs can be serious and can actually rust through the roof of the car quickly. Check for tears in the roof. Do they appear large enough to allow water to enter? If so, they must be repaired. Note this and determine with the seller who will bear the expense.

(10) Check brake lights, turn signal, hazard lights, parking lights, interior lights, and headlights. Have someone sit in the car and use each one as you watch. Note problems. If

any systems are not working properly, don't just assume that a bulb is burnt out. Have the bulb replaced then and check again. Bulbs are cheap to replace. Repairs to electrical systems are normally very expensive.

(11) Check for ease of starting. Start the car cold, and then start it several times after your test drive. Race the engine under both circumstances, and look for blue smoke shooting from the exhaust. Many sellers will tell you that smoke "simply means the carbon is burning off the rings." Don't believe them. Make a note for your mechanic to do the same test to determine the cause.

(12) Open the hood and check the following with the engine *off*:

A. ALL BELTS AND HOSES. Look on the inside of the belts, not the outside. Are they cracked and dry? They will need to be replaced. Make a note.

B. LOOK FOR CORROSION AND RUST ON THE RADIATOR. If there is any, the radiator probably leaks. Make a note for your mechanic to check it.

C. LOOK AT THE RADIATOR COOLANT. If the coolant is rusty, the cooling system has probably not been maintained. Make a note for your mechanic to determine if the radiator needs to be recored.

D. LOOK AT THE BATTERY. Are the terminals corroded? Are the wires wearing through? If so, the battery probably has not been maintained. Check the battery case. Is it cracked? If so, the battery will probably need to be replaced. Look at the battery levels. If even one of the cells is dry, the seller obviously doesn't service his cars—or the battery is definitely in need of replacement.

(13) Leave the hood open and have someone start the car. Have them push the accelerator down gently, slowly

increasing pressure. Do you hear knocks? Knocking sounds can indicate value problems. Make a note. Do you see any signs of leakage on the engine block or attached parts? Leakage can indicate bad seals. Do you hear any clicking or grinding? Both can indicate problems. Let the car run at idle for at least five minutes, and then pull the car forward. Are there pools of liquid? Many sellers will tell you, "Oh, that's only the air conditioner condensation." Likely story. Rub your fingers in the pools. If they are red or brown or clear and slippery, you have problems with the transmission, engine seals, or block. While the car is running, walk back to the exhaust. Is it pulsing? If so, you could have a bad valve. Check this by holding a dollar bill over the end of the exhaust pipe. If the bill is pulled to the pipe, you have *serious* valve problems. Rub your finger inside the pipe. Is there oil on your pinkie? If so, the car is burning oil.

(14) Check the interior of the car:

A. LOOK UNDER MATS AND CARPETS. Are there signs of rust or excess wear? You can live with the wear, but rust indicates both leakage and rust coming through from the underside of the car, which is very expensive and at times impossible to repair.

Again, look for welding seams on both sides of the floorboard. Seams can indicate a wrecked car at best, two cars pieced together at the worst.

B. LOOK UNDER THE SEAT COVERS. Are they just soiled, or are the seats tearing apart?

C. LOOK ALONG THE WINDOWS AND AT THE HEADLINER. Are there signs of stain? Stain always indicates leakage.

D. LOOK FOR MISSING DOOR HANDLES OR CONTROL KNOBS. Are the missing parts important to the operation of the car?

E. CHECK THE HORN, RADIO, WIPERS, AND OTHER ELECTRICAL GADGETS, SUCH AS POWER WINDOWS AND SEATS. Are any inoperative things important to the operation of the car? If so, make a note.

F. START THE CAR. CHECK THE OPERATION OF THE AIR CONDI-TIONER, HEATER, AND DEFROSTER. CHECK ALL GAUGES. If any systems are inoperative, make a note for your mechanic.

G. CHECK THE BRAKES. Don't move the car, but apply strong pressure to the pedal and hold it for at least thirty seconds. If the pedal continues toward the floor, you probably have a leakage in your braking system.

H. CHECK THE CLUTCH (for standard transmission). Start the engine, set the parking brake, put the transmission in first gear, and let the clutch out as you slowly press on the gas pedal. The engine should stall when the clutch pedal is one half to three-quarters of the way up. If it doesn't you probably need clutch work. Make a note.

I. CHECK THE AUTOMATIC TRANSMISSION. With the car idling, and your foot on the break, slip the transmission from neutral to reverse. If you hear a loud "clunk," the transmission bands probably need tightening, at the minimum. Make a note. Slip the transmission from neutral to drive, and listen for the same sound.

J. LOOK AT THE SPEEDOMETER. Are the miles reasonable for the age of the car, no more than fifteen thousand miles per year? If the miles are unreasonably low, ask the *owner* what the mileage was when he traded the car in. If the individual numbers on the speedometer don't line up exactly, the car may have been "clocked," the miles turned back. Most speedometers are virtually impossible to line up if they have been tampered with. Again, ask the previous owner about the mileage.

(15) The test drive. Tell the seller you will be happy to buy the gas, and you will be happy to have him go with you, but that you would like to drive the car thirty to

forty-five minutes. Plan to drive the car on crowded streets and on uncrowded ones; on bumpy roads and smooth; up and down hills, if there are any in your neck of the woods. Don't be satisfied with a drive around the block. Too many problems with used cars don't surface during quick test drives.

A. CHECK THE ENGINE PERFORMANCE. The car should be responsive when cold and warm. There should be no grinding or humming sounds in the car rear end or transmission. If there are, make a note for your mechanic.

B. CHECK THE BRAKES. The brakes should stop you without pulling, fading, or making unusual noises. Listen for a grinding sound when the brakes are applied. Grinding can indicate worn-out brake pads or worse. At an appropriate place on the highway, slow the car to five miles per hour, and apply the emergency brake. If the car does not come to a complete stop immediately, the emergency system is faulty.

C. CHECK THE STEERING. Is there lost motion when you turn the wheel back and forth? The car could have linkage problems. Does the steering wheel jerk and resist when you turn it? Probably there are power-steering pump problems.

D. CHECK THE TRANSMISSION. *If the car is an automatic,* speed up gradually until the gears shift. Is there a clunking sound or a second of hesitation before shifting? Hesitation or jerky shifts could indicate problems with a gear mechanism. Slow down to ten miles per hour and then press firmly on the accelerator. Do the gears shift quickly? If you are driving a three-speed automatic, the car should shift two times. If it doesn't, this could indicate gear problems, too. *If the car is a standard shift,* shift several times through all gears from a standstill. Are some gears hard to enter? Is there a grinding sound? Either could indicate linkage problems.

E. CHECK THE SUSPENSION. Drive over bumpy roads at slow and fast speeds. At a safe point on the road, "veer" the car hard right and left. If either action causes a large amount of bouncing or sway, your shocks may be defective. Make a note for your mechanic. Now, drive back to the lot and check under the hood again. Is there any fluid on the engine? Is steam or any other vapor rising from the engine? Is the radiator hissing? Make notes.

(16) Finally, check the tires. Do they match, four radials or four polyester? If they don't, the tires will have to be changed. Driving with mixed tires can cause excessive tire wear and heating, handling problems, and accidents. Are the tires worn evenly? Look at the rear tires. Are the edges of the tires badly or unevenly worn? If so, your seller has probably placed the front tires on the rear. That's okay, but if any of the four tires show unnecessary wear along the edges, your car is probably out of alignment. Make a note.

These sixteen steps obviously take a good deal of time and attention, but take the time. And don't be self-conscious. Look over each car as if you were going to marry it. If you buy it, that's what you will be doing: living with the thing, warts and all.

Now, look over your checklist. If there are many minor things wrong with the car, don't scratch it from your list. If there is an indication of major things, make sure each of those items is added to the following checklist for your mechanic. Make out a clean, neat sheet for him, and leave room for his notations concerning each item. Leave room also for his cost estimate to repair the car to your satisfaction.

Mechanic's Checklist

1. CHECK THE ENGINE
   inspect transmission fluid
   check points, condenser,
       and rotor
   check spark plugs and
       ignition wire

2. CHECK FAN AND BELTS
   charging system
   power steering
   air conditioner

3. CHECK COOLING SYSTEM
   radiator
   heater
   by-pass hose

4. CHECK BATTERY

5. CHECK BRAKING SYSTEM
   lining
   wheel and master
       cylinders
   drums and front disks
   hoses, bearings, grease
       seals

6. CHECK EXHAUST SYSTEM

7. CHECK SUSPENSION
   ball joints
   tie rod end
   idler arm

8. REMOVE DIFFERENTIAL
   PLUG AND CHECK
   LUBRICANT

9. TEST-DRIVE CAR

IN YOUR OPINION
Should engine compression be checked with gauge?
What are the specific problems, if any, with this car?
What is your estimated repair cost?

What They Cost:
American Cars

NOTE: Manufacturers have been known to change their profit structure on cars without notice. If you *really* want to be accurate, compare the percentages below with those in *Edmund's*.

It's easy to determine what cars cost the dealer. First, find the number or numbers by any car line in the table. For instance, by American Motors Concord are the numbers ".12" and ".17." The number ".12" is the percent of profit in any *base* Concord—one without options. The number ".17" is the percent of profit in *all* options on any Concord. Both the base price and the total cost of all options are listed on the window of every new car sold in America.

To determine the cost of a Concord that lists for $7400, has a base price $6000, and options totaling $1400, simply multiply $6000 by .12 and $1400 by .17; then, add your answers together. For this Concord, the total profit is $720 plus $238, or $958. Subtract the profit figure from the list price, and you will know the cost of the car: $6442.

If a car line has only *one* number by it, simply multiply the total list price of the car *excluding freight* by that number, and subtract the answer from the list price.

Dealers, as we've mentioned, also pay charges for gas, oil, and advertising on each car they order. After you have developed your cost figure, add $75 for these charges, and then add the charge for freight. In our example, the total might look like this:

Cost of car	$6442
Gas, oil, advertising	75
Freight	325
TOTAL COST	$6842

American Cars
Percentages of Profit

	% of Base Car	% of Options	% of Total Car
AMERICAN MOTORS			
Concord	.12	.17	
Eagle 30	.12	.17	
Eagle 50	.11	.17	
Spirit	.10	.17	
BUICK			
Century			.16
Electra			.16
Estate Wagon			.16
LeSabre			.16
Regal			.16
Riviera			.16
Skylark	.12	.15	
CADILLAC			
All models, including			
Seville			.16
CHEVROLET			
Camaro	.12	.16	
Caprice			.16
Chevette	.12	.16	
Citation	.12	.15	
Corvette			.17
Impala			.16
Malibu			.15
Monte Carlo			.16
CHRYSLER			
Cordoba			.16
Imperial			.22
LeBaron	.12	.16	

Newport	.17	.16	
New Yorker	.18	.16	
DODGE			
Aries	.12	.15	
Diplomat	.11	.16	
Mirada			.16
Omni	.10	.14	
St. Regis	.18	.16	
FORD			
Escort	.14	.16	
Fairmont	.14	.16	
Granada			.16
LTD			.16
Mustang	.14	.16	
Thunderbird			.16
LINCOLN			
All models, including			.17
Marks			
MERCURY			
Capri	.14	.16	
Cougar			.16
XR-7			.16
Lynx	.14	.16	
Marquis			.16
Zephyr	.14	.16	
OLDSMOBILE			
Calais			.15
Cutlass (all models)			.15
Cruiser Wagons			.15
Delta			.15
Omega	.12	.15	
Ninety-eight			.16
Toronado			.16
PLYMOUTH			
Grand Fury	.18	.16	
Horizon	.10	.14	
Reliant	.12	.15	
PONTIAC			
Bonneville			.15
Catalina			.15
Firebird	.12	.15	
Grand Prix			.15
LeMans			.15
Phoenix	.12	.15	
Safari			.15

What They Cost: Foreign Cars

It's easy to determine what foreign cars cost, too. Find the number or numbers by any car line in the table. For instance, by Arrow are the numbers ".11" and ".15." The number ".11" is the percent of profit in any *base* Arrow—one without options. The number ".15" is the percent of profit in *all* options on any Arrow. Both the base price and the total cost of all options are listed on the window of every new car sold in America.

To determine the cost of an Arrow that lists for $6400, has a base price of $5400, and options totaling $1000, simply multiply $5400 by .11 and $1000 by .15; then add your answers together. Our Arrow has a total profit of $744 ($594 plus $150). Subtract the profit figure from the list price, and you will know the cost of the car: $5656.

If a car line has only *one* number, multiply the total list price of the car *excluding freight* by that number, and subtract the answer from the list price.

Foreign-car dealers also pay charges for gas, oil, advertising, and, usually, docking fees. The amounts vary considerably from manufacturer to manufacturer, but for shopping purposes, assume $75. Add this $75 to your answer, and then add freight. In our example, the total might look like this:

Cost of car	$5656
Gas, oil, docking	75
Freight	250
TOTAL COST	$5981

If a number has an "A" by it, the car line *does not* have standard profit margins on options. Use the number for shopping purposes, but use a new copy of *Edmund's* if you really want to be accurate.

Foreign Cars
Percentages of Profit

	% of Base Car	% of Options	% of Total Car
ALFA ROMEO			
All models	.155	.17A	
ARROW			
All models	.11	.15	
AUDI			
4000 series	.14	.18A	
5000 series	.145	.18A	
BMW			
320i	.14	.19A	
528i	.16	.19A	
633CSi	.17	.19A	
733i	.17	.19A	
CHALLENGER			
All models	.12	.15A	
CHAMP			
All models	.11	.15	
COLT			
All models	.11	.15	
COURIER			
All models			.13
DATSUN			
210 2-door standard	.09	.15A	
All other 210 models	.135	.15A	
All 310 models	.135	.15A	
All 510 models	.135	.15A	
All 200 SX models	.135	.15A	
All 810 models	.14	.15A	
All 280 ZX models	.155	.15A	
720 Std 4-speed truck	.125	.15A	
All other 720 trucks	.13	.15A	

DODGE D-50			
All models	.11	.15	
FIAT			
Strada, standard	.08	.16A	
Strada, customs	.12	.16A	
All Brava models	.15	.16A	
All X-19's	.14	.16A	
All Spyders	.15	.16A	
FIESTA			
All models	.09	.15 *	
HONDA			
Civic 1300 4-speed			.09
Civic 1300 5-speed			.14
Civic 1500 4-speed			.09
All Accords and Preludes			.15
JAGUARS			
All models			.155
LANCIA			
Beta, 2- and 4-doors	.18	.20	
Beta 3-door wagon		.20	
Zagato convertible	.17	.20	
LUV TRUCK			
All models			.15
MAZDA			
GLC standard 4-speed	.09	.22A	
All other GLC models	.12	.22A	
All 626 models	.13	.22A	
All RX7's	.13	.22A	
All B 2000 trucks	.11	.22A	
MERCEDES			
All models			.20
MG CONVERTIBLE	.135	.18	
PEUGEOT			
All 504's	.15	.17	
All 604's			.17
PORSCHE			
All models			.20

* Sport option group, Chia group, and heavy-duty package have an average mark-up of *30* percent.

RENAULT

Base 2-door Le Car	.10	.17
Deluxe 2-door Le Car	.135	.17

SAAB

99GL	.12	.17
All 900, but Turbo	.16	.17
All 900 Turbos	.165	.17

SAPPORO

All models	.12	.15

SUBARU

All standard series	.07	.16
All DL series	.12	.16
All Brat series	.13	.16
All GLF series	.14	.16
All GL series	.13	.16

TOYOTA

Corolla Tercel

Standard models	.09	.19A
1315 model	.11	.19A
1382 and 1385 models	.11	.19A
1386 SR 5, 5-speed	.12	.19A
1386 black package	.135	.19A

Corolla

1601 4-speed	.095	.19A
1612 automatic	.13	.19A
1614,1615,1617,	.135	.19A
1654,1657,1675	.135	.19A
1676	.135	.19A
1676 black package	.145	.19A
1682, 1685	.135	.19A
1686	.14	.19A
1686 black package	.145	.19A

Corona

All models	.135	.19A

Celica

2162, 2163, 2165	.14	.19A
2175	.145	.19A
2195	.15	.19A
2195 black package	.155	.19A

Celica Supra

All models	.16	.19A

Cressida

All models	.15	.19A
Land Cruiser	.15	.19A

Pickups

7071	.13	.19A
7081	.135	.19A

7095	.14	.19A
7381 and 7382	.13	.19A
7395 and 7141	.14	.19A
7145	.16	.19A
7145 black package	.165	.19A
7441	.15	.19A
7445	.16	.19A
7591	.13	.19A
7691 and 7693	.13	.19A

TRIUMPH

All models	.14	.18

VOLKSWAGEN

Convertible	.13	.20
1751 Basic Rabbit	.08	.20
All 1752 and 1753 models	.135	.20
All 1772 and 1773 models	.135	.20
All Sciroccos	.145	.20
All Dashers	.145	.20
All Vanagons	.14	.20
All Campmobiles	.14	.20

VOLVOS

All DL models	.16
All GT & GL models	.175
All GLE models	.19
All GLE 2-door coupes	.20

Converting APR's to Add-On Rates

USING THE CHART: How many months are you planning to finance? Go to that column at the top of the page. Follow the column down the page until you find the APR *closest* to the one quoted by your financing source. The *add-on* rate for that APR is at the far left. Since the APR changes with the number of months financed, you *must* use the month column used by your financing source to develop the APR.

Number of Months	24	30	36	42	48	54	60	66	72
Add-on Rate									
7.00	12.91	12.88	12.83	12.76	12.68	12.59	12.50	12.42	12.33
7.25	13.35	13.32	13.26	13.18	13.10	13.00	12.91	12.82	12.73
7.50	13.80	13.76	13.69	13.61	13.51	13.42	13.32	13.22	13.12
7.75	14.24	14.19	14.12	14.03	13.93	13.83	13.72	13.62	13.52
8.00	14.68	14.63	14.55	14.45	14.35	14.24	14.13	14.02	13.91
8.25	15.12	15.06	14.97	14.87	14.67	14.64	14.53	14.41	14.29
8.50	15.55	15.49	15.40	15.29	15.17	15.05	14.92	14.80	14.68
8.75	15.99	15.92	15.82	15.70	15.58	15.45	15.32	15.19	15.07
9.00	16.43	16.35	16.24	16.12	15.99	15.85	15.71	15.58	15.44

Number of Months	24	30	36	42	48	54	60	66	72
Add-on Rate									
9.25	16.86	16.78	16.66	16.53	16.39	16.25	16.10	15.96	15.82
9.50	17.29	17.21	17.08	16.94	16.79	16.65	16.50	16.35	16.21
9.75	17.72	17.63	17.50	17.35	17.20	17.04	16.89	16.73	16.58
10.00	18.16	18.06	17.92	17.76	17.60	17.44	17.27	17.11	16.96
10.25	18.59	18.48	18.33	18.17	18.00	17.83	17.66	17.50	17.33
10.50	19.01	18.90	18.75	18.57	18.40	18.22	18.04	17.87	17.70
10.75	19.44	19.32	19.16	18.98	18.79	18.60	18.42	18.24	18.07
11.00	19.87	19.74	19.57	19.38	19.19	19.00	18.80	18.62	18.44
11.25	20.30	20.16	19.98	19.78	19.58	19.38	19.18	18.99	18.80
11.50	20.72	20.57	20.39	20.18	19.97	19.77	19.56	19.36	19.17
11.75	21.15	20.99	20.79	20.58	20.36	20.15	19.94	19.73	19.53
12.00	21.57	21.40	21.20	20.98	20.75	20.53	20.31	20.10	19.90
12.25	21.99	21.82	21.60	21.37	21.14	20.91	20.68	20.46	20.25
12.50	22.41	22.23	22.01	21.77	21.53	21.29	21.05	20.83	20.61
12.75	22.84	22.64	22.41	22.16	21.91	21.66	21.42	21.19	20.96
13.00	23.25	23.05	22.81	22.55	22.30	22.04	21.79	21.55	21.32
13.25	23.67	23.46	23.21	22.94	22.68	22.41	22.16	21.91	21.67
13.50	24.09	23.87	23.61	23.33	23.06	22.79	22.52	22.27	22.02
13.75	24.51	24.28	24.01	23.72	23.44	23.16	22.89	22.62	22.37
14.00	24.92	24.68	24.40	24.11	23.82	23.53	23.25	22.98	22.72
14.25	25.34	25.09	24.80	24.49	24.19	23.90	23.61	23.33	23.07
14.50	25.75	25.49	25.19	24.88	24.57	24.26	23.97	23.69	23.41
14.75	26.17	25.89	25.58	25.26	24.94	24.63	24.33	24.04	23.76
15.00	26.58	26.30	25.98	25.64	25.32	24.99	24.68	24.39	24.10

"The Negotiation" in Abbreviated Form

If You Are Financing, Buying a New Car, and Trading the Old

1. Compute your Available Cash (Loan Cash plus equity in your trade).
2. At the store, copy down all information on the particular cars which interest you.
3. At home, develop the cost and your maximum offer for each car.
4. Check your budget: compare your maximum offer to your Available Cash.
5. Compute your "best probable" difference figure (your maximum offer minus the wholesale value of your trade).

   DEALING WITH THE STORE—
   take the following information with you:
   —the location, stock number, and color of each car
   —your maximum offer and "best probable" difference figure on each car
   —the wholesale value of your car
   —your Available Cash figure

6. Have your car appraised.
7. Agree on the wholesale value of your trade.

8. When you have agreed, make your offer on the car.
9. Check dealer's difference figure (his offer on your car minus the agreed price of his car): compare it to your "best probable" difference figure.
10. Let dealer write it up; check the buyer's order for accuracy.
11. Sign the order, but do not give a deposit.
12. Give a deposit when your offer is accepted. Recheck your difference figure, if necessary.
13. If you are financing at the dealership, confirm the amount to be financed and the APR.

If You Are Financing, and Buying a New Car Without Trading

1. Determine your Loan Cash.
2. Determine your down payment.
3. Compute your Available Cash (Loan Cash plus down payment).
4. At the store, copy down all information on the particular cars which interest you.
5. At home, develop the cost and your maximum offer for each car.
6. Check your budget: compare your Available Cash to your maximum offer.

DEALING WITH THE STORE—
take the following information with you:
—the location, stock number, and color of each car
—your maximum offer on each car
—your Available Cash figure

7. Go to the lot that is home to your favorite car.
8. Take the salesman to his office.
9. Tell the salesman you are prepared to make a firm offer.
10. Make your offer and insist it be taken to management.
11. Check the buyer's order: compare the figure on the order to your Available Cash. If the figure is satisfactory, sign the order, but do not give a deposit.
12. Give a deposit when your offer is approved. Compare the final accepted offer to your Available Cash, if necessary.
13. If you are financing at the dealership, check the amount to be financed and the APR.

If You Are Financing, Buying a Used Car, and Trading the Old

1. Compute your Available Cash (Loan Cash plus the equity in your trade).
2. Decide on three or four used-car sources.
3a. Look for cars with asking prices higher than your Available Cash figure.
3b. Drive each car; use your checklist to inspect each car.
3c. Write down all items that may affect loan value.
4. Call your bank or credit union and ask for
   —the loan value of the car
   —the lowest interest rate and number of months the car can be financed.
5. Determine their "probable profit": compare their asking price to the loan value of the car.

6. Compute your "best probable" difference figure (loan value of their car minus wholesale value of your car).

   DEALING WITH THE STORE—
   take the following information with you:
   —the location, stock number, and color of each car
   —your "best probable" difference figure on each car
   —the loan value of each car
   —the wholesale value of your car
   —your Available Cash figure

7. Leave your car to be appraised and take their car to your mechanic. Take your Mechanic's Checklist and note on the list any problems with the car. Ask your mechanic for an estimate to repair the car to your satisfaction.
8. Subtract the repair estimate from your Available Cash figure and put the new figure in your pad.
9. Return to the lot and compute his difference figure: subtract his figure on your car from his asking price.
10. Compare his difference figure to your "best probable" difference figure.
11. Always negotiate, even if his difference figure is a good one.
12. When the salesman will not budge
    —check his probable profit: subtract your "best probable" difference figure from his final difference figure
    —decide if you can afford it: add his final difference figure, tax, and the payoff on your car
    —compare this total to your Available Cash.
13. After agreeing on price, discuss warranties.
14. Let him write it up. Check the buyer's order, sign it, but do not give him a deposit.

15. If you are financing with the seller, check the amount to be financed and the APR.

If You Are Financing, and Buying a Used Car Without Trading

1. Determine your Loan Cash.
2. Determine your down payment.
3. Determine your Available Cash (Loan Cash plus down payment).
4. Decide on three or four used-car sources.
5a. Look for cars with asking prices higher than your Available Cash figure.
5b. Drive each car; use your checklist to inspect each car.
5c. Write down all items that may affect loan value.
6. Call your bank or credit union and ask for
   —the loan value of the car
   —the lowest interest rate and number of months the car can be financed.
7. Determine their "probable profit": compare their asking price to the loan value of the car.
8. Determine your maximum offer.

   DEALING WITH THE STORE—
   take the following information with you:
   —the location, stock number, and color of each car
   —your maximum offer on each car
   —the loan value of each car
   —your Available Cash figure

9. Take their car to your mechanic. Take your Mechanic's Checklist, and note on the list any problems with the car. Ask your mechanic for an estimate to repair the car to your satisfaction.

10. Subtract the repair estimate from your Available Cash figure and put the new figure in your pad.
11. At the lot, offer your salesman *less* than loan value. Negotiate.
12. When the salesman will not budge
    —compare his final offer to your Available Cash figure
    —determine his "probable profit" figure: subtract the loan value of the car from his final offer.
13. After agreeing on price, discuss warranties.
14. Let him write it up; check the buyer's order, sign it, but don't give the salesman a deposit.
15. Negotiate; compromise; give a deposit when your offer is approved. If necessary, compare the final figure to your Available Cash figure.
16. If you are financing with the seller, check the amount to be financed and the APR.

If You Are Paying Cash, Buying a New Car, and Trading the Old

1. Compute your Available Cash (your cash plus the equity in your trade).
2. At the store, copy down all information on the particular cars that interest you.
3. At home, develop the cost and your maximum offer for each car.
4. Check your budget: compare your maximum offer to your Available Cash.
5. Compute your "best probable" difference figure (your maximum offer minus the wholesale value of your trade).

DEALING WITH THE STORE—
take the following information with you:

—the location, stock number, and color of each car
—your maximum offer and "best probable" difference figure on each car
—the wholesale value of your car
—your Available Cash figure

6. Have your car appraised.
7. Agree on the wholesale value of your trade.
8. When you have agreed, make your offer on their car.
9. Check dealer's difference figure (his offer on your car minus the agreed price on the new car); compare it to your "best probable" difference figure.
10. Let him write it up; check the buyer's order for accuracy.
11. Sign the order, but do not give a deposit.
12. Give a deposit once your offer is accepted. Recheck your difference figure, if necessary.

If You Are Paying Cash, and Buying a New Car Without Trading

1. Determine your Available Cash.
2. At the store, copy down all information on the particular cars that interest you.
3. At home, develop the cost and your maximum offer for each car.
4. Check your budget: compare your Available Cash to your maximum offer.

   DEALING WITH THE STORE—take your Available Cash and maximum offer figures with you.

5. Go to the lot that is home to your favorite car.
6. Take the salesman to his office

7. Tell your salesman you are prepared to make a firm offer.

8. Make your offer and insist it be taken to management.

9. Check the buyer's order: compare the figure on the order to your Available Cash. If the figure is satisfactory, sign the order but do not give a deposit.

10. Give a deposit when your offer is approved. Compare the final offer to your Available Cash figure, if necessary.

If You Are Paying Cash, Buying a Used Car, and Trading the Old

1. Compute your Available Cash (your cash plus the equity in your trade).

2. Decide on three or four used-car sources.

3a. Look for cars with higher asking prices than your Available Cash figure.

3b. Drive each car; use your checklist to inspect each car.

3c. Write down all the items that may affect loan value.

4. Call your bank or credit union and ask for the loan value of the cars which interest you.

5. Determine their "probable profit": compare their asking price to the loan value of the car.

6. Compute your "best probable" difference figure (loan value of their car minus wholesale value of your car).

DEALING WITH THE STORE—
take the following information with you:
—the location, stock number, and color of each car
—your "best probable" difference figure on each car
—the loan value of each car
—the wholesale value of your car
—your Available Cash figure

7. Leave your car to be appraised and take their car to your mechanic. Take your Mechanic's Checklist and note on the list any problems with the car. Ask your mechanic for an estimate to repair the car to your satisfaction.

8. Subtract the repair estimate from your Available Cash figure and put the new figure in your pad.

9. Return to the lot and compute dealer's difference figure: subtract his figure on your car from his asking price.

10. Compare his difference figure to your "best probable" difference figure.

11. Always negotiate, even if his difference figure is a good one.

12. When the salesman will not budge
    —check his probable profit: subtract your "best probable" difference figure from his final difference figure
    —decide if you can afford it: add his final difference figure, tax, and the payoff on your car
    —compare this total to your available cash.

13. After agreeing on a price, discuss warranties.

14. Let him write it up. Check the buyer's order, sign it, but do not give him a deposit until your offer is approved.

If You Are Paying Cash, and Buying a Used Car Without Trading

1. Determine how much you plan to spend (your Available Cash).

2. Decide on three or four used-car sources.

3a. Look for cars with asking prices higher than your Available Cash figure.

3b. Drive each car; use your checklist to inspect each car.

3c. Write down all items which may affect loan value.

4. Call your bank or credit union and ask for the loan value of the cars which interest you.

5. Determine their "probable profit": compare their asking price to the loan value of the car.

6. Determine your maximum offer.

> DEALING WITH THE STORE—
> take the following information with you:
> —the location, stock number, and color of each car
> —your maximum offer on each car
> —the loan value of each car
> —your Available Cash figure

7. Take their car to your mechanic. Take your Mechanic's Checklist and note on the list any problems with the car. Ask your mechanic for an estimate to repair the car to your satisfaction.

8. Subtract the repair estimate from your Available Cash figure and put the new figure in your pad.

9. At the lot, offer your salesman *less* than loan value. Negotiate.

10. When the salesman will not budge
   —compare his final offer to your Available Cash figure
   —determine his "probable profit" figure: subtract the loan value of the car from his final offer.

11. After agreeing on price, discuss warranties.

12. Let him write it up; check the buyer's order; sign it, but don't give him a deposit.

13. Negotiate; compromise; give a deposit when your offer is approved. If necessary, compare the final figure to your Available Cash figure.

Glossary

ADD-ONS: High-profit items added to cars by the seller, not installed at the factory.

ALLOWANCE BUYERS: Customers who care only about the amount of money given them for their trade. Also referred to as wienies.

ASKING PRICE: The maximum amount of money sellers wish to attain; an imaginary figure used by sellers to snare imbeciles.

AVAILABLE CASH: The total amount of money available to an individual buyer, including equity, Loan Cash, and out-of-pocket cash.

"BE-BACKS": Customers who tell a salesman, "Oh, don't worry, I'll be back tomorrow." Sure.

"BEST PROBABLE DIFFERENCE" FIGURE: The lowest price a customer will probably pay when trading.

BIRD DOGS: People who send customers to a particular salesman, usually for money.

BONUS CARS: Slow-selling cars that pay extra commission to salesmen.

BUMBLEBEES: Folks who flit from dealership to dealership, looking at every new car in sight but never buying.

BUMPING: Getting a customer to raise his offer on a particular car. Also called "raising."

CAR QUEERS: People who dream constantly about buying a new car and enjoy hanging out at car stores.

THE CHART: When a customer is paying the highest interest rate for financing allowed by law and also buying life and accident and health insurance.

CHOPPED CAR: A car reconstructed from two wrecked and/ or stolen cars. This procedure, also called clipping, is a specialty of "chop shops."

THE CHRISTMAS CLUB: A technique designed to convince the customer his or her first payment is being paid by the dealership when it is actually being paid by the customer.

"CLOCKING": Turning the car's speedometer back to register lower mileage.

THE CLOSE: When a customer is finally convinced to sign the buyer's order.

CLOSER: A dealership employee whose only job is getting customers to sign a buyer's order.

CREAM PUFFS: Extremely nice used cars; also referred to as "cherries."

DEMOS: New cars driven by salesmen and other dealership employees. Seldom a good buy.

DETAIL MAN: A person who cleans new or used cars, especially a person who "doctors" minor problems with cars.

"DIFFERENCE": The selling price of a new or used car minus the actual wholesale value of a trade-in.

DIFFERENCE BUYERS: Customers who care only about the difference in cost between their present car and the newer car. Also referred to as jerks.

"DIPPING": Borrowing a down payment for a customer, usually from a small loan company.

DOUBLE-DIPPING: Borrowing a down payment for a customer from two lending institutions. Persons who are double-dipped are also referred to as spastics.

DOWN STROKE: The total amount of the down payment, including cash and equity in your trade.

EQUITY: The amount of value left in a used car when the car's payoff is subtracted from its true wholesale value.

FAIRIES: Rainy-day buyers, invariably pipe smokers and other weird types, who actually seem to understand the car-buying process and are not intimidated by salesmen.

FINANCE CHARGE: The total of all charges customers incur when they finance a car rather than pay cash; includes interest, documentary stamps, insurance, and credit fees.

FLOOR-PLANNING: When cars are owned by financing institutions rather than dealerships. The vast majority of automobile dealerships floor-plan their cars.

FLOOR WHORES: Salesmen who don't work by appointment but simply tackle any unattached customer on the lot.

GROSS, BACK-END: The profit to the dealership on the sale of financing, insurance, and "add-ons," such as rust-proofing.

GROSS, FRONT-END: The profit to the dealership on the sale of a new or used car.

HOLDBACKS: Profits built into each new-car invoice but considered "cost" by the dealership.

"IN THE BUCKET": When a car owner has a net payoff that is higher than the true wholesale value of that car, he is said to be "in the bucket."

LEPERS: New or used cars avoided even by the salesmen due to their physical condition or length of stay at the dealership.

LOAN CASH: The lump sum of cash an installment loan will buy; the actual sum of an installment loan that is applied to the purchase, not interest.

LOAN VALUE: The average amount of money lending institutions will lend on a particular car; usually refers to used cars.

NEGATIVE EQUITY: When you owe more on your car than its true wholesale value.

NET PAYOFF: The amount owed on a car minus any pre-paid interest or insurance premiums.

A NICKEL: Five hundred dollars.

"NICKELS": Small dents and scratches on a car.

THE PACK: Extra profit added to the invoice cost of cars by dealers; packs are used to confuse both customers and salesmen.

PAPER MEN: Used-car sellers who finance their own cars regardless of the credit of the buyers.

PAYMENT BUYERS: Buyers who care only about their payment. Also referred to as suckers.

PEACOCKS: Persons who must drive the newest cars, regardless of the price penalty they must pay for the privilege.

RETAIL VALUE: The wholesale value of a car plus the anticipated profit gained from reselling the car.

ROAD HOGS: Used-car wholesalers who travel from dealership to dealership peddling their wares.

SKATING: When a salesman deliberately sells another salesman's customer.

"SPIFFS": Cash bonuses paid to salesman—tax-free, of course.

THE STORE: The dealership.

"SWITCHING": The automobile version of sadism: convincing a customer to buy a car with a larger profit margin; convincing a customer to buy a car with a bonus to the salesman.

TANKS: Large, unpopular cars or station wagons.

"TISSUE": The actual invoice price of a new car.

"T.O.": To turn a customer over to another salesman or manager in order to close or raise the profit on a sale.

TRADING DOWN: Buying a smaller or less expensive car than your present one; trading a newer car for an older one.

"UPS": Customers.

THE "UP" SYSTEM: When "ups" are assigned to salesmen by numbers, i.e., "Okay, Killer, you're up next."

WATER: What remains when the value of a used car is less than the amount the seller has in the car. For instance, if a seller has $1000 dollars in a car with a true wholesale value of $600 dollars, the dealership has $400 dollars in "water."

WHOLESALE VALUE: The value of a used car to someone who plans to resell it.

WRITE-DOWNS: When the value of a used car is lowered on a dealership's book.

Index